To

Ross,

Thanks for your
support. Together we
can make a difference.

J. Barrett

11/25/95

SILENT CRY:

Ray, Deke and Me
The Key To Stopping
The Violence

AN AUTOBIOGRAPHY

by

E.J. Bassette

3B Publishing Company
Chicago Heights, Il.

3B Publishing Co.
1517 Western Ave. Suite 252
Chicago Heights, IL 60411
708/747-6822
1-800-424-EDGE

Library of Congress Catalog Card Number: 94-094600
ISBN: 0-9642800-0-0

Jacket Design: Troy Brown Design, Chicago
Photography: Billy Montgomery, Chicago
Creative Concept: E.J. Bassette

Edited by Derrick K. Baker

Printed in the United States of America

First Edition: October 1994

1 2 3 4 5 6 7 8 9 10

Dedication

I dedicate this book to my parents, Essie V. Bassette and Ernest L. Bassette, for teaching me discipline and the value of life. Mom, your faith has instilled in me the truth that with God all things are possible. Watching and learning from you Dad gave me a living example of what it takes to be a man.

Rising from ghetto to glory

Table of Contents

Foreword

At this, the close of the twentieth century, America is engulfed in a war as devastating as any conflict the nation has known. Every day the casualties mount. And it is not just young men who are filling body bags and crowding county morgues. Innocent women and children are falling, too, victims of the senseless slaughter that is nearly as horrific -- though we continue to deny it -- as the atrocities in Bosnia, Rwanda and Haiti.

While everyone agrees that the nation's cities are in critical condition, there's great disagreement about the causes or potential cures. Conservatives charge that the breakdown of traditional values, the collapse of our national moral code and apathological dependency on the welfare state have brought us to this precipice. Liberals retort that decades of warehousing the poor in high-rise hellholes -- where access to good education and good jobs is inadequate -- and the failure to outlaw the rapid-fire weapons that have made killing even more easy was the formula for mayhem.

Into this debate steps E.J. Bassette, a young man with a more personal perspective on the ills affecting urban America than many of the pundits offering prescriptions for the epidemic of violence. Bassette is a product of the cruel streets of Chicago's near South Side, a community marked by towering housing projects, crumbling tenements and generations of families locked in the vicious cycle of poverty from which many see no escape.

And so it is from the vantage point of one who has survived the unmerciful blows dealt children reared in the forgotten communities of our inner cities that he writes this poignant memoir.

Bassette is not merely a boy from the "hood" writing about the homies and their exploits. He is an American success story, a young man who found direction and used his innate intellectual and athletic gifts to climb out of the urban maelstrom that claimed the lives of his two closest friends. Yet, instead of finding a corporate culture that valued his rare combination of professional polish, determined salesmanship and street smarts, he discovered a cruel truth: that a Black man in the three-piece suit is still -- in the eyes of many -- a nigger. Furthermore, he learned that the symbolic body blows inflicted on him in corporate America stung just as much as the punches he fended off fighting his way through the ghetto.

And as E.J. came to grips with the lives and deaths he has witnessed, he realized that he and WE are not impotent observers of this mayhem. We can and we must do something about it. This is part of his effort.

5

Be forewarned as you venture into these pages that the stories contained herein are not sanitized or prettied up for mass appeal. This is gritty and graphic stuff, the stuff of which so many Black youngsters' lives are made. The protagonists here, including Bassette himself, don't always behave nobly. They live by the code of streets. They do stupid, malicious, randomly violent things -- just as any young people are apt to do when left to their own devices in a stupid, malicious, randomly violent world. The precious few of those youngsters who, by the grace of God, are guided out of their belittling environment often demonstrate, as Bassette has, how able these young minds are when their negative energy is harnessed for constructive use. The vast majority, however, are sucked in the vacuum of hopelessness where they live out their lives in poverty and despair. All too frequently, those lives are tragically short and meaningless.

In part, this book is an attempt to give meaning to the all-too-brief lives of some of those victims -- the young men E.J. knew and loved as brothers. But this is not only a paean to fallen friends, it is a warning to America -- a wakeup call -- alerting us that our time for ignoring the plight of the inner city and its denizens has run out. Now, the catastrophe that is urban America is on the brink of exploding and the rage and violence that is boiling over there will not be contained within the bounds of any city. The L.A. riots offered just an inkling of the devastation and destruction that can occur when the fury of the inner city erupts.

Bassette urges us, as a society, to come to grips with our forbidding impression of Black men and to collectively engage in a national effort to create more positive images and role models for young Black men to emulate and for society to recognize. As one of those role models, Bassette has embarked on a personal crusade to challenge Black youth to reach beyond the barriers of race and class and strive for a new reality in the unfamiliar territory of academic achievement and employment. He is challenging all of us, too, imploring us to reach out to the forgotten children of our cities, to offer them a hand up, a hand that may save us all from a cataclysmic revolt that will make the L.A. insurrection seem infinitesimal by comparison. We must make an effort to hear the not altogether silent cry that is building to a deafening scream. If we listen and act together, we can stop the violence.

Charles Whitaker
Professor of Journalism
Northwestern University
Evanston, Illinois

6

Acknowledgements

In making my dream a reality, I faced many difficulties and adversities, but I've been able to take those lessons and utilize the good in each, weeding out the bad elements. I've had to rely heavily on other people to help me in different areas or opportunities. In order to write this book I had to speak to the families and friends of those who passed and have them recount the tragedies that surrounded the deaths of their loved ones. Writing this book has let me know that I am doing the right thing, sharing a message of hope in what seems like a hopeless situation. I thank each family for allowing me to use the pictures and articles so that you may see the faces behind the names.

During the two-year period it took me to compose this book, Donna and our children have patiently supported me and I thank them for that. I would also like to thank my brothers, Eric and Eddie, who have given me their moral support. My love and thanks to Johnnie Mae Groce, my mother-in-law for her advice, support and love over the years.

To James Anyike, author of *African-American Holidays* and *Historical Christianity African Centered*, I will be forever grateful to you for taking me by the hand and leading me through the world of self-publishing. And to Luke Helm, your support and guidance has gotten me through one of the lowest points in my life and has helped me prepare for my life's work. You are the meaning of brother.

I give special thanks to the people who have worked closely with me typing and revising: Wendy White, a beautiful young lady and close family friend; Eldora Wines, my big sister and friend; Schakina Sept, my cousin now attending Grambling State University; my editor Derrick K. Baker; and again my wife Donna.

I would like to thank some others who have helped me along the way.

Dwayne Staton	John Alexander	Joyce McEwen
Carol Mann	Debbie Hill	Princess Tucker
Rick Corso	Anthony Zeringue	Samuel Huff
Armond McCarol	Micheal Williams	Dr. Tom Drinka
Les Brown	George Fraser	Coach Larry Mortier
Ken Hayes	Mike Ward	Mark Carlson
Rich Sweeny	Bill Flannigan	Marcella Smith
Sammy Hunt	Dr. Phil Withers	Cheryl Rutherford
Robert Hurst	Nola Smith	Millicent Knight
Morgan Carter	Dennis Kimbro	Marvin Long
Coach Torian	Coach Brad Smith	Sabrina Mackey
Pat Debonnet	Eva Williams	D.J. Tolliver
		Elisa Walker

SILENT CRY

PART I
BACK IN THE DAY: GROWING UP IN THE "LOW END"

Interpretation

While thinking about life and trying to understand all its different twist and turns, there's one part of living and experiencing that offers its most interesting face. That face is called interpretation, which is defined as clarifying the meaning of by explaining or restating. For example, two people can see a car accident, and based on the two individuals' perspectives, the story about what happened can be as different as night and day based on which story and what version you hear. Neither person is wrong, but it takes the listener to be keen enough to chose what part of the stories they need (good or bad) to understand what happened.

I know this is true in other walks of life because I grew up in a family in which there is 20 years' difference between the oldest child, Elleana, and me the ninth. Listening to my older siblings talk about being raised is like listening to them have a different set of parents. Even though we cross each others' paths, our version of what happened in our own family is very different.

For example my oldest sister and brother, Elleana and Eddie, were born in the 1940s when Momma was a teenager and Daddy was in his early twenties. I was born when they were in their mid-thirties and early forties, respectively.

I write this to say one thing. This story comes from my eyes. I recount the lives of many people and events in my life that gave me experiences both good and bad. My version of what it took for me to become a man respectful of all women, particularly my own black woman, will come out. My ability to look past all the negative and focus on the positive will come forth. Finally, my belief in a strong family unit that must bond together will be discussed.

So now that you are prepared for this journey let's strap on our seat belts and go into my world.

The Key to Stopping the Violence

Friends for Life

Growing up in the Ida B. Wells projects meant having plenty of friends to play with. When I started school I was in a half-day preschool class at Doolittle Grammar School, on the South Side of Chicago. It was the same grammar school all eight of my older sisters and brothers attended. All my classmates would always play with the toys and my personal favorite was the sandbox. My best friend in the class was Ray Grant. Once the teacher shouted "playtime" we would race to the front of the line to get the shovels and play in the sand. One day me and a new boy in class reached for the same shovel. We fought over it and he won. Then he began hitting me over the head with it.

After that I stayed away from him, but I noticed everyday he was dressed in a blazer and bow tie. After school, one of my older sisters would always pick me up. One day when we had almost reached our apartment, I saw the same little boy with the blazer and bow tie. His mother was straightening out his tie as she sent him out to play. He lived in the next building. We started playing and fighting that day in 1965 and never stopped. That little boy, Ray Grandberry, became one of my closest and dearest friends. And for the next 20 years we laughed about the way he pounded my head with that shovel.

His mother was like any mother would be -- his best defender when he did wrong. Ray and I became one in the minds of many over the years. Ray, the youngest, had two sisters, Vail and Gracie, and one brother, Ivory. His father, Mr. Grandberry, frightened us with his strong and demanding voice. Mr. Grandberry only had to say something once.

Lamar Lewis was the first friend I can ever remember having when I was three or four years old. Mr. and Mrs. Lewis, Lamar's parents, and my parents had known each other for years before we were born. They all had already been living in the projects for close to 20 years. Lamar's apartment building sat between Ray's and mine. I would play with Lamar and two of his three sisters, who were close to our age. We would play on our second-floor back porch with my sister, Evette. Lamar was not quite six months older than me but because his birthday was in September, he started school a year earlier. Lamar would occasionally beat me up over little things, sending me home crying. Lamar was not fat but he was thick and six months was a big difference at that age. When I wasn't crying, he was teaching

9

me how to curse. Lamar would tell me to say "shitball" and I would "shitball, shitball." He would laugh to no end. Then he would say "motherfucker." I would repeat it and again he would laugh and laugh until one day, my bigmouth sister, Evette, heard me and told Momma, "Erski is over there saying bad words." I would deny saying it and because I was only 4 years old, and Momma's baby, she would believe me. I learned at an early age not to say the wrong thing around my sister.

Around 1966, Ray and me were doing what all five year olds do, playing marbles or riding tricycles. The gang element was at its peak in the ghetto. We would sneak across the street to Ellis Park where there were what seemed to be thousands of the Black Stone Rangers wearing red tams. They would take up the entire park holding their meetings. They would pat us on the head as we walked between them and tell us we would be little Black Stone Rangers one day. We always loved the way they spoke, strong. They said, "What's up brothers and sisters." "Peace," or "I'm black and I'm proud." We didn't understand what was going on but I learned to keep my eyes open and listened to everything.

Ray and all the other boys were fascinated with the Black Stone Rangers. We would copy the gang symbols they would throw up, then argue about which was the best gang, the Black Stone Rangers or the Disciples. We'd run around the 'hood playing gangsters because that's what we saw. We would shout out the name of the gang we represented: "Stone to the bone." "D' thang." "Disciples run this MF." Then we would pretend to shoot each other with sticks or pieces of wood. Throwing up a gang sign was just the way it was in the low end.

Changing Times

Black people all over the city wanted to move into the Ida B. Wells homes. It was a well-kept lakefront complex, three and four stories tall, that sat three blocks west of Lake Michigan. There was a definite difference between the row houses that we lived in and the newly built high-rise projects that surrounded Ida B. Wells. We had grass, fences and trees with beautiful landscaping. Ida B. Wells (named after a famous black activist) was known as a haven for black families. Momma and Daddy moved there in 1945, after World War II. They raised all eight of my sisters and brothers there for close to 20 years before I was born. Neighbors watched each other's kids and were allowed to

The Key to Stopping the Violence

spank you. Then they'd take you home and you'd get in trouble again with your own parents. White people would take tour buses through the neighborhood to view the beautiful area. At one time, only working and married couples were allowed to move in. The garbage was always collected once a week, and the janitors constantly swept the backyards. Even though gangs existed, our parents, although not wealthy, were very much in control of our behavior.

In the high-rises, there was a different story. They were 14 floors built to house thousands of people in a small amount of space. A lot of the people moving in were single-parent families. It was almost impossible to watch your kids if you lived on the 10th floor. They always seemed to be dirty and unsupervised. As a child, Daddy would drive us to church most Sundays and Momma's friends would bring us home in the evenings. There were a lot of days and nights when we couldn't get a ride and had to walk through another high-rise project development called the Darrow Homes.

As we walked, people would throw all kinds of things over the porch at us or anyone else walking by. No telling what was going to come down from one of the 14 floors. Things like baby diapers full of shit, glass bottles or even bricks would come down from the porches or windows. Occasionally a large item like a washing machine would come down.

Eventually, the Chicago Housing Authority (CHA) put gates over the porches of all the high-rises in the city to prevent the people below from getting hurt or killed. It was common knowledge that the families in the row houses thought we were better than the families in the high-rises. Momma always said "They (CHA) tried to get us to move into a larger apartment in the high-rise. But I prayed that God wouldn't put us there. I had all you kids sleeping in two rooms." She thinks to this day not moving across the street saved some of her kids' lives.

Although the established families in the row houses always looked down on the people in the high-rises, we still had to go to school with their kids. Soon I began to see Ida B. Wells deteriorating. The grass stopped growing, fences were being torn down, trash and glass weren't being cleaned up. Daddy was the strong silent type. As things continued to change Daddy was always our security blanket at home. He worked during the day, but he was home every night. If there was trouble all us kids looked for Daddy to handle it. One night a man was screaming for his life. His hands and feet were bound by rope and tied to a

11

rail in the hallway. Two thugs had his shirt off and were beating him mercilessly. Daddy, not knowing if they were armed, shouted at the offenders, who then ran away.

A Normal Childhood

One thing Ray always had was fun birthday parties. I felt sad because my family never had parties for me because we were supposed to be religious and dancing and parties were against our religion. But Momma would dress me up to go to Ray's apartment for his parties. Ray and his older brother Ivory never wanted for toys. They had all the fun toys of the '60s, like a wagon, paddle cars, Tonka trunks, and Rock 'Em Sock' Em Robots.

At the party, we would wear party hats and there would be plenty of balloons and food. Mr. Grandberry would always have Ray dance for his company and friends. Vail, Ray's older sister, collected music put out by the Jackson Five and James Brown. Ray would slide across the hard floor in the projects doing James Brown steps for his company. His birthday was at the end of July so it would always be a bright, sunny day, complete with kids running in and out of the second floor apartment with the screen door slamming behind us. We'd eat hot dogs and dance.

I always felt awkward as Ray's father hollered out, "Look at my boy dance. Ray show that stuff." Ray would move across the floor imitating "The Godfather of Soul" and Michael Jackson. Mrs. Grandberry, with that wonderful smile on her face, watched her baby boy turn a year older. They would always ask me to dance, but that was against the rules in my house. I wished my parents were more fun and loose.

On other days we would play in front of Kevin's apartment, another friend, with Lamar, Frankie, Ray and myself fighting over the toys all day. Ray and I were arguing about a toy one day. Up on the second floor, Mr. Grandberry was listening to us argue as I told Ray I'd kick his butt. Mr. Grandberry hollered down for Ray to hit me and kick my butt. We looked at each other as Ray swung and hit me in the face. Mr. Grandberry continued to encourage his son to kick my so and so. I was too scared to swing back because I thought if I did I would be beaten up by Mr. Grandberry.

The Key to Stopping the Violence

Rocky Road

Our parents would dress us and send us out to play in the backyard. Like most boys Ray and me liked to throw rocks, but Daddy had always said no rock throwing because I might break a window or put out someone's eye. One day Ray and me were standing in front of our friend Frankie's house. Ray started throwing some dirt rocks he picked up out of the sidewalk construction. Ray said they weren't rocks, just dirt. That was all I needed to hear. We started throwing "dirt" to watch it explode on the street. Some of the neighbors would come by and say, "You little boys know you shouldn't be throwing rocks." We would stop until they left.

At the stop sign at the corner of 37th and Vincennes we threw throw rocks over the cars when they stopped. At the young age of 5, Ray and I didn't have strong arms but we continued having the time of our young lives until a car drove up and Ray tried to throw over it. The rock smashed into the car window and the driver jumped out and hollered at him from across the street. Ray took off running as the man chased him and I followed the man. Ray was running and crying through the backyard and everybody else was running to see what was going on.

The man caught him in the hallway of Ray's building. There had to be 20 or 30 people around. Ray's father heard the commotion and came down from their second floor apartment. The man grabbed Ray by his shirt and told him to tell Mr. Grandberry what happened. Mr. Grandberry looked at Ray and said, "Boy, did you hit this man's car with a rock?" Ray looked up with tears and said, "Yeah, but Ersk was throwing rocks, too."

All the kids turned and looked at me. Mr. Grandberry smacked Ray upside his head, took him by his belt buckle and threw him up the project hallway stairs. He was cursing and swearing and he said he didn't want his son around me. Then the man grabbed me and asked where I lived. I began crying and said I didn't do anything. By then all the kids ran and beat me to my own apartment. By the time we got to my house Momma and Daddy were already informed by the neighborhood bigmouths. Daddy went through his usual sermon, smacked me on the head and told me to take my pants off. I got a whipping and was told I couldn't play with Ray anymore.

SILENT CRY

Within the next couple of days Ray and me renewed our friendship when we found an old car tire. We tried to play with it without talking. As the day went on we became inseparable. I still laugh to myself whenever I see little boys throwing rocks at cars.

Daddies' Influence

Despite the chaos that often ruled our environment, our fathers still had significant influence over us and how we acted inside and outside of our homes. They also continued to be good role models and were there for us when we needed them. Ray suffered from asthma and Mr. Grandberry would carve notches in a big tree in front of their building. The markings showed Ray how much he had grown and how much he needed to grow to get past the asthma attacks. All the kids would go to the tree as Ray placed the back of his head against it to guess how many years it would take to reach that certain height. As years went on, whenever Ray got into a fight, it was almost a lock that if he was losing he'd stop and call time out because of an asthma attack. That went on for years.

Like most little boys, Lamar, Ray and me would compare our fathers' cars to see who had the coolest one. Because our fathers all parked on different streets, we would walk to each of their cars in the front of our respective buildings and look through the windows.

In 1966 Daddy had a red car that was so old we could see the street under our feet. My older sisters would tell me I was small enough to fall through the holes. One summer day in 1966 everyone in the family was screaming, "Daddy has a new car. Daddy has a new car."

I was 5 years old and riding my scooter when I got the word that Daddy was going to pile us all in the car and take us for a ride. I left Ray and Lamar and sped around the corner on my scooter at full speed and ran right into the side of the new car. I put a scratch on the new ride before we could get in. Daddy gave me a look of disgust, then we all piled in and drove from 37th Street to 43rd Street to show Big Momma (Daddy's mom). It was the best looking car I had ever seen. A 1965 Chrysler New Yorker, tan with tan seat covers and doors with the coolest dashboard I had ever seen. Daddy always got a Chrysler, and Lamar's parents always bought Oldsmobiles. Ray's father always had a green Chevy Impala. Kevin Green's father also had

The Key to Stopping the Violence

a Chevy Impala but a different color than Mr. Grandberry's. Mr. Green's cars always ended up in the extensions striped down to nothing. We would stop on the way home from school to play on and in his abandoned car.

Daddy made few new purchases, but we spent a lot of time looking in department stores like Sears or Goldblatts. All we usually did, however, was walk by the TVs (now I understand why). We would look at the new color TVs, then once home, Daddy would make his own color TV . A color TV in our house was when Daddy put a piece of see-through, multi-colored plastic in front of the TV screen. "Y'all come and watch the new color TV," Daddy would say, as it turned the people's faces green, red and blue. Daddy would get mad if one of us kids said it was fake color.

Wheeling and Dealing

When I was about 8 years old, my next door neighbor was the mother-in-law of New York Knicks N.B.A. basketball star, Walt Frazier. Momma would baby-sit Walt and Marsha's son, Walt Jr. When I would see Walt Frazier, I knew he was important, but I didn't understand until much later in life. He was the Michael Jordan of his day who actually married the girl next door. All the neighbors would gossip about how he bought Marsha new clothes and cars.

Ray and I would find ourselves daydreaming, while looking inside her car saying we were going to play pro ball and be rich some day. One hot summer day Ray and me talked about making a go cart and we needed wood, wheels (usually from an old tricycle), hammers and nails. We saw a little guy riding around on his tricycle. He had to be about 3 or 4 years old. We quickly decided that those were the perfect wheels for our go cart. So Ray and me walked up to the boy and offered him some candy. While I distracted him, Ray loosened the wheels.

The little boy began to cry and we ran away with his wheels. We thought we had pulled the perfect job. We didn't realize that at age 7 or 8, you don't have enough savvy to steal. We didn't think about maybe his parents or the neighbors were watching him.

The little boy lived in the same backyard as us. We took the tires and hid them in the sewer (they were really basements attached to each building) on the side of Ray's building under the kitchen window of the Hudson's. Then we went to Ray's house and gave each other a congratulatory high-five. We would fix the go cart later in the day when the excitement died down. In the meantime, we watched our favorite show, "Speed Racer." We were settled in Ray's bedroom when Ray's older brother, Ivory, came in with a big brother smirk on his face. Ivory said my Momma, Ms. Clark (Walt Frazier's mother-in-law) and the police were outside looking for us. We began to panic. Momma and Mrs. Grandberry were exchanging words about whose son was at the core of the problem this time.

Ray and me went to the porch and the little boy pointed us out as the culprits. Momma demanded that I come downstairs to the first floor and tell the policeman where the wheels were. I said I didn't know anything. Then Ms. Clark said she saw the whole thing and we had taken the wheels. My mother's impatience took over and she said the magic words: "Wait until your father gets home." I looked up at Ray standing on the porch and began to cry. I said the wheels were around the corner in the sewer. The police officer went with us and made me go into the sewer to retrieve them. Momma slapped me and told me to go in the apartment and wait for Daddy. Momma and Mrs. Grandberry then exchanged a few harsh words about keeping us away from each other. By this time, it looked like everybody in the projects was outside watching. I ran to the building and waited in my room until Daddy got home and gave me one in a long line of disciplinary whippings.

Murder: A Mixed Message

The first murder I knew of happened when we were 8. We spent a lot of time on Ray and Ivory's second floor porch. Everyday it seemed like thousands of people walked through the projects going about their business. This day Ray and me were standing on the porch when a man came walking through the backyard. He walked from the side of the playground into our view. Ray told me to look at the man. "He's the dude that killed my nephew," said Ray. I thought, "Yeah, okay, sure Ray."

Ray said they were shooting craps at Doolittle grammar school when his nephew tried to get out of the game. He was ahead at the time. He tried to run, but the man picked up a brick and bashed in his head and killed him. Now as we watched him walk out of view, I knew something was wrong. How could a murderer be walking around? Ray told me that the man had rank (respect) in the projects because he had murdered his nephew.

The Key to Stopping the Violence

Ray even went out of his way to speak to him. I'm sure the man never knew that Ray was related to someone he had killed. As time passed I learned there were many more murderers walking around.

Escaping North to Chicago

At some point every kid asks their parents, "How did we get here?" or "Did we always live in Chicago?" "Did we always live in the projects?" We all would like to know how our parents met and why they behave like they do. This is the story I've learned from my parents.

My Grannie was born and raised in the South where she married a Baptist preacher. Grandfather was one of 10 children (nine boys and one girl). He was the third from the oldest. Even though he was small, word is he was one of the meanest men who ever lived. He met my Grannie one day when he was preaching the word of God. As their relationship grew he also became very abusive. He would continually beat Grannie and lock her in a sub-basement for days at a time. Grandfather would often chase and beat her, then on Sunday preach God's word.

Momma was born in 1925. She was the youngest of five kids. Her father's brutal acts, as well as the fear she had for his aggressive ways, caused a lot of problems for her as she grew older. Because Momma was growing up poor in Alabama, during the late '20s and early '30s, there was little that could be done about these problems.

One day Grannie finally decided she and her kids had suffered enough abuse and packed up and headed to Chicago. Many in the family had gone to Chicago before her; in particular her sister-in-law (Aunt Lucille), my grandfather's only sister. Aunt Lucille opened her door one day to see her sister-in-law with her five kids. (Grannie had lost five other babies to miscarriages.)

Momma lived her preteen life on the South Side of Chicago. She never got over the problems she had to face in those early years. I never knew those problems existed until I was much older. That explained a lot of Momma's decisions and actions. Those problems followed her as she grew up. She never trusted male figures. Her experiences left her cold and confused.

I remember Momma always talking to or about her mother. Grannie was a very fair-skinned, small-framed woman, about 5' tall. She carried large shopping bags full of goodies from the bus stop at 37th and Cottage Grove. The bags would almost drag because they were so big or because she was so small. She would come during the day when me and my sister Evette were playing. She always gave us candy. She seemed old to me because she was so small, and always seemed to be walking slowly. I can't say I ever remember her telling me anything specific, but I remember sensing she was important and felt she played an important part in Momma's life.

My father's mother (Big Momma) and his father, Granddaddy, (who was one of 14 kids) also came from the South. Granddaddy was born in 1900 in Alabama and worked on a white man's plantation as a sharecropper. At the age of 20, he was struggling to find a way to pay off the white owner to put him in a position to leave the plantation. But according to the plantation owner, the blacks owed more money than they were getting paid. So most of the blacks spent the rest of their lives working to pay back the money that they were being cheated out of.

Granddaddy decided there had to be a better way. So he approached the plantation owner, asking him how much he owed. The plantation owner said according to his records Granddaddy still owed him enough money to keep him working for another year. Granddaddy pulled out his own records and said, "No, according to my records you owe me." The white man looked with surprise and said, "Nigger, I'll pay you your money but you got to get off my land today before you teach the other niggers these bad ways."

Granddaddy could have easily been lynched for being what white folks called "an uppity nigger." Granddaddy left that plantation and headed to Chicago with the woman he loved: my Grandmother (Big Momma). Daddy and his brother, Uncle George and sister, Aunt Ann, left the South when they were small kids. But before leaving Daddy remembers black men being killed by the KKK and thrown in the schoolyard for all the little boys to see. Black people were fleeing the South to get away from the wrath of the whites.

Daddy, born in 1919, and his family grew up on the South Side of Chicago and attended DuSable High School. Daddy went to school with the likes of the real estate magnate, Dempsey Travis, former Chicago Mayor, Harold Washington and famous singer, Nat King Cole. Daddy had a choice of girls he could have found happiness with and during one of the parties at the Savoy Ballroom, he saw the woman he fell in love with

The Key to Stopping the Violence

and wanted to marry. Back in those days black people believed that the lighter your complexion, the better you would be treated in society. Momma had very fair skin and long hair, which to a lot of black men represented beauty.

They eventually married and had a daughter and a son. My father was drafted by the Navy to fight in World War II. His brother, George, also fought as a member of the Army. At that time the only thing a black man could do in the armed forces was cook and clean.

As time passed in the '40s and '50s, Momma started showing signs of a person who couldn't handle the family pressures. Daddy said she always said she only wanted one kid, so as they began having two, three and four, she would become sad and cry and say that she hated having babies. Because of their lack of knowledge about birth control, they continued having babies. At one time they had one son and five daughters. Then another boy, Eric, then Evette and then finally me, E.J., No. 9.

My mother and father were the perfect couple on the outside because of their good looks and the strict way they raised their family. But on the inside Momma had a fear of my Daddy and hate for all men who represented power or authority. So much so, that on two occasions before I was born Momma suffered from deep depression.

Treasures In Heaven

Both of my grandfathers died before I was born. My father's daddy died in 1945 at the age of 45. My two grandmothers died before I was 9 years old. Although I was only 3 or 4 years old, I remember the day Grannie got sick. Momma took me and Evette with her and we played in the waiting room of the hospital. Grannie told her other girls to take care of Momma if something happened to her. I remember Momma crying when she heard that Grannie had died. It was then that Momma started seeking a replacement for her mother's daily talks. She went from church to church trying to find someone who could fill Grannie's shoes. After Grannie died she became depressed and had to seek professional help.

Lean on Me

Momma would send us to church on 39th Street for Sunday School, but was looking to change churches. My oldest brother Eddie went to another church for about a year and 1966 was the first year we attended this church. It had exactly what Momma was looking for: a woman preacher. Momma gravitated toward her with love and respect.

In church I had plenty of friends. We would sit for hours in the basement talking about life in the projects. Slap boxing, which was done with open hands instead of fists, was everything back then. If you could slap box, you would get respect. So I used my hands like Muhammad Ali, throwing quick jabs instead of body punches. Down in the church basement I taught my friends how to fight.

Over the years around the projects my family became known as the family that went to church on Wednesday, Thursday and Friday nights. Momma even went on Saturdays to cook. Then she would go back early the next day for Sunday School and morning service. After service she would stay the rest of the day to supervise and help serve the food because she was head cook for the church.

The pastor had to have complete control over her church members or she found a way to get rid of them. Momma said the pastor preached that she would be on the right side of God's throne, across from Jesus Christ. Adults believed her. I enjoyed the church as a kid because I had so many friends there and most of my first experiences with girls came from the girls at the church. At school I fought and argued with the teachers, students, friends and girls, but at church we were one of the favored families. In church, the Bassette family included four of my six sisters, one of my two older brothers, me and Momma. Momma was beginning to lean on the pastor the way she once leaned on Grannie.

We prayed everyday. Momma would pray with some of the ladies of the church via telephone. I would wake up to her praying and shouting about how good God was to let us live another day. Then she would stretch out on the floor, hollering about how God would bless the chosen people in the church. My four sisters and Eric were buying into all of this but I had other interests in my life and was able to keep a balance.

As time passed, the pastor continued to exercise tight control over what her members believed. She would tell the women in the church they needed to get their husbands in the church or leave those devils. I was never caught up in the seriousness of believing the "chosen church."

The Key to Stopping the Violence

One Man Makes a Difference

Elouise, my fourth oldest sibling, met James in high school in the late '60s. They were married in Chicago. James was drafted by the army and had to do time in Germany. After returning to the states, James and Elouise decided to go out and eat right after leaving the airport. The year was 1970. James still wore his army uniform with his young wife by his side. At the restaurant they visited, Elouise noticed a popular Chicago baseball star. The person was none other than Ernie Banks, the short stop for the Chicago Cubs. Elouise convinced her husband to walk over and just speak to Ernie while he was sitting there eating his meal. James finally walked over in his strict military look and walk. He told Ernie, "Mr. Banks, I wanted to come by your table and say hello." And then James, the young military man, walked away. Ernie told him to wait one minute, and then he asked James where he was stationed. James replied that his tour of duty had just ended. Ernie said, "You look like a bright and intelligent young man. Now what career are you going to go into?" James hesitated and didn't quite know what to say because he didn't have any college training. He thought about trade or auto mechanics, but instead of saying what he wanted to say, he responded "Computers. Yes Mr. Banks, I want to work with computers."

Ernie looked at James and said, "I believe you'll do an excellent job in computers." Then Ernie grabbed a napkin from the table and scribbled a name on it. Ernie handed the napkin to James and said, "Give this man a call and tell him Ernie Banks recommended you." Ernie wished the young man good luck and continued to finish his meal. James put the name in his pocket. Once James was settled in, he did give the man a call. The man hired James at a computer company called IBM. and James started there as a stock boy. He's been there now over 20 years as the IBM machine became the biggest name in the world for computers. Ernie Banks was able to touch one young black man's life by both of them reaching out to each other. Elouise and James have been able to raise their kids and live a wonderful lifestyle because James had the courage to speak and be pleasant. To a small kid that one story stayed with me.

SILENT CRY

Stray Dogs: A Boy's Best Friend

When we weren't riding our bikes, playing games or fighting, we watched shows like "Lassie" and "Rin Tin Tin." None of us had dogs. The only dogs we played with were those stray dogs that ran in packs of 15 or 20. We could spot the leader of a pack. Following the leader were smaller dogs that were easy to catch because they would fall behind or get lost from the pack. Like most boys Ray, Lamar, Kevin, Frankie and me always wanted a dog like the ones we saw on TV. We would beg our parents to get us a dog for Christmas, but since that would never happen, we thought of several ways to catch a stray dog, such as getting one of them to follow us or using food as a lure. If that didn't work, we would chase them until we caught one and put one of Momma's clotheslines around its neck. Sometimes we would chase those dogs for blocks. We would try to avoid the ones with patches of fur missing or with foam on their mouth.

We had all grown up seeing dogs and cats abused. I remember watching along with my sister, Eldora, some older homies burn a cat alive. Shooting dogs was a sport. Over in the Darrow Homes high-rise, I would see dogs or cats hanging from ropes on the upper porches. Ray and me, or whoever had an outside hallway, would try to keep the dogs overnight. One time, when me and the boys had a dog, we got mad because we couldn't get it to do all the tricks we would see the dogs do on TV. So what began as fun turned into abuse.

On this occasion I dared anybody to hang the dog. Nobody wanted to do it, so I threw the rope over a tree branch and started pulling on the rope. The dog started scooting backward. I pulled harder, pulling him off of his front feet. I could hear him struggle for air as I continued to show my boys that it was no big deal. All of a sudden, everyone got a strange look on their faces and instantly I knew someone was looking at me from behind. I turned slowly with the rope still tight in my grasp. It was Daddy. I let the stray dog down slowly and handed the rope to Ray. I smiled to keep from crying and told my boys that I had to go. Daddy had the passenger door open for me. When I got in, he slapped me upside my head, took me home, beat my ass and put me on punishment. Ray did get two dogs and Lamar even had a dog for a short while. I never did have one in my childhood. But I did eventually get my kids a dog.

The Key to Stopping the Violence

High-Rise Terror

Like most fifth graders I enjoyed looking for excitement, sometimes forgetting the danger. The lure always became the unsecured buildings that our teacher and parents had no idea we played in. My classmates and me enjoyed playing in the other 7 floor high-rise projects called the extensions across the street from the school during our lunch break. All the boys in class had one hour to get to the buildings and run through the hallways and play on the elevators. We usually had one problem: when the elevators weren't working.

Our favorite games were getting on the elevators, stopping them between floors or turning off the lights and playing on the roof of the elevators. After the elevator would stop between floors we'd open the doors and leave enough room to squeeze out. We would climb on the top of the elevators, jumping into the inside before it reached the top. We grew accustomed to the writing on the walls and the urine smell of the elevators. We thought that was the way things were supposed to be. Often we pissed in the hallways ourselves.

Once I was making a jump out of the elevator with about 5 feet of room where the elevator should have been. We were playing 5 1/2 floors up in the building. After I jumped, I started to fall backwards. I lost my balance, almost falling into the elevator shaft. Luckily, one of my classmates grabbed me by the coat and pulled me back. I surely would have fallen five floors to my death. But instead we continued to play as though nothing had happened.

I often heard of boys getting caught between the doors with the elevator crushing them or cutting them in half. I never thought much about the danger until I became older and realized how far it would be to fall five stories or how lethal it would be to get crushed.

We spent time talking shit about "juicing" girls in the dark hallways. My friends would tell me how much ass they were getting on the elevators. I knew I wasn't getting none but I'd lie right along with them. The only fear I had was of the gangs that lived in the buildings. They were usually made up of grammar school dropouts, some as young as fourth-graders. They looked like baby convicts. I wasn't so afraid of the smaller ones because I knew I could beat them. But I had to deal with their brothers, cousins and often the whole damn family. One building seemed as if it was full of criminals and gangsters.

SILENT CRY

Bad blood usually stuck together, so we wanted to avoid those buildings. But as shorties we didn't think that all they had to do was walk to the next building where we were, and kick our asses.

One cold winter day the gangsters caught about 10 of us as we headed to play on the elevators. They were my worst nightmare because once they came after you, your life would be miserable. We all started running. I ran the fastest. As we ran toward Ellis Park my friends stopped one by one, panicking or screaming, saying they weren't running because they hadn't done anything. I was so far ahead I could have run across the park toward my building. But I, too, stopped because I didn't do anything, either.

The thugs left everyone else and kept me in the middle of the field. They started kicking my ass and dragged me through the snow. With a face full of snow I remember being near the street as they continued to kick me. A punch landed dead between my eyes. All I could see was white lights and stars. They dragged me back into the building and walked me up seven floors. They said I was going to die. I pleaded for my soul. On the fifth floor, a little boy, probably 4 or 5 years old, was coming down the stairs when one of them said, "This is my little brother." One of the thugs asked him, "Didn't he take your money?" The little boy, not playing along, started crying and they started beating me again. They said I made their little brother cry.

After getting to the 7th floor they decided to kick my ass down each and every floor, some in front punching me in the face while others kicked me from behind. I started pushing forward and screaming at the top of my lungs for someone to help. They beat me until we reached the first floor. Finally a lady opened her door to see what was going on. I crashed through, knocking her out the way. At the same time I begged the lady not to put me out. She saw how bad I had been beaten. She said her son would be coming home and he would walk me home. They stole my hair pick. I was glad not to have to go to school that afternoon. I have never forgotten that experience.

A Mother's Nightmare

Lawrence Green was one of the older teenagers in the backyard. Kevin, his younger brother, was one of my homies who I had known since we were 4 years old. Kevin's mother and

24

The Key to Stopping the Violence

father had lived in the neighborhood for years. We all thought his mother was beautiful. She had long black hair and a pretty smile. Mr. Green had a dark complexion and was on the chubby side.

Kevin and Ray lived in the same building at 3717 S. Vincennes. Lawrence was a teenager when Kevin, Ray and me were young, but he would always look out for his little brother. Lawrence was truly one of the good boys, staying away from the gangs, and trouble with the law. Lawrence wanted Kevin to be tougher because he thought it was easy to intimidate Kevin and make him cry.

A few years after high school, Lawrence got married. Kevin, Ray and me would talk about how Lawrence and his wife never seemed to get along. They had only been married a month. We would go over to their new apartment at 3653 S.King Drive, which was about 3 blocks away. I would always ask Kevin why Lawrence seemed to have changed. He used to be full of fun and laughter when he lived at his mom's apartment. But lately he would barely play with us and always seemed to be irritated.

One summer day in August, 1972, Ray, Kevin and me went over to visit Lawrence at his first-floor apartment. We played with the family cat while his wife, Collette, paced around the house, not saying much. She seemed to be on the anxious side. Kevin asked Lawrence what was wrong a few times until Collette took Lawrence in the back bedroom and they began arguing about us going home. She said she wasn't in the mood for company and that she wasn't a kid and didn't want to entertain kids. We sat there pretending we didn't hear the argument, and continued to play with the cat. Finally around 9:30 p.m., we had some cookies and candy and Lawrence sent us home.

The next day I came out and I looked for Ray and Kevin. When I found them, they were on the front porch. They both had tears in their eyes. They said Lawrence had been killed. According to the police and Lawrence's wife, he left the apartment about 10:50 p.m. to go to Alco Drug Store at 35th and King Dr. The store stayed open around the clock and was a favorite for getting late night snacks. His wife said he went out to get some ice cream and never came back. The police concluded that someone caught Lawrence between 35th and 37th streets, robbed him and dragged him into a car and beat him to death.

SILENT CRY

Then they dropped off his body in the Northern suburbs, with a black plastic bag over his head.

Lawrence was not a drug dealer, and he wasn't into gangbanging. But, because he was a black male, the police figured the crime had to deal with gangs or drugs. This left his family and neighbors in shock. The newspapers covered the story as the "Second south side black found slain in north suburb". At the funeral it was said Lawrence's face had been beaten so bad it was distorted. My parents didn't allow me to go.

Ray, Kevin and me went back to where we last saw him at the apartment. We saw bloodstains near the back door on the back porch, which didn't make any sense if Lawrence wasn't murdered there. We started telling each other his wife killed him because we could sense something was happening the night before. We urged Kevin to confront his mother with what we discovered. We also told Mrs. Grandberry and some of the other grownups in the backyard. No one believed us because we were just eleven year olds. Lawrence's then-widow moved into the projects with Lawrence's family. She tried to keep Kevin away from Ray and me. At the funeral they said she didn't show any signs of remorse and when the police broke the news of Lawrence's death, she didn't seem sad. Her reaction was not normal.

These events prompted the police to reopen the case with more questions about the circumstances surrounding Lawerence's death. They found bloodstains that had been washed off the couch, furniture and walls. There was blood on the porch and leading to the alley. It matched Lawrence's blood type. The police later arrested his wife. After her arrest, she testified to her involvement in the murder of her younger husband. Lawrence was 20 and she was 23. She also named her lover, a CTA bus driver, as her accomplice.

The murder went like this: After Kevin, Ray and me left that night, Lawrence and his wife continued to argue. Lawrence left for a while. While he was gone, his wife called her lover, who came to the apartment and hid in the closet. When Lawrence returned, his wife led him to the couch. Her lover slipped out of the closet with a wooden 2x4 board and hit Lawrence from behind. They put a bag over his head and repeatedly struck Lawrence in the head and face until he was dead. They loaded his body in the trunk of the bus driver's car, cleaned up the apartment and dumped the corpse in a North all white suburb. It

The Key to Stopping the Violence

was an experience that changed my life and affected Ray and Kevin. They later became bitter and hardened about Lawrence's tragic death. We should have received counseling or had an adult discuss the murder with us.

Back in those days, our parents handed out discipline, but they never talked to us to find out what we were thinking. They never knew our thoughts about the murder.

1974, two years later, became the deadliest year in Chicago history with over 900 murders. We were 13 at the time. That murder record still stands to this day.

Caught in the Crossfire

As we got older things in the projects continued to deteriorate. We couldn't see it because we were in it. One night Ray, Frankie, Hank, a friend who lived in the building behind me, and the rest of us had been playing in the backyard when night fell. I always had to go in once the street lights came on. I would get upset because I knew a lot of the fun and action started at night. After school I wasn't allowed to go out until after my homework was completed. By this time some of the boys had already flunked a grade or two. Putting them behind in school.

For me weekends consisted of cleaning up the urine and shit in the hallways near our apartment. Sometimes when I would leave to handle my newspaper route in the morning, the funk in the hall would hit me. The nasty person would wipe their ass with their own underwear and leave them behind, too. Half the day would be gone before I got out to play. Only when I got older did I realize that my parents were teaching me pride and respect for property, as well as protecting me from the streets of Chicago.

One evening the boys talked me into walking across the park to the playground where the sandbox was located. We would use the sandbox to do flips, with a piece of board as a platform. Some of my boys were excellent gymnasts. Night fell and I knew I would get in trouble with Daddy if I didn't get back home soon.

The park was completely quiet, except for us talking and laughing. Suddenly we saw a man running toward us. As he zigzagged across the baseball field, we heard the familiar sound of gun shots. We ran for cover as the bullets hit the dirt behind the man's feet. The others dove headfirst in the sandbox, while Ray and me ran up the sliding board in the tunnel. Looking up, I

27

could see fire coming out of the rifle pointed out of a sixth floor window. I heard someone say, "I'm out of here." It was M.C., who took off across the field -- right in the path of the bullets. I looked up again and everybody else started running, including Ray. They ran as the shots were still ringing through the night. I was left there in the sliding board tunnel. I curled up and said a prayer. Then I took off running across this empty field hoping that the bullets being fired wouldn't hit me.

Once I got across, I met up with the rest of the fellows. We talked about what had happened and how it happened. We would later laugh about how I was the last one at the playground. I knew that we were caught up in the crossfire that could have taken a life. Sadly, as we laughed, I knew something wasn't right about where we were living. I don't remember getting in trouble that night for coming in after the street lights came on.

Fatal Swim

One Sunday back in the summer of '73, Momma and Daddy took Evette and me to the lakefront. It was one of the rare times I remember church being out without an evening service. I ran up and down the rocks by the water, striking fear in Momma because she thought that I would fall in. We lived three blocks from the lake. There were plenty of people out riding bikes and playing in the parks.

As we sat on the rocks looking out at the boats and water, three older boys in their late teens walked within 15 feet of us and started throwing rocks in the water. Their girlfriends came and joined them. The boys went back to their car and returned wearing swim trunks. I saw a "NO SWIMMING" signs painted on the rocks. So I asked, "Daddy, should they be swimming with those signs being there?"

Daddy told all three boys to be careful because swimming was not allowed. They ignored him and one boy jumped in and started to go off in the water while the other two continued to play around with the ladies, and drinking beer.

The first boy got out of the water, and one of the others jumped in. He began to swim away from the shore. Daddy stood up and shouted, "Don't get in trouble because I haven't been swimming in 30 years since I was in the Navy."

The two boys on land laughed as we continued to watch the other one in the water. I kept thinking, "Why would they go out there?" Daddy said the lake could be fine one moment, but

The Key to Stopping the Violence

you could get sucked in at the spots where the water becomes like a small whirlpool. As soon as Daddy stopped explaining how undercurrents worked, the boy in the water starting hollering, "Help me, help me. Oh, my God." Daddy stood up and hollered to the other two to pull him out. They laughed as one boy said, "That's my little brother. He's just showing off. Nothing's wrong with him. He swims like a fish."

By this time the boy was thrashing in the water. Then we watched his head go under water as his hands reached up. Daddy hollered "Damnit, that boy is drowning. Get him out of there."

The two boys frantically dove in the water as we watched the drowning boy sink out of sight. His brother swam to the spot where the boy was drowning, and hollered that he couldn't see him. Then we watched the boy float to the surface with his hands extended over his head. His body looked as if he was asleep. Daddy hollered, "Right behind you, there he is. Reach out, you can grab him."

The boy yelled back, "I can't see him, where?" As quick as his body came up again, it started to go back down as we sat there unable to do anything except watch. The boy's body slipped into the dark dirty lake.

Daddy hollered to the two boys that he would be coming up again a third time. Then almost like clockwork, the boy's body came back into sight. His eyes were closed. The boy reached out and grabbed until he had his hand. We screamed with relief. As the other boy swam toward him, the first boy hollered "Oh my God, I can't hold him."

He couldn't hold on to the boy's hand. We could see the drowning boy submerge until he disappeared out of sight.

The sight of his sinking body was being carved in my mind forever. I was watching a death in progress and couldn't believe my eyes. At this point, the boys in the water were hysterical. Daddy ran across Lake Shore Drive to a pay phone and called the police. People began coming from everywhere as life guards, boats and helicopter rescue teams arrived. The fire and search rescue team finally found the boy's body about an hour later. They pulled him out as people looked on with shock. His body had turned a strange color. The two boys came over and shook Daddy's hand. They thanked him for everything. Momma and Daddy never talked about this incident after it happened. When I got back in the 'hood, the brothers wouldn't believe me because the story sounded made up. Momma, Daddy, Evette and the relatives of this young brother knew differently

SILENT CRY

Coming Out Alive

One summer day in 1974, Ray's dad, Mr. Grandberry, came home with the terror of three men in his voice. "Ray, Ivory get up here." They stopped playing softball with the homies. I already knew what the problem was. Mr. Grandberry had told them they had to get rid of the dogs, Thunder and Max.

Mrs. Grandberry allowed them to have the dogs because she figured that was better than seeing Ray playing with the alley dogs we'd find. We all wanted a dog to grow up with. But like Daddy, Mr. Grandberry played everything by the book and had threatened Ray and Ivory with taking the dogs away. Mr. Grandberry argued it was against the rules in the projects to have them, anyway. Mrs Grandberry wasn't around as he started screaming at Ivory about getting rid of Thunder and Max, both of which had become more than just Ray and Ivory's dogs. They really belonged to all the boys in the backyard. Carl's dog had been shot dead after they let him out to piss. Mark's dog had been killed by a car.

Ray felt his father didn't like anything that made him happy. By this time in Ray's life he had been in and out of the hospital because of an ulcer. Ray had lost a lot of weight and had become very angry. He was constantly worried about his mother.

Mr. Grandberry would beat on Mrs. Grandberry as the boys tried to stop him. That usually led to their beatings. Ray often blamed his ulcers and rage on Mr. Grandberry's actions toward them. That day Ray had been talking about how he wouldn't let his father take his dogs. We talked about what we would do to him until Mr. Grandberry got home and called Ivory in the house. Then as we stood on the first floor we could hear Mr. Grandberry hollering at Ivory about why he hadn't taken the dogs to the dog pound. As he hollered, Ray said they weren't taking his dogs. He started looking as though he would cry. Kids were coming from everywhere saying, "Ray, go up and help your brother." Or "Your father ain't shit. He's going to make soap out of your dogs."

We all got behind Ray and started going up the hallway to the second floor porch. Ray carried a stick. We were going to stop this mean man once and for all. As we walked up on the porch Ray looked through the screen door and saw Ivory standing there with Mr. Grandberry calling him everything but

The Key to Stopping the Violence

the son of God. Mr. Grandberry looked from the living room and saw all of these faces staring at him through the screen door. Ray hollered out "You're not taking my dogs." His father barreled toward the door yelling, "Who in the hell are you talking to?" Ray let out a loud scream. We hesitated for a few seconds not knowing what to do. I hollered, "Run, he's coming." All the kids took off running toward the hallway door. Mr. Grandberry hit the door like a bat out of hell with his arms reaching for Ray. Ray stayed out of his grasp. Because Ray kept stumbling over so many people Mr. Grandberry caught him at the bottom of the stairs. I felt like there was nothing I could do for my friend, so I did what everybody else did -- I went to the door to listen.

Ray had been terrified of his father his entire life. After things calmed down Mr. Grandberry took the dogs to a lady on 47th and Drexel. Later that day Ray had a plan. We were to go to this lady's house to steal Thunder and Max and then we'd take them to Kevin Green's house out further south. So we began our journey to retrieve Thunder and Max. Just me and my boy against the world.

We walked about seven blocks south to 39th Street through the Darrow Homes projects, crossed 40th Street until we came to another section of the projects on 43rd and Cottage. We had already been walking for what seemed about an hour and a half, not anticipating problems along the way. When we got toward the front of the projects, a brother standing in the courtway hollered, "Hey cuz, do you have a cigarette I can get from you?"

I shouted back, "Sorry cuz not here."

As we continued to walk, the brother called out to us again. "Don't I know you MF's from somewhere?"

I looked at Ray. The guy started coming our way. I whispered to Ray to run on the count of three. We took off running around the projects toward a residential area a few blocks away. We ran through an alley and stopped because we figured we had outrun him. We continued on our journey to get Thunder and Max when about 40 yards away we saw three men running our way. "Don't that look like the same nigger from the building?" I asked Ray. "That's him."

One dude had a chain and the other two had sticks. We took off running in the opposite direction but to our surprise at the other end of the block was about six other thugs running at us with chains and bricks. Everyone in the projects knew you

31

never crossed the lines of someone else's turf. In our quest to save Ray's dogs, we had lost sight of the golden rule of how to survive in the low end.

I told Ray to run toward the three boys, figuring that if we had to fight, fighting three thugs sounded much better than fighting six. As we ran toward them we cut into the vacant lot. This wasn't the first time I had been chased and I knew I had to help Ray keep up with me because he had lost a lot of speed from that ulcer. We ran across streets and dodged through people and parked cars. I spotted a fence and I told Ray to jump over. There was a dog in the yard and I figured it was a Rottweiler or a Doberman and those thugs wouldn't come after us. It did stop them long enough for us to knock on the glass door. An old lady answered and we frantically told her that they were after us and wanted to beat us up. She asked where we were from and we told her Ida B. Wells projects. This lady let us into her house and she made us undo our braids, picking out our afros; she thought that could have been the problem.

I wouldn't let the lady call my house and neither did Ray. She said we could wait until her son got home and then he could take us home. We sat on the porch where people were gathered around saying that we would eventually have to come off of the porch and that we were going to get our asses kicked. Girls in the neighborhood said we could leave the porch because the dudes were gone. But we saw them peeping around the corner. The lady's son did come home and we asked him to drop us off two blocks from the backyard at 39th and Vincennes to make sure our parents didn't see us in a stranger's car.

We were only 13 years old and about to enter our last year of grammar school. We realized as we went back into our 'hood that journey could have cost us our lives.

The dogs did make it back because Mr. Grandberry eventually left. Ray and me often reflected on that day as being one of the closest calls in our lifetimes.

Artis Gilmore, Chicago Bulls

"Hey man, Big Artis Gilmore from the Bulls is down at the Parham's backyard!" was the call all us kids heard one summer day down in the projects. As everybody dropped what they were doing, Ray and me joined the pack of kids running to see this basketball giant we had only seen on TV. There must

The Key to Stopping the Violence

have been hundreds of brothers and sisters already around waiting to see him for themselves.

We all crowded at the Parham's family screen door trying to peep in before what they called the main event. Finally this 7 foot giant with a 3 foot afro and beard came walking to the asphalt basketball court in the Darrow Homes projects. He was accompanied by some of the older Parham brothers. The Parhams had been in Ida B. Wells as long as my family and were known throughout the projects for their basketball talent. The Parhams had enough basketball players in the family to play against anyone in the projects and win. Several of them played college ball and some played semi-pro. We knew it was just a matter of time before one made it to the big time.

Artis had come down to play some of the brothers in the 'hood in a pick up game. The brothers Artis was playing against were straight up thugs and gangsters. The crowd and the thugs seemed to be more energized when the thugs were brutalizing Artis with elbows and forearms to the chest. They were making a name for themselves by trying to be the one who stopped Artis from slam dunking on them. There was plenty of shit being talked on the court and in the crowd as men hollered out to Artis that the best black athletes would never get to him because they were in jail or already dead.

During the game, Artis looked over at his car and noticed he had left his window down. Some kids were in his car, jumping on the seats, rummaging through his glove box and blowing the horn. He stopped the game, as they scrambled to get out. He caught one shorty with his garage door opener. He snatched it and rolled up his window and locked the doors.

Artis stood around as Ray and I moved close enough to get a good look at his thighs. We were pulling on his leg with at least another 100 kids, asking for money. Ray and me started tugging at his shorts real hard and hitting Artis with our elbows. There were so many kids around him we knew he couldn't tell who it was.

We could see Artis was totally out of control with all these kids and adults asking for money. He finally made his way over to the ice cream truck. He bought lots of ice cream and told the ice cream man to throw it out to the hostile crowd. Black folks young and old were punching and throwing down to get that ice cream. Artis left the scene but did continue to make it down to the projects for periodic visits.

SILENT CRY

One day, about 20 years later, I had a chance to meet Artis Gilmore at a party at the Cotton Club on the South Side of Chicago. "Hey Artis, I remember when you used to come down to the projects when I was a kid," I said. One of Artis' hands wrapped around my entire neck. "You're lying and I don't like people that lie." I was standing there saying "Oh shit!" "Artis, you know the Parham family. You would visit and buy ice cream for all us kids."

"You're right, I'm good friends with the Parhams and I always gave to help people," he remembered.

Eat and Run

Whenever Ray and me got bored we would catch the bus and head downtown to find some action and fun. To this day when I see little shorties downtown asking for money or just running around having a good time, it always reminds me of the boys and me.

One rainy day, when Ray and me just wanted to hang, we asked Hank, to walk to 35th Street by the Lake Meadows Shopping Center to wait for the Cottage Grove CTA bus to take us to the Loop. When people got off the back door, we'd sneak on. Once downtown, we would go to Sears. We would go to the TV section and play with the controls until one of the salesman chased us away. We also hit the candy area in the store, filling our pockets with candy while we moved around. Then it was on to Goldblatt's, where Hank would steal hats and shirts.

After working up an appetite, we walked up and down State Street and Michigan Avenue to find a restaurant. We found a pizza place and stood at the window watching all the white people eat. Hungry, we decided to go in, and surprisingly the waiter escorted us to a table. "I'll have a large pizza," I said as we laughed among ourselves, knowing our intentions. Fifteen minutes later the pizza arrived and our eyes bulged over its size. We ate that pizza like it was the first food we had in a long time.

"How are we going to pay for this?" I asked the fellows. Just then Ray says, "Man, I gotta use the bathroom." He walked toward the front of the restaurant. The next thing I knew Ray was standing outside on the street, licking his tongue out at us. Hank hadn't noticed Ray yet, so I said to Hank, "I'm gonna go see what's taking Ray so long." Then I walked out and we both were standing, free, shaking our butts and licking out our tongues at Hank to get his attention. He finally looked up and realized he

The Key to Stopping the Violence

was alone, soon to face the check. Hank broke for the door but the white manager caught him and shouted for security to go after us.

Ray and me took off through the crowded streets of downtown Chicago, laughing, confident they would never catch us. We hopped a bus back to the projects, on the way wondering what lie Hank was using to get out of the jam. A few hours later, Hank came home. He gave them so many fake names and telephone numbers that they finally let him go.

In those days Hank always seemed to owe Ray favors. Sometimes that meant stealing a hat for Ray from Goldblatts. A couple of days later Ray and me found a loaded gun in the sewer. We spent the next two days showing off our new "toy." We showed it to some of the older homies, and one of them tried to take it. The gun had two bullets as Ray and me played keep away by throwing it back and forth. That night after I went in, Ray showed it to everybody in the hood. They started acting crazy with it and by the next morning one of them had fired the gun in the direction of a man walking through the park.

At the time they thought they shot somebody but we never heard of anybody being wounded. The next night they went to the lakefront and tried to steal a bike. A second bullet was fired in the air. I never saw the gun again. I'm glad no one was hurt from that stupid experience. In '94 Hank is in jail for an alleged murder. Although mantaining his innocence, his eligibility for porale is not do until after the year 2002.

The Paper Man

Gip was a legend because he kept boys off the street, working in an old building at 36th and Cottage Grove that he converted into the paper branch. He was a short man, about 5'9" with powerful legs and a fairly large stomach. He had a gun on each hip and a pistol on his lower leg. He carried so much money that his pockets bulged as he walked. His head was shaved bald and the sun beamed on his light brown complexion. All of us kids ran around him when we saw this great figure walking up the sidewalk toward my building. He could hardly take a step without all of the adults stopping him to speak.

Gip was in charge of one of the largest newspaper home delivery services in Chicago. When my brother, Eric started his job I helped him deliver his 150 plus papers a day. I was no more than 9 years old and we would get up at 5:30 in the

SILENT CRY

morning to deliver the *Sun-Times* in the projects. Eric delivered to half of the courtways and I delivered the other half. He paid me $3 a week and he made $20.

We would walk through the cold at 6:00 a.m. across Ellis Park to 36th and Cottage Grove. By the time we arrived, Gip had already opened up and let the alley dogs out for their piss. Sometimes Gip's brother, who was a wino, stayed there or some other homeless person found refuge at the branch. Gip would get the wood stove burning to heat the cold branch. Each paper boy had his own papers stacked in wooden stalls. We all had an account book with each account on a large ring. Selling the *Sun-Times* was a tradition in my family dating back to when Eddie, my oldest brother, worked for Gip as a kid.

To work for Gip was an honor because he was a father for boys who didn't have one and a brother to others. Gip was never approached the wrong way by anyone, in part because of the two six shooters on his hips. If your route was to far too push a buggy, you had to be driven around your route. That was done by one of the many unemployed winos who constantly hung around the paper branch with their cars. Cliff, a wino who lived around the corner, was a skinny, tall, light-skinned man who was probably in his 30s but looked 50 or 60. His cars would always be missing a side window or two, and they were covered with plastic. His alley dogs would shit in the car, so we would throw newspaper over the mess, then jump in.

Most of Cliff's days were spent with the hood of his car up and him trying to fix something. Us boys never understood why his cars would never exceed 25 miles an hour. We would putt-putt along and usually have to get out and walk because the car would stall. Cliff and the rest of the winos would sit under a tree drinking and talk about how much sex they were getting. The winos always referred to them as ugly bitches. Sometimes they would come by the branch. It was shameful how ugly these ladies were. Most of them were prostitutes with teeth missing or they had huge, noticeable scars where they had been abused. They would come around to ask the winos for money, and even though the winos were broke it made them feel important to holler and curse at the women. Then the winos would run to Gip and ask for an advance in pay, which they spent on the women and wine. Gip would tell the winos to keep those nasty hoes away from the paperboys and the branch.

By 7th grade I was given my own route next to my brothers. I delivered before school, and on Wednesday, Thursday

The Key to Stopping the Violence

and Friday night I collected from my customers. I would usually take Ray with me to collect. Ray and I would have fun with customers letting us in their apartments, so we got to know different people. We often pretended to be brothers, although I was taller than him. The older people would tell us how nice we were and gave us tips for great service. Then there were certain customers who never paid on time. They pretended to be broke, and some of them had such nasty houses we didn't want to go back. That was the group of people that usually got their Aid checks (ADC) on the 3rd and 15th of the month. Some of my homies hated me being their paperboy, because I knew whose Mommas' had Food Stamps. We were poor, but you didn't want yo momma gettin no Aid check. Homies would sig on your family for days. I learned from Eric to take pride in getting all the money from each customer. I would collect more than $150 a week, then return the upfront cash that Gip had given us in quarters, dimes nickels and dollars to make change for the customers.

Gip had a photographic memory and kept precise records. He knew each paperboy and what he owed. If you were short, it came out of your paycheck. We all learned how to work, count money and hustle. The paper branch became a home away from home. Sometimes Ray and me played around too much and irritated the older people. Gip would take his guns out of the holsters and sit them on his big desk. If he thought someone was cheating him or if a stranger walked in off the street, Gip was quick to point those big guns in your direction. No one ever thought about robbing him. Gip didn't tolerate thieves. He did fire a shot between me and Ray's head one day to stop us from playing around; scaring the hell out of us.

Across from my route was the first McDonald's in the low end on 39th Street. It was also the only one I've ever seen closed and torn down. The area was so bad we knew that we were going to get robbed after we bought our food. After making collections, Ray and me would go to the backyard to get the homies so we could go back to McDonald's in a group of six or seven for protection.

But after we came out they would steal our food anyway. You would see thugs peeping around the side of the McDonald's. A thug would kill you over a hamburger sandwich. Their strategy was to pull you behind the store, rob you and kick your ass. Some of the boys from the Darrow Homes high-rise would do anything to get our food but they would never come to our backyard. We knew going in we had four blocks to make it back from McDonald's, which was on neutral turf. We would put the food under our arms like footballs then count to three and burst out the McDonald's door at the same time. If we made it through the first level of thugs, we had to make it through the second set in our own projects. Each block was full with thugs who wanted to take your food or beg you out of it. With my speed I never thought twice about being the one caught. But if Ray was caught I knew I had to stop to fight because we never let each other fight alone. We may have fought each other, but we never let other people fight us. They later closed the McDonald's because of burglaries and robberies.

Soon it was Ray's turn to get a paper route. I remember the day Mrs. Grandberry walked to the branch to meet Gip. Gip knew Ray because he was always at the branch with me. Ray was excited to finally get his own paper route, but he was always afraid of something happening because he covered the building where Lawrence Green was killed. Ray constantly worried about everything. I helped him with his route and he helped me with mine.

As we got older it became more dangerous because certain people knew we were paperboys and wouldn't hesitate to try to rob us. One night we took Wesley Chamberlain (Pro-Baseball, Boston Red Sox) with us on Ray's collection route. That's when some grammer school dropouts wanted to rob us. They started following us, so we ran to one of Ray's customer's apartment on 36th and King Dr. After several minutes, we thought the thugs had left, so we continued collecting. When we got to the next account, They came running behind us. We left Wesley to block the hallway door and I told Ray to knock on his customer's door. I begged the customer to let us go through their back door and from there Ray and me ran across the Madden Park baseball field to our backyard, leaving Wesley behind to find his own way back. We knew that because he was younger and had no money, the thugs wouldn't bother him. The next day Gip sent one of the older boys with Ray to collect.

Running For Glory

Roy Parker was one of the greatest running backs to come out of the Chicago Public League -- or anywhere else for that matter. The star halfback for the Wendell Phillips High School Wildcats, he was selected to the 24th annual high school All

The Key to Stopping the Violence

American football team. Playing for the Wildcats from 1973-75, Roy totaled approximately 3,000 yards and 39 touchdowns in two seasons. He was one of the best running backs in the city and country. Roy ran a 4.3 in the 40-yard dash and by 1975 was considered the best football player in Illinois. Coming out of high school he was the second most heavily recruited running back behind future NFL Hall of Famer Tony Dorsett, who played for the Dallas Cowboys. I, along with countless others, considered Roy a mentor, friend and role model.

Fortunately, only being in 8th grade, I was selected to go to Wendell Phillips High School for a special program in advanced math and science. I would do my paper route and then head to the high school. Then I would walk back four blocks north to grammar school. I would see Roy walking to school with his equipment and I would volunteer to carry his football helmet and pads. I soon became obsessed with carrying his equipment and listening to him talk about how many colleges were recruiting him. He treated me like a younger brother. I eventually got tired of walking to Wendell Phillips High School, and with no parental encouragement, I dropped out of the advanced math and science program.

That fall Roy was ready to go to college. He had more than 1,500 colleges after him, and he chose Eastern Illinois University. Although I didn't know anything about Division I and Division II college football programs, as a curious 13-year-old I wondered why he chose Eastern. It was the same school my brother, Eric was going to. Before Roy went to Eastern he got married to a girl from the extensions (high-rise). She was only a sophomore in high school, and attended Lindblom. The next thing I knew people were saying Roy was back home. I remember running up to him with Ray, Lamar and some other guys. Roy told me the unthinkable: He quit the team and came home. I couldn't understand why. Later he came back to the paper branch as captain and that's when he told me the reason. Roy said he went to Eastern because it was close to home, only 2 hours away, and that the school promised him that he would start his freshman year. The president of the university had promised Roy that if there ever was a problem, Roy could call him. During his first college game, Roy ran an 80 yd touchdown. The coach wouldn't let Roy start in the second game. So Roy decided to go to the president's house. Opening the door, the president said he didn't know who he was.

SILENT CRY

Pride stepped in and Roy decided to leave football forever. At about the same time Gip became ill and Roy took over the branch. But the *Sun-Times* home delivery dropped off. Roy would say he would never play football again because he accomplished all his athletic goals. Four years later, Roy showed me letters from professional teams and college programs that still wanted him to play. He worked for the phone company for a while until Roy let the streets of the low end take over. Roy's luck started going from bad to worse, and he never got back to his dream.

Manchild

The thing that I enjoyed most about the projects, was that there were always plenty of things to do. The girls usually played hand ball or jumped double dutch, while boys played football and baseball. On some days, Mr. and Mrs. Lewis, Lamar's parents would play in a game of soft ball with us. There were always enough homies out in the summer to get a good 16" softball game going. Since there were no organized leagues around the area, each backyard formed its own team, with the coach being one of the older players. I spent many hours with Lamar and his brother Rocky, Ray and his older brother Ivory, Wes Chamberlain, and his three older brothers, Larry, Juan, and T. C.,along with my older brother Eric, and all the rest making teams up to play against other teams and backyards. We would go to the park to play hardball or have good games right in the backyard with 16" softballs.

Dudes were always stylish when it came to softball. One of our team's biggest rivals was the Comets, who lived across 37th Place. Their team was headed by Curtis. As our players, like Eric, Rocky and T.C., got older and started playing other sports, Lamar, Ray, and me joined the Comets and we played the Parham's teams on Cottage Grove and the Red Sox with Ricky Wright and Roy Polk from the extensions. We would have classic games at Madden Park or Ellis Park.

Curtis was a very smart but intense person. Most of us were 13 to 16 years old, while he was about 17 and treated us like his little brothers. There was always some resentment or conflict on the team because Lamar, Ray and me were not from the same backyard as the other players. But Curtis would always find a way to teach us discipline and teamwork. Curtis was a star player

The Key to Stopping the Violence

in High school, where he played third base and sometimes pitched.

As we grew older Curtis really came to like Ray and me. He said he liked the way we hustled as paperboys and how Ray and me always looked out for each other. I can't say he felt the same about Lamar, maybe because Lamar ate so much. Ray sat on the bench but Curtis would put him in to pinch hit.

Curtis started trying to get us into tournaments in other areas like Washington Park and some West Side parks. He would always make sure our parents knew where we were. Even though he lived in the backyard across the street from us, we never saw or heard much about his parents. One brother said his parents had died in some kind of accident, which left Curtis and his older brother living in the projects alone. Curtis was like a grown man to us, and it was only when I was older that I understood he was a teenager trying to make a difference.

The things I remember most about the Comets baseball team was the practices Curtis put us through. He would have us running the bases and taking hitting practice. He showed us how to steal bases and how to slide properly. He taught the outfielders how to hit the cutoff man. Being a first basemen, I would have to run to the mound if the ball was hit to center or right field. Curtis was a baseball wonderboy and he made us do everything at full speed. Lamar was not his favorite because he didn't show the same interest as Ray and me, Lamar was thinking more about football. Ray, Lamar and me would sit in the playground and talk about how we would be sports heroes and make it out of the projects. Ray would tell me we would write a book because nobody would believe all the adventures we had. The book would be called "From Ghetto to Glory" he'd always say.

Curtis would practice us so much because we were never in any tournaments. Practice became a way for Curtis to keep us together. Curtis called the team together one day and said we were going to play some white boys in an all star game. He said we had to go down to 39th Street west through Mayor Daley's neighborhood, which was all white. Curtis said he was only taking five players and we all had to bring our own gloves, bats and helmets. All of our lives had been spent in the hood. Now we were going to a foreign area. Curtis said the area was very racist and we all had to sit together on the CTA bus with bottles and knives in our baseball bags. Curtis said that this was the area where Dr. Martin Luther King Jr. was spit on and thrown bricks at during a Civil Rights march. "Once we pass 39th and State street, we are entering Daley's territory and all the honkies are racist," Curtis warned us.

We rode the bus all huddled in the back, packing knives, bottles and bats as weapons, waiting for some white people to attack. I remember being paranoid because Curtis talked about how good the white boys could play because the white man had the best coaching and baseball fields. He reminded us that our baseball diamonds were full of glass and rocks but we had to use that to beat them on the field.

When we got there the first thing I noticed was their uniforms. We always had T-shirts because we couldn't afford uniforms. Their parks looked as nice and well kept as the professional parks. We started the game as the visiting team. I batted third in the order and hit a single, then stole second base. With two outs, I tried to steal third but got a late jump. Curtis had taught us to be physical and if someone blocked the base, knock them out of the way, and knock the ball out of the opponent's glove. While running to third base I saw that the white boy had the ball at least three steps before I got there, so I laid a forearm into him, knocking him to the ground. As he got up his face turned red and he charged toward me yelling, "Fuck you asshole." The benches cleared, but no punches were thrown. I went back to the dugout with my big Jose Cardinal(Chicago Cubs) afro hanging from under my cap. Curtis said I could have started a race war; he took me out of the game. Ray and Lamar did play but we lost the game and returned to the low end with out another incident.

We had another tournament to play in and Curtis still had it out for Lamar, so Lamar went back to sleep, not making it to the game. Ray had to finish his paper route, so he was going to be late. I got there around 10:15 a.m. Curtis took me in the bushes, slapped me around and punched me in the face. "The only reason I did that to your ass is because we didn't have nine men here at 10:00, so we had to forfeit the game." He apologized as I stood there with a tight face from being used as a punching bag.

Like most of the older guys Curtis would always smoke reefer. I always wondered where he got money to buy food for us or baseballs until we realized he sold reefer to take care of himself. Seeing him smoke never affected Ray, Lamar and me because almost everybody did it. Selling joints was the No. 1 way for teenage boys to make money. Everyone knew the Bassettes didn't smoke reefer. I only thought about two things: baseball and football. Ray loved Curtis because he showed him the support and belief he needed to play baseball.

The Key to Stopping the Violence

Long Ride Home

Curtis would have the Comets practicing at Washington Park on 55th Street instead of Madden Park on 37th Street. He was trying to get us more organized and competitive. I had never seen black kids with uniforms until we started going to Washington Park. We would walk from 37th and Vincennes to 37th and King Drive and then wait for a jitney (a cab that ran up and down King Drive) for 20 cents. Lulu, a heavy set lady who always drove new Cadillacs, was a jitney driver who lived in our backyard. She was the first person I ever saw with a phone in her car. I don't think it worked, but she had a big phone in the back window. LuLu was the auntie of Louis Clayton, who played football with Roy Parker at Wendell Phillips High School

Ray and me would ride the jitney down to Washington Park with our baseball gloves and bats. I had just bought a new 10-speed bike for $100 with money I made as a paperboy. This was the first big purchase I had ever made with my own money. I remember going down to Montgomery Ward with Momma and Eric to pick out the bike and being so frantic that I wanted the floor model because it was the last one they had in stock. I added two mirrors and a bike pump with a tool bag that hung off the seat. Eric locked up his bike outside of Ward's. After I bought my bike, we rode home along the bike path near Lake Michigan. Momma took the bus back to the South Side. We were in 8th grade and 10 speeds were taking the place of the banana seat polo bikes. We went from riding in packs and sliding through dirt on concrete to going for longer rides on the lakefront.

Ray's mother had already gotten him a 10 speed, but Ray would rather ride the old polos we put together from old bike frames that we'd find on the street. I had seen a number of 10 speeds and mini-bikes taken over the years. Being in the wrong place at the wrong time could always mean your bike wouldn't be yours anymore.

Curtis called a practice at Washington Park one evening and some of the fellas said they were going to ride their bikes down to the park about 25 blocks away. I rode with them. Ricky Wright decided to ride his bike to the park, too. If I was going to go with my prize possession, I needed to be with people who were willing to fight, if necessary. Ricky was not afraid of much. I knew a nice new bike would be tempting for a lot of people, especially if the bigger dudes saw a little shorty on it. We went down to Washington Park with no problem and found all the homies for practice.

After practice, Rick and I headed home as the sun was setting. As we got close to home Ricky wanted to stop at the 534 building to visit some of our friends in the high-rise extensions. I was still only allowed out after dark when I was on my paper route or at church, so I told Ricky I had to go. I decided to take a short cut through the building's backyards instead of staying on 36th Street. This way I could made it home a few minutes early. I was about 5 minutes from my building and just before I crossed the street to my backyard my bike pump and baseball glove fell under my bike. I peddled for another 15 or so feet before stopping and turning around. I had a strange feeling that said, "Leave them." But I peddled back anyway and as I bent over and picked up my stuff I heard some footsteps as two men came running around the corner. One of them stopped in front of me and grabbed the handle bars. The other man circled around and grabbed the back seat. The one in the front said, "Hey little man, this is a nice bike. You gone be giving it up today." I wasn't getting off. The man behind me said, "If you don't get up I'm gonna knock yo fucking' face off." I grabbed the handle bars as my body language said, "You have to take it because I ain't giving it up. The man in the front said, "I see we have a crazy motherfucker on our hands." Out of nowhere came a right fist that crashed into my jaw. Then a second fist forced its way past my lips and into my mouth. I bit his hand and tried to rip off his fingers as he screamed. The one in the front was pulling the bike and the one in the back tried to put me in a choke hold. All I could do was hold on to the bike for dear life. I began to shout for help. The one in the back was shouting to the one in the front that this little son of a bitch is tougher than he thought. Finally they dragged me off the bike, but I grabbed a nearby tree with one arm. Blood was rushing down my chin from a busted lip and my face was tight from the punches. I didn't let the bike go. No one was in sight.

During the struggle my prized possession was being torn up. Finally, they overpowered me and got the bike. Then the one in front jumped in front of the bike while the other man had me around the neck. I threw an elbow to his stomach to escape. The other man was trying to peddle away but couldn't because he had on a pair of 3' inch platform shoes. That gave me a chance to catch him before he could get any momentum. I grabbed the back tire and lifted the bike, almost throwing him head first. As I was

The Key to Stopping the Violence

pulling the bike I saw my friend's little brother on a first-floor porch. I shouted for him to get his brother or mother. He was only 3 years old, so he sat there not knowing what to do. Then a lady I knew, Ms. Ratcliffe opened the door and I pulled the bike -- and the two thugs -- toward her. They came in and she tried to calm everybody down. We were all shouting at each other. My face was full of blood and my shirt was bloody. I said they were trying to steal my bike. They told her I stole it from their little brother and they were trying to get it back. So I told her I lived across the street and I knew her sons. She looked at me and knew I was telling the truth, and said, "Let's call the police and let them see who's right or wrong." She started to call the police, and as I sat down at the table she turned around to ask them their names. They opened the back door and ran. Mrs. Ratcliffe asked me if I wanted the police. "No, I just want to get home," I answered.

My new 10 speed was all scrapped. The mirrors were broken and the spokes were bent. I thanked her for what she had done and she sent me on my way through the night. Once home Momma and Eric were waiting for me and I told them what happened. They prayed for me but the incident gave Eric another reason to tell Momma why she shouldn't let me go anywhere by myself. The next morning I brought the bike down the stairs and it looked even worse in the daylight. I was retaping the handle bars when Ray rode around the corner on his 10 speed. He did what any good friend would do: try to cheer me up. He laughed at the story as I showed him how I had fought these two guys to a standstill. Since we lived three blocks from the lake, we decided to ride from 39th Street and the lakefront to the museum at 57th street. I knew I couldn't ride fast because Ray was still recovering from his ulcer and didn't have the power to keep up.

We decided to head toward the 39th Street bike path past the El Rukn Temple. Ray continued to joke about the two thugs who tried to take my bike. He said that story had to be in our book, "From Ghetto to Glory." As we approached the Hyde Park neighborhood, I told Ray I wasn't going to ever give up my bike. Ray was laughing, talking about how my bike still had speed even though it had been damaged. I was telling Ray to put his bike in first gear and ride up to the top of the hill ahead so he could ride down as fast as he could. Because of his weakness, Ray only made it up halfway, then he stopped. I hollered down to him to try to make it up but he had already gotten off and started walking. As Ray continued to walk, I continued to tease him

45

about not making it all the way up, as I stood at the top of the hill, near the bridge. I noticed two guys riding one bike. A black dude on the handlebars and a white peddling. Ray was still not even halfway up the hill. Out of nowhere the black dude jumped off the handlebars and grabbed me from the back. He said he wanted my bike. The first thing I thought about was to get Ray out of there. I knew if those two men couldn't get my bike the night before, I wasn't giving it up to no punks from Hyde Park. I hollered to Ray to get out of here. He looked up and turned his bike around and started back downhill, the black dude told me to get off the bike. I said, "Fuck you. If you want it, take it." The white boy hadn't said anything yet. The black dude decided to take a swing from behind and hit me in the mouth, just like the man did the previous night. Like the last episode, I tried to bite his damm fingers off. He was screaming for his life when the white boy decided it was time to leave. He begged his accomplice to leave and he finally let the bike go. As I was speeding away down the bike path I turned around and yelled, "Yo Momma's a ho". They vowed to catch me again one day.

Ray had a pretty big headstart. As I scanned the bike path, I couldn't see him. Then I looked toward the expressway and there was Ray riding on the emergency ramp like the wicked witch from the "Wizard of Oz." I tried hollering but he was so far away and the noise from the cars drowned me out. So I cut across the grass and angled in front of him. We made eye contact and I told him to continue to 37th Street. When we got to 39th Street I told him how I got away. I teased him by saying they would have had my bike and anything else they wanted by the time he got back to 37th Street for help. We laughed about this story for years to come. Ray and I would later sit around and tell Mrs. Grandberry. She loved to hear the story and I loved to tell it.

Cold Cool Sick Crazy Curtis

In spring of 1975, Curtis's senior year, something happened to him. The word was that   one of the school's all-time great baseball and football players, was selected to play third base. That left Curtis on the bench, which was not where Curtis wanted to see himself. He and the coaches had a falling out and not only did Curtis quit the team, but he also dropped out of school. That fall, as I was entering Lindblom High School, we heard that Curtis had been put into a mental institution, suffering from a

The Key to Stopping the Violence

nervous breakdown. We knew that all Curtis had was baseball and the Comets. That was the crutch he leaned on. We hadn't heard much more about Curtis until toward the winter of my freshman year when out of nowhere Curtis knocked on Ray's door. Curtis asked Ray, Lamar and me to come outside into the cold dark hallway. He had a strange look on his face, especially his eyes as they seemed to bulge out of his head. Curtis got real close in our faces and started telling us how they had bullshitted him and how he was supposed to be the main man on his high school baseball team. His intensity heightened as spit started hitting us in the face from the force of his words. He started telling us he was Satan and that he had met death and not even death would take him because he was already dead and that this life didn't mean anything to him. Curtis pulled out a black pool ball and said it was used to kill white people. He held the ball in his hand to show us how he hit white people in the temple. We asked Curtis what did all this mean as he shouted, "Don't you understand. My name is Ice Cold Cool Slick Crazy Curtis." He hollered it out again: "I'm the motherfuckin' Ice Cold Cool Slick Crazy Curtis," his words rang through the dark, cold drafty, hallway. As he continued his rampage he pulled the scarf back from his neck and there was a scar from his right ear across his neck and almost to his other ear. We jumped back in shock. Curtis said the devil won't even take his soul. He had tried to take his life and give it to the devil because there wasn't anything to live for. Ray's emotions were thrown for a loop because he knew Curtis was suppose to play professonal baseball. Plus Ray saw all of our heros fall one by one. I later heard Curtis went back and forth to the mental institution. Like millions of others, Curtis's potential was never realized or recognized. He thought sports was the only way out of the low end.

My Brother's Keeper

Martin and Damen lived at 38th and Cottage. They would come down to our backyard. People came from all around to play in our backyard because we had a perfect baseball field. We painted the bases on the concrete and a batter's box and foul line alongside the wall. First base was directly by the tree in front of my building. Second base was on the other side of the baby swings. Third base was toward Frankie's house, with the painted foul line going up the side of his building. Home plate was painted on the ground with Ray's building behind it. Left field

47

was beyond the trees and Hank's building was the left field wall. We pretended that our backyard was Wrigley Field. The porches on the second floor was where the bleachers were, and people would watch. The banister was our dugout. We played 16" soft and rubber ball until we couldn't see the ball anymore because of darkness.

Martin was the youngest brother and Damen was the oldest. Martin was quiet and would come down to the backyard to visit Lamar's sister. I knew them before they started coming down because I was their paperboy. Damen and Martin didn't look alike; Martin had a darker complexion and Damen was light skinned. Martin was taller than Damen. They would always come down together and leave together. One day we heard that Martin had killed Damen over a piece of chicken. It was said that it started as a regular fight between two brothers then escalated when Martin took the chicken from Damen and ate it. Martin picked up a knife from the kitchen table and killed him. I wanted to see if it was true. It was. Damen was dead and Martin was placed in a juvenile home. But within a year, he was back in the neighborhood. He played ball with us and nobody mentioned what happened. It just became another thing that happened at the low end.

Comiskey Park: Bat Day

Growing up in the low end of Chicago meant we were within walking distance of Comiskey Park, home of the Chicago White Sox. However, all of us grew up Cub fans, admiring Ernie Banks, Billy Williams, Ron Santo, Don Kessinger, Randy Hundley, Fergie Jenkins, Glen Beckert, Ken Holtzman and coach Leo Durocher. We followed the '69 cubs when they lost the pennant race to Tom Seaver and the New York Mets. Everybody wanted to be baseball players in the early '70s, when the Cubs added players like Jose Cardinal, all the homies wanted that big afro. I wanted to be Ernie Banks, hitting that 500th home run in Wrigley Field. We would wear Cubs hats and made our backyard into Wrigley Field. Ray's dream had always been to be a major league player. Sundays after church, I couldn't wait to get home to the backyard, where a game was taking place, either a 16" softball or rubber ball game. Since Eric and I always got home after 2:30, we got to the games late. I would practically race from church through the Darrow Homes projects to play in those games. They were willing to put someone else out of the game if

The Key to Stopping the Violence

you were a better player because everyone wanted the best people on the field. We occasionally broke the neighbors' windows with the baseballs. The games kept us out of serious trouble. Every now and then gangbangers would run through the middle of our games with shotguns and other objects of destruction. We would all scatter in different directions, taking cover while the police and security tracked through looking for the men. Those events were so common we would be back playing as though nothing happened within minutes. Athletic skills meant a lot because some of the dudes with the best athletic skills also ran others parts of the community.

Baseball was not allowed because they said it could result in broken windows. But we played anyway. Security guards would walk around and patrol like police officers to enforce the rules. For years, they would send us in a frenzy as we tried to gather our bats and balls, running from them. If they did take your bat they were allowed to keep it until your parents came to the main office and picked it up. We knew our parents wouldn't go through the hassle of going to pick up a bat or glove, so the best thing was not to get caught.

As we grew older we all had our favorite bat, and most of them came from the annual "Bat Day" hosted by the White Sox at Comiskey Park. Momma believed that Sundays were only for church and to serve God, so to her going to a game was a sin. But for me Ray, Lamar, Frankie and all the other fellas, bat day was an event we wouldn't miss. Each year I knew I would have to beg and cry until finally Momma would pray and check with her Bible to ask God for a sign. While she waited for a sign, I cried until she would reluctantly tell me that it was out of her hands and I should go and ask Daddy. As my parents were getting older I knew they couldn't keep to those rigid rules they used with the other kids. Daddy always said yes, which sent me running to Ray and Lamar with a big smile. We knew all day was going to be a blast because "out of sight" meant "out of mind." We were never big Sox fans, but these Sundays were special because we were getting free bats. Mr. Grandberry would have his work cut out for him with all of us to watch.

After the long walk to the park and going through the turnstyles to pick up our bats, we made our way to the upper deck balcony. Once we sat down -- always, it seemed, behind a giant beam -- we compared our bats. We thought that they gave the black kids the smaller bats and the white kids the bigger ones. That gave us an incentive and excuse to look for people with the so-called "good bats." First we'd go to our seats with Mr. Grandberry but it wouldn't be more than 10 minutes before one of us said we had to use the bathroom. We'd leave one by one, leaving Mr. Grandberry by himself. We'd look at the white kids walking around with their bats and we headed for the place where fights would break out every year over bats: the upper deck by the catwalk. That area by the scoreboard became a place where all the frustrations of two races would be taken out. Up there were the white kids from Mayor Richard J. Daley's neighborhood and the black kids from the projects east of the Dan Ryan expressway. Whites and Blacks knew this was a section where they could fight without Andy Frain security being involved. We would all have about two bats each by the 7th inning. We would be gone for innings at a time, only returning to Mr. Grandberry for him to hold more bats. Sometimes he would be furious with us for being gone so long because he knew we were up to something.

We gained our props with each other by taking the bats from the bigger white boys. The way we got the bats consisted of running behind a unsuspecting white boy and snatching the bat and outrunning him. Our thrill and goal was to come home with enough bats to play with the next year. The white boys were just as vicious in taking the black boys' bats. Of all the years we did that, I never saw anyone get seriously hurt; usually little more than words between the groups were exchanged. Security became aware of our confrontations and started coming by to keep a handle on things. We would figure ways to get bats home but we had to leave some behind because security maintained a high profile to scare people from taking more than one bat out of the park. Every year Ray always had the most bats.

"BeBe's Kids" at Great America

The Ida B. Wells projects would sponsor field trips to places like Great America once a year. Buses loaded with inner city kids would leave for the suburban amusement parks like the now-closed Old Chicago or Great America. I would have to make a scene in order to get my parents to let me go, but once on that yellow school bus I, along with the rest, acted like formal training was not a modern-day experience. The buses were full of hundreds of black kids with only a few parents from the community center. There was no way they could keep all of us in check.

The Key to Stopping the Violence

Once we entered Great America, we went for the ride we wanted to get on with no regard for the lines, nor the masses of white people. We knew we could intimidate the white kids, and we often did. If Ray and me wanted to get on the roller coaster, we couldn't believe people would wait in line for an hour and a half for one ride. We would walk up and break the line by "bogarting," pushing, elbowing, jumping over rails, whatever it took. Hell, we could get on rides in 10 minutes.

One time we jumped on the water boat ride as white kids and grownups shouted out things like, "That's not fair" or "You're cheating," as though we didn't know that. We thought, "What in the fuck do you think. We're jumping in front." After riding the boat ride we would jump out then jump back in before the attendant could stop us, laughing, knowing that there was nothing they could do. One time there was a white boy in the front of the boat as we jumped on, leaving his friends standing there on the platform. We dumped cups of water on his head as he sat like a statue, water running down his face. Ray and me jumped out of the boat before it stopped and ran off the platform laughing.

I now realize we showed the side of ourselves we thought white people wanted to see. Those trains around the park were perfect to jump on and off through the ride as the conductor screamed at us. We made park security earn their money. Midway through the day there would be a load of brothers being sent back to the buses by security. You could be sure that by the end of the day, someone would have stolen a huge stuffed animal. We knew security was no match for kids who had seen and done it all. Before the day was out, half of the kids would be on the bus and not allowed in the park again. But that next year, we would be back just like the disruptive BeBe Kids made famous by the late comedian Robin Harris.

Pitching Pennies

It seemed that Eric and me were the only two brothers in the Ida B. Wells projects who didn't pitch pennies. Momma was always against it or any other form of gambling, so I tried not to do it out of respect for her. Plus I knew Eric would be right there and he wouldn't allow it. There was a side to me that didn't want to gamble because people would want to fight if they lost a quarter or if they were cheated. Most people who pitched pennies eventually wanted to shoot craps and that's when you were usually in over your head or with the wrong crowd. So I would sit on the banister and watch as Ray, Lamar and my other homies pitched pennies.

I saw many fights break out over pitching two pennies on the sidewalk to see who could get closest to the line. The one who pitched closest picked up all the money.

Revenge

As we were growing up the one thing about Ray I admired and feared was his ability to never give up in a fight. If a person fought Ray and won, they never really won because he was going to find a way to get them back. Ray earned this reputation at a young age and he demonstrated it one time during a fight with a boy named Sherman. Sherman would come and visit the low end every summer, so picking on him was as normal as scratching an itch. Your reputation was built on fighting and a lot of shit talking. If you could talk a homie down, that was better for you because your words did what your fists didn't have to do. There was always a group of brothers you could bluff. Some you had to slap box and some you had to fight. In each building, backyard or block, you had bad boys, fighters, and gangsters. Our backyard was full of athletes. We attracted people who wanted to play softball, football and other sports, but that's not to say we didn't have our gangsters too.

Ray was known as a fighter. Sherman had been afraid of Ray for two summers. Then for some reason, Sherman stood up to Ray during a fist fight. Normally I would have jumped in to defend Ray in fights but because it was Sherman, I decided to stand back and let it go. They were fighting over money that was bet while pitching pennies.

As the crowd gathered around to instigate, Ray threw a flurry of punches that got the best of Sherman. Then Sherman closed his eyes and let one punch go that hit Ray on the jaw, knocking him to the ground. Just then Mrs. Grandberry came to the screen door on the porch and had Ray come in. That punch was talked about in the backyard for the next several days. Nobody knew Ray better than Lamar and me; we knew that wasn't the end of it by any means. Ray never said anything to us about it. He let everybody brag about how Sherman kicked his ass and how he had lost his props.

About three days later, when we were playing softball in the backyard, Ray and Sherman were on the same team, along with Lamar and me. During our team's at bat, we used the banister to

The Key to Stopping the Violence

the basement as the dugout, with the next batter standing in the painted circle in the concrete batter's box. Sherman had started pitching pennies nearby with some of the dudes not playing with us. Ray's turn to bat was coming up next. Lamar and I sat there on the banister as Ray picked up the bat to start warming up. Lamar looked at me and said, "Ray's about to do something."

I could tell by the way he was swinging the bat and looking over at Sherman. Before we could react, Ray was walking toward an unsuspecting Sherman, who was bending over with his left hand on his knee to pitch a penny. Ray pulled the bat back like he was winding up to hit a baseball and unloaded right in the middle of Sherman's back. Bam! The noise stopped all the homies in their tracks. Sherman, in a delayed reaction, screamed. We didn't know if Ray had broke Sherman's back until he took off running in the opposite direction until he was out of site. Ray calmly dropped the bat and walked away. I had always known that Ray had a mean streak that made him hell if he was against you. But you had a dependable ally if he was with you.

Later that summer I watched Ray fight Ivory for hours, not giving up until Ivory slammed Ray to the concrete and broke his foot. Ray managed to bite Ivory in the chin and left teeth marks in his brother's face that are still there to this day. Both Ray and me were always seeking attention from our older brothers. They would both constantly ignore us, telling us to play with each other instead of spending time with us themselves. This caused anger and resentment in both Ray and me toward our brothers, making us want to fight other people and our own brothers.

Peer Pressure

Ray and me spent so much time around each other I knew all of the things he liked and hated. He became increasingly aggressive after his father left home. All Ray's life, when Mr. Grandberry addressed Ray it was in a hostile tone. Now him and Ivory were the men of the house. I could tell Ray was looking for attention from other males weather the attention was good or bad. He became increasingly attracted to the underground life that permeated the 'hood, that is the world of the gangbangers. Whenever we talked about some of the things going down in the 'hood, Ray took the side of the thugs and gangsters. I would take the side of the person being hurt. If there was a fight, he loved for the bad guy to win.

SILENT CRY

We would sometimes sit on the bannister and talk to the gangsters, in particular, was a fair-complected man with blond hair. Him and his boys had become notorious for having gunfire exchanges with the police. His family lived across the street from Ray. There was a shoot out across from the meat market store at 37th and Cottage Grove. The store was frequented by people from three or four different projects. Once the gangsters had a long shoot out with the police and managed to escape.

The next morning we sat and talked about the incident. Ray marveled at how they stood up to the police and got away. I was in eighth grade and the gangs were making a comeback. There were always gangs, but they weren't as prevalent or as organized as the Blackstone Rangers or the Disciples had been. But each building or area still had a gang presence. At school we had some members of the Blackstone Rangers; people like Lil' Ma' who was one of the young leaders of the Stones of the '60s. MooMoo lived in Lil' Ma's building and was one of the up and coming gangbangers. Ray was attracted to MooMoo and Lil' Ma. He would give them respect and try to be noticed. He made it his business to get close to them. Ray even started liking Lil' Ma's sister and started hanging in the 565 building.

I was amazed at the difference in his attitude toward me. Lamar and Frankie noticed that Ray was running with the boys in the 565 Building and that he wasn't around after school anymore. Some of the 565 boys were in Ray's 7th grade classroom. When we played baseball in the backyard, Ray was nowhere to be found. Then one day, I saw Terrence and Big Boy with Ray coming out of his apartment. They both lived in 565 and were part of the gang. I caught up with Ray later and asked what was he doing with them. Ray tried to convince me not to worry because he was their leader. How long could that last, I asked him, being the leader of a gang at age 13. That was the last conversation I had with Ray for a long time until one day during lunch at school.

Instead of playing football or baseball in the schoolyard, I decided to go to Walgreen's in the Lake Meadows shopping center across from the school. Ray, Terrence and Big Boy, along with several more of their boys, approached me in the store. I was walking toward the candy section to buy a candy bar when Ray and the rest of them cut in front of me. Ray moved out in front as his boys backed up. Out of nowhere, from Ray, came a right fist to my jaw. I had tears in my eyes, not so much from the hit but because I knew Ray was put up to it by the 565

The Key to Stopping the Violence

gangsters. It was part of his initiation -- turn on his best friend. I didn't swing back.

"You can do this because you're my brother. But if any of you other punk motherfuckers try it, your ass is mine," I said. The others backed off and they all walked away slapping Ray five and talking shit. I went on to Ray's house and told his brother, Ivory, and Mrs. Grandberry that I was worried about Ray.

I continued to hear about the things the young gangbangers were doing to people. Later in the school year I was on my way out of the school building at 3:15. I noticed Ray's gang members peeping around the building as one of them called my name and said, "Your boy is going to get his ass kicked when he comes out of that building." I turned around and went back in the school. Ray stood there not knowing what to do. He explained that they had turned on him because he wasn't part of their Building 565. Even the older gangbangers had called him out because he was considered an outsider. They had threatened him, so he was not about to leave the school building. I told him that I had just seen them, and we could go out the back way. Ray and me, along with a older girl named Rhonda, walked to our backyard safely. I was loyal to Ray even though he had turned against me earlier.

Blinded by Gunfire

Like Ray, I had some enemies at the school. For some reason the Booker boys had started in on me. When we chose baseball teams during the morning and lunch, I would jump up as one of the leaders. The best players always chose the teams; that's where you earned your props.

In the beginning of the year I didn't know who the Booker boys were. Jimmy Booker was in 8th grade and Maurice Booker was in 7th grade. I associated with the athletes, the brothers played sports rather than fight. The Booker's were dudes who could fight -- and play sports. Fighting and bullying became their sport. Jimmy began starting fights with me as the year progressed. Every time we got ready to fight, his boys stepped in to break it up. It got so bad that everyday I anticipated the Booker brothers coming after me. They had the backing of some brothers who had hearts of stone. Whenever a person had backup, it was tougher to deal with them. By midyear they started to organize a gang to fight against the older gang Ray belonged to. Ray led the younger gangsters and MooMoo was over the big gangsters.

SILENT CRY

One day after school about 12 of them surrounded me in between the big school and little school. Jimmy called me a pussy in front of all of his boys. I tried to walk away as the circle closed in. I told him I would be a pussy today. Then he called me another name but I refused the potential ass kicking by continuing to agree with him. They all expected me to jump bad so they could eat me for lunch. I looked Jimmy in the face and said, "I'm whatever you say today but we'll see what I am without your boys." As I walked though the circle Jimmy pushed me and said, "Your day is coming soon."

The Booker boys and the people in their extension building were fighting MooMoo and those in the 565 building. The gangs were pairing off as all the gangs carried zip guns to school. The pressure was starting to mount for shorties to declare a gang affiliation. Me and most of the athletes were neutral. I was aggressive but not a punk, and I was smart enough not to join a gang. I was also smart enough to take the long way home and leave school at different times to avoid the trouble. I often kept chains and sharp objects in my locker for protection.

We would come out of school sometimes and see 30 gangbangers blocking the street waiting to get some kid. One time the fighting broke out and MooMoo's boys were looking for the 510 gangsters. Ricky Wright and me were walking from school and got caught in the middle of the fighting. We ran to the first extension building we could find and hid on the fourth floor. Ricky was one of the most intense, competitive friends I had but he like me was not for the gangbanging.

After we thought the coast was clear, we stood up to look out of the fourth floor window and saw about 30 gangbangers outside the building looking for the 510 gangsters. One gangbanger saw us and hollered, "Those motherfuckers are on the fourth floor. Let's get them." I got ready to run when Ricky stopped and said there wasn't anywhere to run. They were coming up both hallways. All we would do was piss them off by going up higher. We stood there as we heard the footsteps running up the stairs. All we knew was that we weren't the gang members they were looking for.

MooMoo was the first on the scene, with his pistol in hand, as his boys ran up to us ready to do bodily harm. MooMoo said, "Damn they ain't who we're looking for. You niggers lucky today." They turned away and went on looking for their prey.

One thing about the projects was that you were only afraid of what was happening right then because there was always so much

The Key to Stopping the Violence

conflict at any given time. You could have five or 10 enemies and not even know it. So we treated the fourth floor incident as if was just another day, one more thing to talk about.

Later that night, I talked Ray into going with me to Lake Meadows to collect the money from my paper route . Another thing about the projects was that all of our enemies lived only five minutes away. Usually thugs who fought you would not come to your turf. They would wait until they caught you in the backyard of their building in the school yard. Walking to Lake Meadows, we had to pass all the backyards and buildings of our enemies. We walked north past the 565 building, figuring no one would see us or recognize us because it was getting dark. The 565 building was located close to Doolittle grammar school. After passing the building we heard a familiar sound: pop, pop, pop! I could see the sparks coming out of a gun as the shots rang into the night air. "Run Ray," I hollered as I instantly took off. "Run!" I hollered again to him because Ray seemed to freeze. He let out a loud scream as though he had been spooked. Ray didn't get a good look nor did I. We ran two blocks north to the private upscale 400 Building in Lake Meadows. Once there we hit 20 or 30 buzzers until someone buzzed us in. Now our hearts were racing because we didn't know if they were shooting at us or if it was just random gunfire. We didn't know if anyone had followed us. We calmed down and I told Ray we would go ahead and collect our money.

The Lake Meadows buildings were always so quiet that the silence would scare us, especially in the hallways. It was the exact opposite of the projects. As we walked down the stairs, we heard other people running on the stairs. "Did you hear that," I asked Ray. "Yeah man, there's somebody else on the stairs," he answered. So we ran down to the next floor and heard somebody say, "Let's check down on the next floor." That scared the hell out of us. We ran down as many flights of stairs as we could then dashed out into the hallway where we got on the elevator. All of the buttons had been pushed to stop on every floor. We were breathing heavily from anxiety and exhaustion. Ray kept saying "they" were going to catch us. I told him to beat on as many doors as possible until we got someone to let us in.

One lady said no and an old lady said she couldn't but would call security. So we stood against the wall at the end of the long hallway in anticipation of the security guard. Once there, he assisted us down the stairs to the back door. We took the long way home south past King Drive to 38th east around Madden

57

SILENT CRY

Park and home. We never knew if those shots were for us or who did the shooting. I had to go back to Doolittle for the rest of the year to graduate. Because of these two incidents in one day, Ray never went back to Doolittle East grammar school. After that, he transferred to a grammar school on 95th Street. It was the same school Kevin, Lawrence Green's brother, attended. Ray did come back to see me graduate. Maurice Booker was murdered in 1993 by 15 gang members. He was beaten to death in the head while having his face smashed with poles and bricks. This was the price they paid him for using their drugs while selling for them.

Home Life

At home, life was becoming a nightmare because Momma had almost been raped coming home from church one Wednesday night. A man caught her on the side of our building, put a knife to her throat and dragged her into our back hallway. He was trying to force himself on her, but luckily he decided to snatch her purse and run. That event caused Momma to deepen her love for God and the people in the church. Unfortunately, her idea of a friend became anyone who attended her church. Everyone else was fast becoming devils. It was evident that she was tired and worn down by all the kids and all the years. She continued telling me she couldn't handle me getting in trouble in and out of school.

Eric had become just as childish always pitting Evette and me against each other. Everyone thought he was this perfect person, but I saw more and more a confused person. When Momma and Dad left for work Eric would often beat me up. One day I climbed out of the third floor window to get away from him. I threatened to jump as my legs hung out over the ledge. Another time, Eric threw a fork at me and it stuck in my neck. I never told my parents about these incidents because I loved my brother too much. As he got older, he stopped doing anything the other older guys were doing like talking about girls and sex. When I would mention the topic, he would tell me to shut up and don't talk that way. Most of my sisters were marrying guys from the church. Pastor and Momma seemed to be doing a lot of matchmaking.

Many of Momma's ways at home seemed to be geared to what we weren't doing and her anger was generated by pressure from the church to bring in more money. Dad started asking Momma where all her money was going. He wanted her to help

The Key to Stopping the Violence

with some of the bills. She acted as if he stole from her and hated the fact he asked her to pay the phone bill. The pastor's message still included encouraging the women to get their men in church.

My parents didn't have good communication in their relationship. Little by little, Momma's decisions were based on emotion and not logic. After church, I would go up to the kitchen and get free meals. One particular Sunday, I decided to go up early and I overheard Momma talking to the other cook, her best friend, "Girl, I'll get a divorce if you get one. I'm tired of being married to that devil." I knew things were going bad. I was about 12 years old and the only thing I could do was get mad. I stormed in the church kitchen and asked Momma why she would say something like that about Dad. He was paying the bills and in my estimation wasn't doing anything wrong.

I used to wonder why Daddy enjoyed sitting in the car in front of our building, not coming in for hours sometimes. I was amazed and hurt at the fact that Momma would defend the church -- her foster family -- before she defended her own husband and children. On Sunday she would be so tired of cooking for the church that she wouldn't want to cook at home.

But what my parents did do was dish out discipline. I continued to rebel from the church. Mom began to get evil at home. Her prayers were geared toward getting the devil out of me. She started grabbing me and trying to pray the demons out. At the age of 14 and 15, I would let her slap me but that belt action was not going on. And she would get on me and Evette about anything and everything. She even begin to tell the church that I was acting sinful at home, so the preacher started separating my friends from me.

At one Thursday evening church service Mom began shouting as if she were totally overcome by the Holy Spirit. As she shouted down the aisles, she worked her way over to me. Then, in the midst of giving God his praises, she cut her eyes toward me and said in a low threatening voice, "I saw you come in late. I'll handle you when you get home." Then she shouted away from me, continuing to give God his praises as if nothing had happened. I began to ask Daddy if it was necessary to go to that church. At one Thursday night service, the pastor kicked out my sister, Eldora, her husband and friends. My other sister, Evette, and her boyfriend left. I had already started figuring ways to avoid the church, which caused more and more problems with Momma. She and Eric jumped me one day at home. Eric hit me from the front and Momma from the back and the two beat me and accused me of being a devil.

Everyday in the house was like hell once Momma came home from work. She would cry and shout every morning after Daddy went to work and accuse Evette and me of betraying her. Once she started whipping me with a belt in my sleep and that was a messed up experience to feel pain and then have your subconscious pain meet your conscious pain and go on until you wake up screaming at being hit.

All this time from as early as I could remember people were telling me I was bad. I admit to being active but my heart was always full of love and compassion. I didn't smoke or drink and my parents wouldn't let us party or play records. We never turned on the TV before noon and always fasted on Tuesday, Wednesday and Thursday. In other words, I went to school starving in the morning.

My mother was a religious fanatic. Eric and some of my sisters went along with it. I was trying to make sense of why Momma chose the men she did for my sisters to marry. Why couldn't we dance or play records? Why didn't we own a grill to barbeque on holidays? Why did Momma seem to dislike her two younger kids? Why did Momma fear Daddy?

I couldn't understand what Momma's hate and near fear of Daddy was about. Why did he let himself be used as disciplinarian and not let his kids know him? We all feared him because he was put in our face by Momma. When I started asking Daddy if I had to go to church, I didn't let him know that the deacons of the church had been holding me and chasing me around while the older ladies prayed for me, pushing and pulling on my face to release the demons while Momma stood over to the side crying and praying. I didn't want Daddy to find out and get mad. This confusion in the home caused problems for me at school and in building trusting relationships.

Loving Advice

Because my class didn't have a homeroom teacher for most of seventh grade and all of eighth, the structure of our classroom went downhill. I had been on the honor roll most of my grammar school years, but we became the worst behaved class in school. I tried several times to get into Mr. Johnson's homeroom class despite the fact that he was the toughest teacher in Doolittle. My efforts were in vain. I knew inside that something was wrong

The Key to Stopping the Violence

I wasn't learning anything. There's something about kids that will prompt them to take advantage of situations even if they don't want to. There are kids in gangs who don't want to be there, but feel they have to. My personality drives me to be the best at what I do, be it good or bad. The lack of classroom structure allowed me to show off in class, fight, cause confusion, be destructive and not study. Inside, I knew it wasn't the best thing or the right thing for me.

In eighth grade we were assigned a homeroom teacher who was afraid of his own shadow. I would get in his face and stand on his feet and dare him to push me or stop me. My classwork consisted of everything but work. Most of my day was spent trying to feel on the girls' butts, fighting or having some of the girls braid my afro. Finally, we got a new principal and assistant principal who came to rid the school of gangbangers and troublemakers. My teacher turned me in to the assistant principal, who told me that I would be in the Mosley "bad boy school" by the end of the week.

He called Momma and she said that she would not come up to the school again because she was tired of me getting in trouble. I pleaded with her not to send me to Mosley because I was eligible to take the test to attend Lindblom Technical High School, the No. 1-ranked academic school in Chicago, which Eric was attending. I wanted to go there ever since I was in sixth grade. That's when Eric took me to a football game and introduced me to all the people he knew at the game. In order to be admitted to Lindblom, you had to be one of the top eighth graders in your school, do well on Lindblom's admission test and the state test. In eighth grade, I, along with Troy, Denise, Donna and Caroline took the El to Lindblom to take the test. I never prayed so hard to pass a test in all my young life. For whatever reason, I never once thought about going to school anywhere else. I was one of the people to pass, which made the first half of my dream come true.

I remember being excited and enthusiastic about being selected to go to the most prestigious public school in Chicago. Many of the accounts on my paper route were teachers at my grammar school. I had to collect from Ms. Washington, a black woman, who was one of Doolittle's best teachers, and had taught most of my siblings.

Like most of the teachers at Doolittle, she compared me with all of my sisters and brothers. They all said I was the worst of the litter. The night I told her I passed the Lindblom test, we were standing in the doorway to her apartment. She handed me the money for her *Sun-Times* delivery bill and said, "Bassette, don't go to Lindblom. You'll never make it there. Those are not your kind of people. Those people want to achieve. Go to Wendell Phillips High School You can make it there." I said, "I'll make it at Lindblom. Don't worry. I'll make it." She shook her head in disgust. I learned at a very young age to believe in my own dreams and not the dreams others had for me.

Maxwell Street/"Jew Town"

The summer after graduation we were wearing our big afros, stacked shoes and walking suits. The Jackson Five and the Sylvers were the groups on the move. We were wearing Converse All-Star gym shoes, bell bottoms and silk-flowered shirts with wide collars. Everybody was doing the dance called the Bump. Shaft and Superfly were in and we were wearing the clothes we had to have.

"Jew Town", north on Maxwell and Halsted streets, was the only place to get these clothes. When I was a younger, Eric would take me to Jew Town to pick up his Converse All-Stars. Back then, Daddy would force me to wear $1.99 P.F. Flyer gym shoes. When Ray and me got older, we would always go shopping there ourselves. The area was full of life with street merchants and the crowds of shoppers.

We could buy watches from both white and black people, who had 10 or 12 on their wrists, or jackets, flowered shirts and sunglasses. Anyone who shopped this area regularly knew that most of the items would fall apart when it got home, but it was the excitement that I enjoyed. I remember going down to buy my first pair of Converse for $15. Ray and me caught the bus and once there, we both picked out a white pair. Man, they were so cool with the star on the outside of each ankle with "Converse" written on it. Anybody who had a life wore Converse with the shoelaces tied like a spider web and the tongue flap down.

Then we'd take out our braids and let our gigantic afros blow in the wind. Girl's liked the afros that would blow with the wind because that was a sign of "good hair" and nobody liked a brother with a nappy 'fro. We admired the older brothers with the Converse without the laces tied. Daddy would practically inspect my shoes to see if the laces were laced up. We copied the brothers wearing them with blue jeans, white T-shirts and nicely picked afros.

The Key to Stopping the Violence

We thought the world belonged to us. Ray was a master at getting the store owners to drop their prices on clothes or whatever. He could haggle over prices for what seemed like hours. It usually lead to an argument, with him calling the owner a cheap Jew or having us put out of the store. Ray would win in the end by telling the owner he could get that cheap shit down the street.

The stores were always full of black people trying to get a better price from the white man. We never left without having our favorite polish or hamburger with grilled onions. After we finished shopping on one of our trips, we ran into Lil' Shawn and his brother, along with some thugs from the Darrow Homes project. They talked Ray and me into hanging out with them instead of heading home. First they wanted to hop on the back of the bus instead of paying, which wasn't that bad because Ray and me had always done that. The only problem was that you had to do it when the bus was crowded and the bus driver couldn't see you sneaking on. These thugs wanted to do it when the bus was only half full. When we tried, the bus driver threw us off, so they decided to walk on Roosevelt Road, headed east. While walking, one of them spotted under the bridge, a huge parking lot for people who park their cars and go downtown. There were about 50 cars parked below us. One of the dudes picked up a brick and threw it and the brick crashed through a car window, exploding like a hand grenade. Suddenly, everybody started throwing bricks over the bridge, listening to the sound of exploding glass. We laughed and walked away, not thinking twice about the damage we caused. We continued walking to the next bus stop to try to sneak on the bus again because it was crowded with passengers. But this driver, like the first one, threw us off, so one of the thugs suggested we run ahead of the bus and wait with bricks. When the bus got up to us we threw bricks at the front and side windows. As the windows were breaking we were laughing while the passengers ducked for safety. From there we ran in different directions with Ray and me splitting from the rest of the pack. I don't know how much damage we caused that day.

Ray and Lil' Shawn continued to do things as the years went by, but I never saw those thugs from the Darrow Homes projects again. Lil' Shawn's brother is now doing life in prison for killing a lady and her unborn baby. As the summer after graduation continued, Ray and Lil' Shawn started stealing brothers' radios and bikes and breaking car windows. I sat on the banister and

SILENT CRY

told my boys I wanted to go to Lindblom to play football. They would leave me sitting there and before they left to cause havoc, they would say, "This is the last time." But they kept coming back with other people's items. I made my decision and tried to stay with it.

"Pizza Pizza"

My brother Eric always seemed to hate having to take me places, for years he had found a way to avoid taking me with him. One night he decided to take Ray and me to a night game at Comiskey Park. He and his friend, John, had extra tickets. The year was 1975, I had just graduated from eighth grade and Eric had just graduated from high school. He would be headed to college that Fall. When we got to the game we watched the first couple of innings and then Ray and me did our usual walking around the park. This was a regular game, no frills or prizes and my only intention was having a good time. It was a cool night and the park was about half empty. As we walked around the back of the park in the right center field upper deck section, we saw the different vendors selling pop, hot dogs, beer and pizza. Each of these men was hollering out what they sold. The sound of all these items would make you want some even if you were broke like we were. The pizza man walked by yelling, "We have pizza, pizza get yourself some pizza." Ray hollered, "Pizza, pizza, give me some pizza."

The vendor, a middle-aged white man, turned around, came back to us and asked, "How many slices will it be?" Ray went into his pocket to pull out some money but his hand came out empty. Ray asked me for some money and I checked both pockets and didn't have any either. We looked at the pizza vendor and said, "No thanks." I turned around to lean on the rail looking down at the lower level and as the vendor walked about 10 steps away, Ray called out again, "Pizza, pizza, give me pizza." The vendor turned around, walked back to us and I looked at Ray with confusion as he pretended to have some money. The vendor responded, "Either you want pizza or not." Ray said he didn't have any money. By this time, I had turned away from them because I had nothing to do with the vendor coming back. The pizza man walked away again as I rested my chin against the rail and began to daydream, looking through the rails out on to the field. Again Ray hollered out, "Pizza, pizza, give me some pizza." The vendor came back without me

The Key to Stopping the Violence

knowing what was going on, cocked his foot and landed a kick square up in the crack of my ass. At the same time he was cursing and saying, "I'll teach you nigger kids to fuck with me."

I was a 14-year-old kid getting kicked up the ass by a white man who probably had kids my age at home. I was in real pain at first and then I turned into a real nigger, cursing back at him. I told him that he had just fucked up in the worst way. It was one of the first times Ray heard me use profanity. The man started to take off his vendor pizza oven and we ran off. Ray was laughing so hard he couldn't control himself. I was suffering from pain and embarrassment. We ran to the Andy Frain security and told them what happened. They blew us off like a few black kids with problems. I told Ray that the vendor's white ass would not get away with this. We had to take things into our own hands.

First, we had to locate him, so we walked around the entire ballpark searching. While we were looking, we were planing the damage we were going to do. Finally, we found him. We stood at a distance hollering things at him. We continued to bother him until he couldn't do his job effectively. Several times, he had us running because he was either coming after us or he was trying to point us out to the Andy Frain security.

This happened the entire game until we found him about the sixth inning on the lower deck, selling pizza to some fans. He didn't notice us behind the wall where the aisle leads into the seats. All night we had been throwing things at him, like cups and litter. I noticed someone had left a half cup of beer on the steps. I picked up the cup and closed the top by folding it over. Because I was a first baseman, I had a pretty accurate throwing arm. We stood behind the wall, peeping out and waiting for him to get in the right position.

As I waited, I told Ray we would have to leave the park because it was going into the seventh inning. I looked up and hollered, "Pizza, pizza give me some pizza." As he looked up, the cup was headed straight for his head. It happened so fast he couldn't react as it smacked him in the face with the same velocity that he had earlier kicked me in the ass. It splashed all over him as he fell off balance. Ray and me took off running back up to our upper deck seats.

Eric and John wondered where we had been and we told them we would meet them at the front of the park on the other side of the expressway, by the Robert Taylor projects. Luckily, they were ready to go because the Sox were losing, as usual. Ray and me walked ahead of them quickly trying to leave the park because we knew that the pizza man and security would   be looking for us. We made it out and it became another story we shared with the boys in the low end. My limited experience with white people was not good.

PART II
Inner City Public Schools Under Siege

Wrong Side of the Tracks

My freshman year of high school was a new experience for me. Mom rode with me to the parent/student orientation in late summer. This gave me a chance to see the other 1,000 freshman entering Lindblom, where I met Clark, captain of the varsity football team. The school had close to 3,000 total students. Mom showed me the best way to take the bus from Cottage Grove to 35th Street where I would then ride the old elevated train south to 63rd and Ashland. From there I would catch the 63rd Street bus west to Wolcott and walk two blocks north to the school. The trip took about one hour. Lindblom was all white in the 60's then in the early 70's blacks started coming. The neighborhood switched over also. Between 71' and 75' all of the whites had moved out. But, Lindblom's academic standards stayed the best in the city.

When school started I met Raymond, who lived in the Ickes Projects, also on the low end. We went out for the freshman football team together and rode the train home together after school. Catching the elevated train at 63rd and Ashland, we rode the last or the first car and watched the Englewood red train as it made all of its stops. We would chase each other from car to

The Key to Stopping the Violence

car while the train made its almost 90 degree turns over the Dan Ryan expressway as well as the 39th street turn. By the end of the ride we would be running through all the cars, kicking, wrestling and punching.

One day while playing between the El train doors I stood hiding because I didn't know which car Raymond was in. I was looking through the glass trying to find him and while my back was turned, Raymond sneaked up from the opposite direction and kicked me in the back, causing me to lose my balance. As I was trying to catch myself, I felt the train begin to make a 90-degree turn. The force of the train pulled me toward the expressway below. At that moment I knew I would fall to my death, out of nowhere a man grabbed me by the back of my coat and pulled me back into the train car. Then he proceeded to slap the shit out of me. He asked me if I was crazy and told me to sit my so and so ass down before I got killed. Raymond was laughing and my heart was racing. I knew this man had saved my life. Did it stop me from playing on the trains? No. At that age I didn't think anything would stop a kid from believing he'll live forever. We continued to play on the trains.

We would also pull the emergency door handle to stop the train in the middle of its route. This forced the doorman to check all the doors before starting the train again. The platforms were also great places to play and run around. I felt comfortable with Raymond because we both were from the low end. We would ride to the end of the line on the north side and back, passing Comiskey Park, past Wrigley Field. One time I tried to show off in front of some girls I knew by pulling the emergency door handle. Before the train could stop, I jumped out onto the platform, but I didn't know the momentum of the train would make me keep running toward the other end of the platform toward a coming train. All I remember was making myself fall as I hollered and hit the platform hard. I tore my pants and scraped my knees as I tried to act like I knew what I was doing. The girls said I was crazy. I took that as a compliment. There were plenty of times when I didn't know when to stop and say enough is enough. I was always looking for attention.

Deke: A New Journey

The junior varsity football team was where I first met Garry Dean Kennedy in my freshman year of high school. The first thing I noticed about him was his knocked knees. He was light-skinned but very thin like me. The most vivid memories I have about Deke, which is what we called him, happened during our freshman year when two incidents occurred. The first was when Coach Sims was talking after practice one day about an upcoming game. Coach Sims was a very emotional coach who demanded respect. He was very stern about discipline and ordered everyone quiet. Some of us were on one knee and some standing. He started telling us one of his many tales about football and life. We all listened with intense interest.

During his talk, he began to move some players away from one player. He then took a few steps backward. All of a sudden he started running full force toward one player. Coach Sims jumped about six feet in the air like he was going for a slam dunk. In the middle of his leap he yelled, "Damnit, I told your ass to pay attention." He landed on the player with a double karate kick to the shoulder pad. The player was Deke, a little skinny freshman.

Coach must have knocked Deke 20 feet in the air, then ran over and picked him up with one hand and dragged him back to his original spot. Everyone looked with amazement. My eyes almost popped out of my head as I thought, "I'm glad that wasn't me." I waited to see Deke's expression or to see if he would cry or fight back. But to my amazement, he just got up and stood there as though nothing had happened. You could hear some of the sophomores snickering. I thought Deke was a punk after that.

The second incident with Deke was later on in the football season. The freshman had some of the worst football equipment in the world. The helmets were old; some were cracked and the gold paint was scraped off. The shoulder pads were missing straps. The uniforms had holes in them. Lindblom wasn't a sports school, and being a public league school, they didn't put much effort into buying football equipment.

Coach decided he wanted us to paint our helmets for the homecoming game. He had different people collect the money so we could buy gold spray paint. I hooked up with my friend, John, and John had put some money together with Deke. Up until this point, I had never heard Deke talk much. When I got the can of spray paint, I noticed that it was almost empty. So I looked at John and said, "Hey, man, I want my motherfuckin' money back." Out of nowhere, Deke shouted, "Man, I'll fuck you up if you talk to my cousin like that again."

I looked at him and said, "Yeah, right." I noticed that he had a temper like me. That brief incident made me look at Deke

The Key to Stopping the Violence

like myself: a person quick to look out for his own. Before that, I thought of him as a light-skinned, howdy doody type.

Prep Bowl: Weekends Back in the Hood

Back in the low end I still hung with Ray and Lamar on weekends. Every year the city high school championship football game was held at Soldier Field. The game featured the top Public League city team against the second or third place Catholic League team. Lamar and I were in high school and Ray was in eighth grade. We had never been to Soldier Field and wanted to go to the game to see the stadium and have fun. When we got there, we started walking around, looking for things to do. On one side of Soldier Field we noticed all the whites from the Catholic schools and on the other side was all the blacks from the Public League. We started off running through the tunnels, then we started bumping white people as we ran. Ray walked over to an old white man using a cane and kicked him dead up his ass and walked away. Lamar and me couldn't believe it, so we all ran around the stadium to get away. Ray later told me he kicked him in the ass to get back at the white pizza man who kicked me a year earlier.

Soldier Field was full of hundreds of black kids just like us. We wore skull caps, Eskimo coats and gym shoes or combat boots. From there we ran into some neighborhood hard core gang members who knew us from the 'hood. On any other day these brothers would have tried to stick us up but today we all had a common enemy: white people. We thought about the way they had treated us when we were in Sox Park and how they would fuck with us if we were in Mayor Daley's neighborhood. Now they were in what was considered a neutral area.

Me and Lamar's idea of "getting" them meant running through the tunnel and hitting or bumping real hard into crowds and knocking people over. But the gangbangers had a different twist: They started catching people in the tunnels and robbing them. They would catch a white boy in the tunnel push him against the wall and then ask him for his reefer and money. I was amazed that all these white boys had drugs on them. Then how a white person would buckle down under the pressure and give up his drugs without a fight. Back then everybody was smoking reefer. That wasn't of interest to me but I realized that drugs wasn't just a black thing.

SILENT CRY

The gangbangers knew the white boys couldn't tell the police. The white boys were scared but furious. In one instance, the gangbangers surrounded some white boys and one of them didn't want to part with his reefer. He claimed he didn't have any. Ray stepped between the gangbangers and took the guy's hot chocolate out of his hand and threw it in his face.

While the white guy was screaming hysterically, Ray calmly went through his pockets, removed his goods, including money, and proceeded to take his head and repeatedly knock it against the hard concrete wall of the tunnel. Me and Lamar grabbed Ray as he gave the gangbangers all of the reefer. They praised him for being so intense. That's when I knew Ray wanted approval to be a bad boy. But I also knew what was happening in his home life that made him act that way.

We decided to split from the gangsters because we had done enough that day. We never did watch any of the game. The cold weather began to get to us. Lamar, Ray and me decided to hit the bus stop so we could make it home. We talked and laughed about what had happened while waiting. We had walked back toward Michigan Avenue to catch the Cottage Grove bus when Ray spotted a white lady on the other side of the street, leaving the game with her son who looked about six years old. Her son held a pennant from the Catholic team school playing that day. Ray went over to them as the rest of us watched from across the street, not knowing what he was going to do. Ray snatched the pennant out of her son's hand. She grabbed the pennant and they began to tussle. I hollered over to Ray to leave them alone. Ray kicked the lady in the stomach and snatched the pennant from her and broke it in two and walked back across the street. The lady cursed as she walked away with her son, who was crying. We hopped the bus and went home, back to the ghetto where those things were part of a "normal" existence.

Sophomore Year

Life became a little easier at Lindblom because I started to know a few of the students. All the students of the same backgrounds were starting to find each other. When you're young, everything you do is for what is called "props," which means respect or proper credit. I would often see a brother they called Dubb in the hallway on the third floor of the school. The third floor was where freshman and sophomores usually hung out. Dubb seemed to be a very cool and controlled person.

The Key to Stopping the Violence

At that time, he was much larger and heavier than me. The tripped out thing about Dubb was that he would carry a Bible around and sometimes wore a priest's collar. His personality was that of a serious person with comical attributes. There were all kinds of people to meet, the get high drug crowd, the cool playboy types, the bookworms and the athletes. I was a ballplayer, so the football players where the boys I liked. The only problem was that we all lived in different areas in Chicago.

There were a few football players that played freshman ball that were already on the sophomore team, there was Deke, Carl Estelle and myself, and a few others. During the spring ball, I began to notice that Deke had a lot of talent. He was a linebacker and his favorite tackle was dropping at the last second and knocking a running back's ankles off. I became what I always wanted to be, a running back. But at first, I found it a little harder than I'd imagined. There is always a time in a person's life where that person will look up and come to grip with reality. I came to grips with football's reality in a drill that made me think, "Is this game going to be this hard?" In the drill, Coach had the running back get on his back and lay the football to his side about a foot away. Then he placed a defensive man about 10 yards away with his back toward the running back.

There was about a 10-yard boundary on each side of the players. When Coach blew the whistle, the running back was supposed to get up, grab the ball and avoid the tackler. It was a drill for quickness. The defensive man had to turn around as quick as possible and knock the shit out of the runner. And it just so happens that I was the first to get picked for the drill. When Coach blew the whistle, I had gotten one leg off the ground and one hand on the ball. The defensive man knocked the living shit out of me.

No Rhyme, No Reason

Ray was back at Wendell Phillips now as a freshman. The fellows would walk up to Alco Drugs because it stayed open all night and because they sold half pints of ice cream. Sometimes Ray, Frankie, Mark, who lived on 39th St., and me would walk there to buy ice cream for Mrs. Grandberry. We would avoid going through the extensions because I had become the cautious one. Instead, we would walk through the more "upscale" Lawless Gardens. That always seemed strange to me. One area was dominated by people on welfare and across the street was a working middle class area with security guards in the buildings.

Lawless Gardens consisted of three high-rises and smaller townhouses on the sides. As we walked Ray decided to throw rocks. It was no big deal because we always threw rocks to see who could throw the furthest. Only this time, Ray decided to pick up a brick and throw it through a big picture window. Frankie, Mark and I had a delayed reaction, then we ran. As the brick crashed through, lights inside people's apartments clicked on to see what the noise was. I took off running north toward 35th Street. Ray followed me. Mark didn't run and Frankie ran south toward home. From about 40 yards away, we saw the security guards pick up Mark. I asked Ray why he did it. He never said why but, reasoned it didn't make any difference. We were in the middle of it now so we might as well try to get out of it, he explained. So Ray and me ran to Alco Drugs and once we got in the store a police car pulled up and stopped in front. They didn't see us go into the store. As we turned, we noticed a familiar face in the back seat of the car. It was Mark. That's when I began to worry.

Ray seemed to get juiced from all the action. We purchased the ice cream, then figured the best way to go home was the side street, and then down King Drive to avoid the main street. We started walking and about a block into our trip home, we spotted a police car, so we ran up in a hallway of one of the nearby apartment buildings. We continued to laugh and walk. Ten minutes later, the same police car circled the area and came back.

We immediately dropped to the ground and crawled under a car. The police car stopped right in front of us and started shining the high beam light on the buildings and the ground. We could hear them talking in the police car as we held our breath. They stayed there for what seemed to be 10 minutes, questioning Mark about our whereabouts. I had never been so afraid. The police car finally pulled away and we knew that we had a long way home. We were running and hiding all the way there. After almost two hours, we finally got about a quarter of a block from Ray's house. I was tired and in trouble because Mom had not wanted to let me go to Alco in the first place, but I had told her I would be back in an hour. That was almost three hours ago.

Then a second problem popped up: flashing lights in front of Ray's apartment. I told Ray I couldn't have them going to my house because Daddy would kill me if the police even knocked

The Key to Stopping the Violence

on the door. He had preached for years to me about not being with the wrong crowd. He didn't want me out on the streets at night, so I knew it would be real trouble in the Bassette camp if I had anybody in a suit, especially a blue one, at my apartment. So Ray did something I will never forget. He looked at me and said, "Ersk, as far as I'm concerned, you weren't here tonight."

I ran toward my building and went upstairs and went in. Momma started hollering at me for not coming back on time. But I begged her to keep it down because I didn't want to wake Dad. On the other front I was praying that the police wouldn't come up to our door looking for me. I shed a silent tear of fear because my greatest fear was Daddy. The police never did come but the next morning. I learned how easy it was to get out of trouble with single parents. Ray lived with his mother, Frankie lived with his mother and Mark lived with his grandmother, so none of them got in trouble. We laughed about it the next day because they knew they had a license to do whatever they wanted. They were all the men in the house as fithteen year olds. I was jealous then because I had to go in when night fell and I would get in trouble for anything an older person or neighbor said I did something wrong. But my dad was the backbone of my existence.

I realize now that he is a part of what saved my life. When a young man can respect his father's words that young man will go on to do great things. If the Black man is not there to guide his son, the streets will give him false direction. Black boys will continue to have no positive image of what they should be, unless their fathers provide it for them. I love you Dad.

A Family Disunited

At a Thanksgiving service in 1976, the pastor separated my friends from me because I was a "sinner." They said I would grow up to be like my Dad.

I sat there and watched and listened as the other 15-year-old boys were ordered to leave their seats as their mothers called them away from me. I wanted to be like Daddy, a man who worked everyday to take care of his nine kids, never stayed out of the house and showed us by example. Then the pastor loudly announced to the congregation that I would turn out to be no good. My family was sitting right there in front. The rumor was told to my friends that I would wind up in jail. I knew then, at 15, that my days in the church were numbered. There was no room for strong-minded people who questioned what was going on.

Momma had told them I made $25 a week as a paperboy. I was giving $2 each Sunday and they wanted me to give more, but I refused. I later found out that all of the adults who questioned the church were also thrown out in the name of God. All of the people who didn't believe that the money was being put to the best use were thrown out, including a few of my sisters.

Momma: Never to Come Back

Even though Eric attended Eastern Illinois University he would come home for holidays. In 1976, my sophomore year of high school, Evette was a senior at King High School. Momma had really began to scare us with some of the things she was saying and doing. All she talked about was that she was in a house among devils and that since Eric was gone she was the only person in the house praying to keep the devil out.

Momma started saying she couldn't handle us anymore. The verbal and emotional attacks accelerated. Most of this was going on while Dad was at work, so he was unaware. At that point I started talking more to Dad, and Momma began noticing our relationship. She told me that she wasn't pleased with this friendship.

One morning, sometime between Thanksgiving and Christmas, Momma had decided not to drive to work in the family car, a '65 Chrysler. I had just completed my paper route and walked in to give Momma a kiss and ask her if she wanted me to walk her to the bus stop. At that moment she lost her balance and I asked what was wrong. Momma said she would be alright. She was under too much stress and she was putting it on herself. But she was still Momma and I loved her even if her life was making things miserable and confusing. I would still do anything for her.

I walked her to the bus stop and came back home to get ready for school. When I returned home from school that evening, Dad was sitting in the living room with a strange look on his face. He told me that Momma was in the hospital. He said that she lost consciousness on the bus and someone called an ambulance and rushed her to the hospital.

Evette, Dad and I left immediately for the hospital. Once we entered the room, she began screaming that she didn't want

The Key to Stopping the Violence

Dad in the hospital room. She started crying, saying if he came in she would die. He didn't understand why his wife of 33 years would deny his presence. I could tell he was hurt and stressed. The doctors found that Momma was a diabetic and her blood pressure had shot up. That was the reason she had been complaining of feeling tired and drained. We found out 16 years later that she had also had a heart attack without knowing it. But she continued to say that it was a sign from God and that he told her she could not come home or she would die. She said that God wanted her to get away from the non-prayers and devils in our family.

Earina, one of my older sisters, called Eric in school. After two weeks in the hospital Momma was released, and what she did next changed the course of our family history forever. Instead of coming home she went to Elaine, another one of my older sisters, and her husbands one bedroom apartment. Instead of Eric coming home for Christmas to be with us, he broke the camel's back by supporting Momma's logic and also stayed at Elaine's house.

Momma still allowed me to see her and went so far as to ask me to move in, too, but I questioned what they were doing and why would we leave Dad when he hadn't done anything to us. Momma would say it was God's doing, that our entire homelife was turned upside down. Then a week later Momma called and asked me to come to the church. She, Eric and me sat on the small side of the church. For the second time Momma asked me to leave Daddy to come live with them.

I sat there with Momma, crying from confusion and fear. No no one assisted her in making the right decision. They just went along with her. It was one of the saddest times I could remember. I said, "This was some church that had separated us and our family was being split because of these people." I stated how they had tried to separate me from the friends I had grown up with. Plus Dad hadn't done anything to deserve this treatment. Sure he was quiet, but he put food on the table. How could I stay here, I asked. I told them there was not enough room at Elaine's for Momma, not to mention me.

I didn't know Momma, Eric, Elaine and Eraina would turn against everyone not associated with the church. I did not know Momma would not speak to me for 10 years.

I ran home and Dad and Evette met me at the door and he asked what was wrong. I told him what happened. As I cried, he looked and laughed, which made me even more upset. He even called me a baby. I ran upstairs even more confused because I had just defended a man I loved but who I didn't know. That was my first understanding of what all that trauma could do to people. Up to that point Mom was always the person I went to. Dad was the worker and the breadwinner, in his generation men didn't show emotions. Was Dad covering up his own feelings or did he think men didn't cry? That put me in a state of anger and embarrassment because I was trying to do the right thing for my family.

Deke and Me -- A New Brother's Love

Weekends were the time I would find myself feeling sorry because Momma wasn't around. Traditionally, the weekends were when we had Sunday dinners and family around. Now the house was always quiet and the loss of family brought on constant depression. Momma and Eric were gone, and Evette was talking about getting married. My girlfriend decided to break up with me and I didn't seem to fit into the Lindblom crowd. I would lay around the apartment on Saturdays and watch the "Wide World of Sports" or old movies. Dad started working more and more overtime on Saturdays, so I spent a lot of time alone. Dad couldn't cook anything but greens so he always made these giant pots of greens or black eyed peas, which he expected us to eat for weeks at a time. I didn't look forward to dinner. Evette never seemed to be around because she spent all of her time with her boyfriend or talking about getting married.

One afternoon the phone rang and I answered to a voice that said, "What's up Ersk. This is Deke. How do I get to your crib? I live down on 37th and Vincennes, down close to Cottage Grove." I explained in detail.

Deke shouted through the line. "I'm going to stop through but before I do I want to know if you have some eggs at the crib." I put the phone down and looked in the refrigerator. We had some.

"Good, then I'm gonna bring some pancake mix and milk. Meet me at the bus stop."

Deke got off at Doolittle School and caught the CTA bus around Cottage Grove to 36th Street. I met him there and he said he was down on my end of town taking care of some business.

So we went to the apartment and started mixing stuff up, I mean cooking a meal. After about an hour we had stacks of

The Key to Stopping the Violence

pancakes, bacon and eggs all ready to eat. We sat there in the living rooms and ate all this food. During the whole time I was puzzled as to why this brother had come over to see me. Deke started saying that he knew something was wrong with me at school but he didn't know what. I sat back on the couch with a feeling of really being important because no one at school had ever shown concern over anything I did or felt. I told Deke it was tough going to a school out of the neighborhood. He expressed the same feelings about Lindblom.

"Ersk, I thought you said you could cook," he then said. "You tried to poison me."

I had burned half the pancakes. We laughed, and he fell asleep on the couch while I was on the floor watching one of those black and white matinee movies. I drifted in and out on the floor thinking about how nice it was to have a friend I could relate to. After about an hour Deke woke up and said he had to get home so I walked to the bus stop with him. For the first time in a long time I looked forward to school on Monday morning.

The Beginning of "Thee Family"

I thought about leaving Lindblom and going back to the low end and Wendell Phillips High School or dropping out of school completely. It was a bright day in late February or early March. The sun was out and everything was looking nice. Usually the weekends were pretty quiet but that afternoon somebody was banging on my door. Dad and me were living alone now. Most of the mothers in the neighborhood thought Momma had died. They figured Momma had done what a lot of people predicted to me and Ray for years: They always said we would worry our mothers to death or kill them from stress. So out of embarrassment I never spoke about her or any of my other brothers and sisters, only Evette.

I was a sophomore in the spring semester and I wasn't having the best of times at Lindblom. I felt like an outsider because I came from the projects. I believed most of the other students came from nice neighborhoods with big houses and lots of money. That, coupled with the problems at home and lack of support, made me very insecure. Additionally, just being a teenager made for a miserable existence.

For the first year and a half, I was very uncomfortable. But at the same time, I still had the single most important thing to me in my life: football. Even playing on the freshmen and

SILENT CRY

sophomore football team my friendships with the brothers on the team was at rock bottom. I wasn't used to having friends who seemed so distant. None of us lived in the same geographic area. In the second semester there was a group of brothers that took auto shop during the same period. The big deal in the classroom was who was going to make the varsity football team. There was a lot of competition going in the classroom. From growing up I didn't like jealousy or envy because those things alone can bring on fights, anger and sometimes death. But on the other hand I wasn't going to let any body punk me. I thrived on the competition.

In my sophomore year everybody was trying to make a name for themselves. In auto class there were some of the roughest boys in the school. Everyday we went through a competition of who was going to be the best at this or that, which eventually led to arguments and near fights. Once I was challenged by a brother in class so I had to give him a 37th Street ass kicking. The brothers in class starting giving me my props, especially one of the more vocals brothers: Deke. But this day when I heard the knock on my second floor door became a historic moment because the two brothers at the door made me feel loved for the first time in a long time.

Dad answered the door and called me downstairs with his usual strong, deep voice. He said there were two boys at the door for me. To my surprise, it was Dubb and Deke, two of the homies from my auto shop class. They stood in the hallway and asked if I could make a quick ride with them. They waited in the car. Dad started asking me a bunch of questions about who they were, where they lived and how they had a car. Dad had all these new responsibilities he never had before. He didn't know them and this was the first time he knew of anyone coming to the low end from school to visit. I assured him that they were boys from school and that the car probably belonged to Dubb's or Deke's parents. Dad's concern was valid because I was only 15. But he let me go.

I jumped in the back seat as we cruised around, Dubb leaning coolly over the steering wheel, driving with one hand. Dubb was leaning so much I wondered how he could see over the dashboard. He decided to cruise south to Washington Park where we watched some brothers play softball for about 10 minutes. Deke was joking about how I had taken old boys face off in that fight at school. Then Deke told Dubb it was time for Dubb to be getting back home with his mother's car. Before they dropped me

The Key to Stopping the Violence

off Deke joked with Dubb that he was supposed to wash the family car. Instead, Dubb had decided to pick up Deke and then decided to come down to the low end to see me. I still smile about that day because it left a feeling of friendship and brotherhood that will never leave me. After that weekend me, Dubb and Deke became inseparable in school.

One Fight, We All Fight

Auto shop became a place where all the action was happening. The teacher was a black man named Mr. Davis, who was new to the school. He was a wonderful teacher and loved to work on any car. While he worked the class would usually be out of control. Whenever a student asked him a simple question, Mr. Davis would elaborate for hours. Deke and I got a kick out of asking him to explain the origin of the screw driver. He would sit you down and start taking you back to when and how the caveman developed it. He was one of the few people I felt comfortable telling about my family life, as he returned the same. " Bassette, you remind me of my youngest son T.D.," he'd say. "I think you both would get along well." Later that next school year I did meet his son.

Most every one of us in the auto shop class was trying to out for the varsity football team. I was one of the sophomores that the varsity coaches wanted to take a close look at. After the long winter drills we finally got our equipment. Dubb and me left for home during a sock-hop. Whenever there was a party at the school it attracted all types of people from other schools. Lindblom had a reputation of being a school full of punks because it was known for books not sports. But I wasn't no punk and some of my new friends weren't, either.

On the way home on the bus we had our football equipment. The equipment was our pride and joy because we had made the varsity football team. When I got off the bus to catch the train, I left Dubb on the bus. As I walked east across Ashland street, Dubb came running behind me, saying there were about eight thugs on the bus who tried to jump him. Without hesitating or looking around, I said, "Dubb, I got your back."

As soon as I spoke all eight surrounded Dubb and me while telling him to give up his watch. I jumped in and one of those motherfuckers stole a punch to my jaw. That's when the fight broke out with eight against two. The only way they got the watch was because one of the thugs grabbed Dubb by the arm and another grabbed it off. I had taken some good punches in the face but it was worth it for my new friend. Dubb thanked me for not leaving him, but that was natural where I was from. I told Dubb the next day we would go home together. When we got to school the next day we told Deke and the other brothers in the auto shop class what happened. I told Deke we would never go home alone again. Deke stood there with tears in his eyes because he felt he let us down. Deke said, " there will never be such thing as a fair fight; if one of us fight we all fight." We were just 15 year old sophomores but we were not going to be fucked with outside the school. At the same time the God Father movie was playing and Deke loved the scene about them all being just one family. And thats when he said the three of us in the auto shop would be a family. Deke, Dubb and me ran though the school halls calling ourselves a family.

That's when us three decided to form a brotherhood to protect ourselves from the elements of that neighborhood. Thee Family was founded in that auto shop classroom in spring 1977. The founders of this unique and prestigious brotherhood were Garry (Deke) Kennedy, Charles (Dubb) Adams and E.J. (Big Daddy) Bassette. Protection of each other brought us together. We searched for more brothers throughout the school like us, we soon inducted what were known as forefathers: Vince (Mr. C.) Currington, Eric (Rick) Lee, Robert (QB) Cook, David Mitchell, Rick Snipes, Ronnie Jackson and Darryl (Sherlock) Shaver, and a host of others.

In fall 1977, during the football season, Thee Family went through what was known as the "reconstruction period." We added mild mannered, but true-to-life brothers Victor (Vick Comma Slick) Simpkins, Carl (Ewee) Estelle, Anthony (T.D.) Davis, Dan (Mercury) Bronson and Ralph Stuart, and a host of others. Thee Family rule of life was simple, "If one fights, we all fight!" We would never let a family man go down alone.

Promise to Dad

Dad and me were still trying to recover from our family going from a apartment full of people to just us two. Dad was also trying to be a mother and a father. Now I admit he was just as afraid of his new responsibilities as I was of mine. One of the things Dad had to get used to was the fact that football had become the most important thing in my life. I expected him to

The Key to Stopping the Violence

be at my games.   It also meant that I couldn't work before or after school because of my practice schedule.

That was a hard pill for Dad to swallow because work was his opinion of manhood. Plus, he felt I should pay my own bus fare back and forth to school. I promised Dad that if he paid my weekly bus fare, I would make my football activities pay off by earning a scholarship to college.

Bus expenses were $12.00 a week to get to school. Dad agreed to pay $10.00, so twice a week, I would have to sneak on the bus or train. Usually timing my jump over the CTA turn style running at full speed to avoid being stopped by the train attendant.

Hard to Say Goodbye

While life in high-school was moving on, the low end was becoming more violent. A friend I grew up with had just been killed. After Ray told me the news I reminisced about what I remembered about our shared experiences.

After classes during grammar school, boys would play hockey at the tennis court. We had Roy Polk and Lil J., Ricky and Ronnie Wright, Lamar and Rodney Cole and the rest. This was during the glory years of Bobby Hull and Stan Makita, when the Chicago Blackhawks were a big deal in the ghetto. Everybody had those hockey games with the metal ball and the little plastic men. During the winter, we would let the water run from the side of the buildings before school and by the time school was out we would have the backyard full of ice.   That's where we learned how to ice skate and use our sleds. Usually in the fall we played hockey on roller skates at the tennis courts. We would tear the tennis nets down and use the open fence as goals. Momma didn't let me run straight outside after school because I had to do my homework first, so I couldn't   play as much. Anyway, I was not nearly as good as the regulars.

Everybody in the 'hood took pride in their hockey sticks. Knowing how to play the game was an art in itself. We knew every player on the Blackhawks, every player in the leagues and who the fighters were. Brothers were losing most of their front teeth from hockey before eighth grade. There were two players whose names would always surface as the best players in the 'hood. We predicted they would be the first black hockey players in the NHL: Roy Polk and Lil J. These brothers had so much finesse and stick handling ability that they could use anybody on the court.   Roy would take on the entire opposing team by himself. Seeing him go one on one was like seeing Bobby Hull make a backhanded shot.

Roy Polk, they said, was twice as good on ice skates as he was on roller skates. Roy was also a good baseball player. As he continued to grow, he didn't hide that he wanted to be the first black in professional hockey. In the summer we played on rival baseball teams: the Comets and the Reds. The Polk family lived in the 534 building where Ray and me enjoyed hanging out.

One day in eighth grade, Ricky Wright, a grammar school friend, and I decided to cut classes and started on our way to the lakefront. We ran into Roy, who was a freshman in high school, and he walked with us to the candy store across Cottage Grove, next to the paper branch. Ricky and Roy bought some cigarettes.   We heard a hit song called "Bennie and the Jets" blasting on the radio and still to this day when I hear it, it reminds me of Roy. Roy was an easy going kid who had a good career in front of him.   He and Lil J. would play in hockey Leagues around the city where the whites had never seen a black person on skates play with Roy's flair and charm.

Once we entered high school, Ricky played baseball at Dunbar. Lamar and Rodney played football at Wendell Phillips, and Roy continued to play in hockey leagues. Because my school was out of the neighborhood, I had to devote more time to travelling and after school it would be impossible to get back and hang out.

One late summer day about two weeks before my junior year of high school . Back in the hood, Roy and some old friends were gambling. Roy and the boys got into an argument about some money. A friendly game of shooting dice led from one thing to another until arguments broke out. The argument was over a few dollars that someone decided to stand up for. As the argument heated up one of the Mason brothers came out to see what was going on. People said there were about six or seven Mason brothers who didn't start anything but didn't take any shit off anyone. Roy asked one of the Mason brothers what he had to do with the conversation. He told Roy it was his business because of the noise in his area.

People stepped between Roy and Mr. Mason, but a punch was thrown and landed on Mr. Mason's face. Mr. Mason left and a few minutes later he and two of his brothers returned. Roy and the boys ran two blocks toward Roy's 534 building. They were laughing, talking and catching their breath. The Mason

The Key to Stopping the Violence

brothers caught up as everybody took off running, while Roy hesitated and looked around. That hesitation gave the Masons an edge. Gunshots rang through the first floor. One hit Roy in the back as he tried to run out the door and down the stairs. He fell on the grass in front of the building. Roy's older brother held Roy as Roy asked him if he was going to die. His brother said "No" as Roy died in his arms.

Roy was 19 years old and left behind two brothers and two sisters, and a wonderful mother. He was a young man with a dream but never escaped the projects. Roy knew hockey and to this day I can still see Roy Polk's fluent moves on the tennis court. I saw Lil J. recently and he looked like life had gotten the best of him.

Ray went to Roy's funeral but I couldn't make it. He said they played "It's So Hard To Say Goodbye" from the movie "Cooley High."

Football, Junior Year

Before the football season started we got a new player on the team from a suburban school. The coaches said he was a stud. In the locker room the first day, Deke and Vince started fucking with him as I came in between them. Later he became a valued part of Thee Family and the brotherhood. T.D's father was our auto shop teacher.

Wendell Phillips High School was again emerging with bona fide football players like Mitchell Brookins(Buffalo Bills), Lamar Lewis, Rodney Cole, Chris Hinton(Minnesota Vikings), and Munchkin. Munchkin first came to my attention because Lamar always talked about his teammates at Wendell Phillips. Wendell Phillips High School had a tradition of success, from the powerhouse teams of Marty Murry, offensive guard Louis Clayton (who grew up in my backyard) and Roy Parker from the city championship teams of 1973 and '74.

Although Ray didn't play football he was involved with the team. Wendell Phillips High School practiced across the street from our backyard in Ellis Park. But because I was always attending practice at Lindblom, the only opportunity I had to see them was on Sunday practice or days when they practiced but we didn't.

In my first two years of high school, Lindblom was not in the same division as Wendell Phillips High School, which was in the powerful Red South division. But my dream was to play against my boys. Mitchell Brookins had come on the scene as one of the premier running backs during his sophomore year. He ran so many touchdowns on junior varsity that they moved him up to varsity. He was the next great runner Coach Bonner showcased in a long line of talent after Roy Parker's era.

In the 1976-77 season, my sophomore year, Lindblom had a great football team with senior running backs Darnell Harper and K.T.; linebacker Frank White; and juniors Jeff Dillard, Michael Williams and Ronald Norwood (Swan). They won the White division and by finishing in first place, Lindblom High School moved up to the Red division for the first time in recent history. This timing was perfect for me because now I would get a chance to play against my childhood friends.

We went into the season my junior year with Wendell Phillips High School as our first regular season opponent. I earned the starting halfback slot and had the opportunity of my life to make a dream come true. But first we had to play two preseason games against Robeson and Marshall High School The first game was at Gately Stadium, which was packed, and I was going to be one of the featured backs along with Ralph Stuart and Jeff Dillard. On the first play from scrimmage, Ralph ran a play 40 yards. Then on the next play, he ran a touchdown. Our next possession we faked the same play, and I ran a reverse for 65 yards. After coming back to the sideline, the seniors told me I ran like Harp, No. 33, who played before me. I went on to run for more than 100 yards. Later I found out legendary Coach Bonner of Wendell Phillips High School was in the stands scouting us for the first regular season game.

I suffered a bad ankle injury in the second game but the Wendell Phillips High School team wasn't aware of it. I would come to the 'hood and they were preparing for their game plan. Lamar would tell me that the whole week consisted of a "key on No. 33 defense." I had worked so hard to prepare myself for a game I wanted to play in so much, but I couldn't. When the game started I dressed anyway. The whole time Lamar and the others hollered over at us as we got our asses kicked.

O.J. Simpson: Hero

O.J. Simpson was my hero since his early days at USC. I tried to pattern myself after him and Terry Metcalf of the St. Louis Cardinals. Walter Payton was coming on as a Chicago

The Key to Stopping the Violence

great, especially the year he almost broke O.J.'s single-season rushing record.

But what made me admire O.J. was when he was on the cover of *Ebony* magazine with his wife and kids. I would sit and look at that picture literally for hours, saying that I would find that one black woman and stay with her forever. My room was full of pictures of all the football players, but O.J. took up the most space.

The older players on the team started calling me "Slow-J," which was a generic version of the real thing. Then after a time they settled for the name "E.J." and I've been using it ever since.

After O.J. and his first wife separated, he popped up with a white woman on his arms. To me that meant status and elegance. So, before I left for college, I told all of the girls I dated that I would go to college, become a superstar and marry a white woman.

I saw O.J. do it and if he did it and I knew he knew what he was doing, then I would do it.

Deke's Image

We gained popularity during the football season from the pep rallies and being in Thee Family. But one incident made Deke bigger than life and changed his whole image and that of Thee Family.

Deke was in the lunchroom with some of the brothers as they went to the line to get their lunch. Thee Family was gaining popularity because we would wear sweaters and ties to school every Thursday. Deke was taking a drafting class the next period so he had the drafting board with him during lunch. A girl in the lunch line decided to get smart with Deke and the other brothers in line. As she hollered and walked toward them, Deke reacted and put his board between him and her. She accidently walked into it and fell to the ground. Deke panicked and ran in the football locker room. The rumor started that Deke knocked this girl over the head with a drafting board. Deke became the most popular Thee Family brother. He became a villain in the school, and upper and lower classmen admired and feared him. We all fed Deke's ego as we praised him for what happened. Thee Family played on that one incident, which time showed wasn't the best thing to do.

SILENT CRY

In another incident that helped shape his image, Deke would always go to a college campus to visit his cousin. He said on the campus they called each other "Dogs." So he became "The Deke Dog" and I became "The J Dog." All the brothers start calling ourselves dogs and the sisters loved us. We became more and more popular in school and our fun got increasingly outlandish. We were intelligent brothers with street sense. We didn't necessarily go out to start any trouble, but being in the inner city, trouble was often un avoidable.

Those who didn't know Deke began to fear him. I knew the real Deke. In the city we had to be tough because the environment was tough. He did alot of nice things people were not aware of. Deke became a brother to me, when my own blood brother wasn't around. Each year Deke would call me on my birthday and surprise me by taking me to the McVicker's Theatre downtown to watch three karate movies for $1, and he paid.

Trouble Starting Fast

After the football season my junior year the 'hood around Lindblom was exploding with thugs coming around and robbing students. They always hung out at 63rd and Wolcott or 63rd and Damen waiting to start their assaults. The senior football players along with Thee Family would walk up to the corners after basketball games and stop at the hamburger shop on the corner of 63rd and Wolcott. This was a usual gathering place for us in the winter after a game. One night I was walking with seniors, Swan and Luther Hunt. Swan was from the low end and even though he was tall, skinny and awkward, he had no fear of the area. That night some thugs decided to throw snowballs at some of the students walking on the other side of the street. There were five or six of us in the first group, but we knew that another 20 or so would be coming along five minutes later. As we started walking by the thugs, a snowball hit the ground in front of us. Luther made a snow ball and threw it back. This was an invitation to fight. The average Lindblom student was passive when it came to defending himself, but we weren't. They were caught off guard by a snowball coming back toward them. They threw another and another one went right back at them. By this time words were exchanged between Luther and the thugs. We told Luther to ignore them and let's get something to eat.

The Key to Stopping the Violence

We went in the corner store and ordered as more ballplayers and students came in. Some students mentioned that there was a gathering of thugs outside the store. I looked at my Thee Family brothers, with that look of anticipation. Luther, who was known for his explosive temper, said he was going outside to see what was going on. The next thing we knew, he was in a fight and we all ran out of the store to help. The girls stayed inside. After we broke up the fight, we went back inside. The thugs started saying they were after Luther's ass. Luther was out of control with anger, so we got our books and we headed toward the other side of the street. That was when our Low end experience came out of Swan and me. Because of the thugs on the other side of the street, some of the senior ballplayers started to panic. I told Luther to walk between Swan and me. We pushed Luther into a store to wait for the CTA bus. The thugs were all around, our girls were crying. The thugs wanted Luther but couldn't come in the store because the owner wouldn't allow it. I went outside to speak with one of the thugs and he said my boy Luther was going to get killed. He pulled back his coat and there was a gun in his belt. I went back inside and let Luther and Swan know the thugs were packing guns. That changed the whole equation. When the bus came we planned to let Luther get on first so he'd be safe. We could see a bus about three blocks away and before the bus stopped at Wolcott, people were scrambling to get on. Swan and I couldn't get Luther on the bus because the big ass football players were pushing to get on even before the women. That left me, Swan and Luther last to get on. I was between Luther and the thugs and Swan was on the other side. Finally the opportunity arose and I pushed Luther on. He and the thugs were passing words and I stood as a shield between them. I was afraid I might get shot at any moment. The bus door closed behind me as I hollered to the bus driver to quickly take off.

With a bus packed with students who thought they were safe, I started to make it toward the middle of the crowded bus the thugs were trying to get in through the back door. They were beating on the door and calling Luther. Just as the bus started moving, a loud bang exploded in the night air that made everyone drop to the floor. Someone had shot the window right in front of me. Then another window burst on the other side of the bus. There were screams of panic. During the chaos, the bus driver stopped. People were crying and screaming and a girl started having a seizure. I fought through the students to make it back to the front of the bus and screamed at the driver to drive the fucking bus before I drove it myself. He panicked, so I grabbed him by the shoulders with the intention of throwing him out of the seat. At that moment, he put his foot to the peddle and the bus started moving. I told him to drive to Ashland Avenue, which was far enough away. I also told him to radio for help because someone was having a seizure.

Thee Family brothers, Deke, Vince, Rob and me met with Luther and Swan, the next day and decided to have a walkout at Lindblom, demanding police protection. We later got on the 63rd Street train with brothers getting off at their different stops. Swan and me rode back to the low end talking about all the fucked up shit that was wrong in the city, like how we went through this in the projects and now we were subject to it again in a so-called residential area. We continued to talk about it after we got off the train and I walked to his building at the 540 extensions. I went home but before I left him, I told him we would go to school together the next morning. That night I called Deke and Vince because we knew we needed protection. The next morning we met and took a different route to school. Once there the entire school was buzzing with what had happened. Thee Family was ready because the previous night when I talked to Ray I told him what happened and that I would need a gun. He told me he could get me a gun that belonged to his mother's friend. He got it, but I told him to hold off because I knew if I had it I would use it. I told him to keep me in mind. I also let him know that I was willing to bring some of the low end brothers up if that could solve some problems. Ray had no problems with this. I never did have him come up.

One of the other brothers brought a .38 pistol to school as Thee Family started to take matters in our own hands. The best and brightest black students in Chicago attended Lindblom, but the school board and Chicago police department were not willing to get an extra patrolmen or bring buses up to the school for us. We figured we would have to protect ourselves. The thugs had guns and we needed guns. After we got in school, Luther called the time of the walk out and I had the privilege of pulling the fire alarm. Once the 3,000 students were outside, Luther stood up and talked about our rights as we all listened. I enjoyed the fact that I was behind the scenes of this worthy event. Students stayed out and the school closed for the day. The next day Lindblom was in the newspaper and Luther's name was mentioned. There were rumors that some peoples names were on

The Key to Stopping the Violence

a hit list, but we went on with our lives. One of Thee Family Brothers had the gun and carried it around school. One day we sat at The lunch table and I heard a Thee Family member asking a female next to him to feel how hard it was. I felt like it wasn't any of my business, but I looked to see what was so hard. To my amazement, it was the loaded .38 pistol under the table pointed straight at my private with his hand on the trigger and her hand stroking it as if it was his dick. I jumped up and asked him what in the hell had he been drinking that day. But as usual if this brother could make an impression on someone, he would.

The walk out never did anything except gain a few days of attention. We were one of the top schools in Chicago, you would have thought they would have taken better care of their students and teachers.

War on Students

Once inside the school things were okay, but Thee Family was being molded by the things that continued to be intense around Lindblom. We had to accept the fact that war had broken out in the Englewood community. There was a growing number of cases of students and teachers being robbed. Teachers' cars were broken into. Because we left the school later than other students, I decided to go home with the people I felt were more likely to fight if a situation arose. Swan, Deke, Vince and some of the other brothers were definitely the right people to be with since things were happening so often

This particular day we had stayed for a basketball game. Swan had just finished saying that if he was approached by someone, he was kicking some ass. I was thinking that all I wanted was to graduate, go to college and play football. But there were school-related obstacles in the way and I wanted to make it out. I thought I had gotten away from it when I enrolled at Lindblom instead of Wendell Phillips High School As about seven of us were ready to leave the school and walk to the bus stop. Swan joked about how he had taken enough bullshit with the thugs. He stopped at a trash can and pulled out a stick to show how he would protect himself at any cost. Our Family brother had stopped bringing the gun to school because Deke thought he would wind up killing us before he shot a thug. We felt it was to our advantage to take our chances against the street instead of bringing the gun. That night, as we left the school through a side door, I decided to get a stick of my own, but they all were broken. So I followed everybody out the door. Once we walked out, the door locked behind us and out of the night two men approached us with guns drawn and pointed at our faces. "This is a stickup," they hollered. Just as they said that one student took off running around the corner. My heart dropped as the guns moved back and forth in each person's face and they shouted for us to drop our books and turn around.

Swan said, "I'm not dropping shit" as he walked toward them with his stick. The robbers were startled. "Death is the only way your punk ass is going to get some money from me," Swan replied. One of the thugs cocked his gun and pointed it straight at Swan while his accomplice tried to grab his buddy as he told him not to shoot. Swan told us to walk toward the bus stop, which was two blocks away. Everyone started walking slowly. I had been the last to come out so I was the last one to begin walking.

As I started walking away I heard one of the gunmen say, "Don't take another step. I felt those guns pointed at my back as I walked with my shoulder tight as though that would stop the bullet. I walked slowly with the fear of death present. But in that environment there was nothing else we could do. As we walked away, the robbers continued to holler that we would see them again.

My life had become a continuous nightmare. After I got to the low end, there were two men who started following me. I ran so fast they could not catch me. I had avoided my second confrontation of that cold night.

Virgin Man

Like most young men, there comes a time when we feel our manhood is tied to how much sex we get. And like most young men, we lie about what we are getting in order to impress our friends or even other girls. Inside we are really embarrassed with the fact that we wouldn't know what sex was if it slapped us in the face.

I was in my junior year of high school when I first encountered that moment of truth. I was sitting at a girls' basketball game with my ex-girlfriend, Kim. We had struggled off and on because of our strange break up. While Kim was questioning me on my latest choice in women, Carrie, who was a sophomore. Another young lady, Desiree, took a seat on the

The Key to Stopping the Violence

right side of me. Desiree was a senior . She always seemed to be spacing out as she walked around school. The one thing all the boys noticed about her was that Desiree had a body to kill for. Desiree combed her hair straight back and never wore any curls in her hair or styled it. Desiree was known for putting people in their place. The word was she was weird or a dike. One thing the fellas knew and talked about was the fact that Desiree had an ass for days. Brothers couldn't hold back saying what they would do for her to get that boy out of her. I was among the guilty. I always told Deke in history class what I would do to Desiree, who was safe to me because I knew there was no way in God's heaven that I could get close to her.

There's a saying that things come to you when you least expect it. That's what happened when Desiree sat next to me at the basketball game. As I talked and laughed with Kim, Desiree leaned over and said, "E.J., you are a fine brother." I smiled and looked toward her with my usual cocky attitude and said, "Thanks, you're not the first person to say that."

A few minutes later, Desiree leaned my way again and said there were some things that she'd like to do to me. I smiled, not taking her seriously. That's when Kim said she had heard what old girl was saying and that Desiree sounded serious. I said that Desiree was just talking shit and that she didn't mean anything. As the game progressed, Desiree got more intense and persistent with what she wanted. Kim got insulted and moved away. Desiree started asking me if I could go home with her that night. I told her no because I had to go home with Thee Family brothers since we always caught the bus together after dark. Desiree said she had driven to school with her mom's car and she would take me home with her and then she'd drop me off at home.

I panicked because I realized at this point she was serious and I was running. Finally she asked if I was afraid. I said no, but continued to turn her down. I finally got away from her and once out the gym I admitted to intimidation but felt like a stud. I saw Vince Currington coming in the gym and I told him about what had just happened. Vince walked up to Desiree, pulling me with him, and said to her, "Give E.J. your phone number. And E.J. give Desiree your number and call each other." That's exactly what I did the next day. Desiree gave me instructions to her house and I caught the CTA bus out south. After getting there, Desiree asked me to go down in the basement with her. As

SILENT CRY

I followed her down, she assured me that no one was home but her grandpa.

After about 15 minutes of conversation, Desiree asked me to take my pants off. I pretended not to hear her, but she became more forceful. "Take your pants off," she commanded for the second time. At the same time she was taking off her pants and her underwear. Of course I was full of tension and excitement as I lowered my pants. Desiree laid down on the sofa and opened her legs, as she told me to come down on the sofa. I hesitated and she pulled me on top of her. From there she took my private and put it in her and she started to scream for me to work my body. My eyes began to sweat as I let out a big scream. I'll never forget it because the whole experience lasted about 20 seconds. Desiree looked at me with disgust and hollered, "Get the fuck off me." Then she kicked me in the chest and knocked me to the floor. At the top of the stairs stood her 80-year-old granddad watching me get my first piece. I'm sure in his mind he was saying, "I could last longer than 20 seconds."

Desiree ran upstairs, yelling at her grandpa to close the door. I laid on the floor, put my pants on, not really knowing if it was as good for her as it was for me. Of course I couldn't wait to get to school Monday to tell Deke, T.D. and Vince how I made a woman out of Desiree. She never spoke to me again in her life.

Fight for Honor

We were seniors in Lindblom and Thee Family was kicking it in full gear. We had started the football season and "let the games begin" was our attitude. I had worked hard over the summer to make sure I was ready. Usually right after homeroom I met Deke and T.D. in the crowded hallways. We would holler through the crowd to look at that piece of booty or grab one of our many female admirers. We had a saying: "There ain't no man like a Thee Family man." Women loved us because we were wild, fun and unpredictable. Vince, Deke and me always led the charge when it came to bullshitting.

Monday morning started off as usual. Walking out of homeroom I could see Deke's bald head shining in the light. But as I walked up to him, eager to start clowning, I noticed Deke was standing there with his hands partially covering up his face. I noticed tears flowing down his face. My mood instantly went from playful to serious. I asked Deke what was wrong. He

The Key to Stopping the Violence

replied as though his vocal cords had been restricted, mumbling that Vince's older brother, Bennie, had been killed on the West Side close to their house.

Vince C. was one of the most important Thee Family brothers. Vince had two bothers -- Bennie, who was a year older than us, and James, one year younger. Vince's father was the reverend of a West Side church and his mother was one of the most pleasant women you would ever want to meet. Vince was known for being loud and live, with a knack for spending Thee Family's money in the bank. We knew Vince had embezzled money from us. He was our treasurer and his personal affairs became part of Thee Family, but our love for him was greater than our hate for his spending habits.

Once Deke broke the news about Bennie we rallied Thee Family together to spread a blanket of love and support. At this time we had close to 40 members in our club. Vince and Bennie's family, the Curringtons, lived in a huge house in Austin, near suburban Oak Park. The house had so many rooms Rev. Currington boarded up the unused bedrooms. Deke called it the Adams family house.

Vince's family would always spend Sundays in church and then after church, they would have a huge family dinner at home. Bennie was always a quiet young man and stayed to himself. Vince's unconditional love for Bennie was the love you could only have for an older brother.

That Sunday, Mrs. Currington cooked dinner as she did every Sunday. Bennie had decided that he wanted some food from a fast food joint about three blocks away from their church home on Lake Street. Mrs. Currington expressed her displeasure with him wanting junk food instead of eating his regular dinner. But, Mother Currington gave Bennie her last $20, and the last words she spoke to her son were "Bring my change back, it's the last money I have. "Bennie gave her a kiss and started on his way. It was about 4 p.m. and darkness had not yet set on the poor west-side community. The rib joint was close to the train tracks over Lake Street. To get to the joint, Bennie, 19, walked past drug addicts and prostitutes. Bennie entered the small storefront joint and ordered his food through the bulletproof window that secured the storeowners from being robbed at gunpoint. After Bennie ordered, some ladies, kids and men came in behind him. Bennie paid for his food and after getting it and his change through the plexiglass window, he walked toward the door. Two men came in and ordered Bennie to hand over the

SILENT CRY

dollar bills in his hand. Bennie said it wasn't his money to give and tried to walk out. One man grabbed for Bennie's hand and tried to pry the money out of it as the other man joined in the struggle, restraing Bennie from behind. Bennie struggled with the two men, dropping his food, but fighting with the money tight in his fist. While in the store the men tried to appear as though they were three friends fighting over food.

The owner hollered for them to take the fighting outside, not knowing that Bennie was fighting for his life. The two men forced Bennie out the door as he desperately screamed for help. The people inside turned their back, not trying to stop what they saw. The two men were joined by a third as the fight escalated into a big-time robbery. They were fighting a determined, Christian man who had the force of God and his family's love behind him. Bennie was brutally beat, hit and kicked in the face as these three criminals continued to try to take his mother's money. The fight moved the four men a block from the fast food joint. Bennie's suit and coat was torn off. Bennie fought alone. No one stopped to help him, but he still would not give up his mother's last money.

The fight continued for more than 30 minutes, then one of the men pulled out a .38 caliber pistol and shot Bennie point blank in the head, leaving him there on the curb to die. The police arrived after the fact and found Bennie's body laying on the street corner. His hand was tightly closed with blood coming from his knuckles where the skin had been torn off by hitting the building and wall during his fight for life. The police found the money Bennie had fought for, still clenched tight in his hand. The MF's who killed this young brother killed only for the thrill of murdering. Bennie died in the honor of his mother's request.

Back at home, the Currington family ate dinner, unaware of the nightmare that was taking place only a few blocks away. As Mother Currington later prepared them for bed, their son and brother lie dead in the morgue. The house was big enough that Bennie would usually come in and go to his room. It was not unusual not to notice him. At 4:00 in the morning when the police came to the door and asked if Bennie Currington was her son, Mother Currington said yes and she told one of the kids to go upstairs to get Bennie, assuming he was there. But the police stopped them and told Mother Currington and Rev. Currington there that they wouldn't find Bennie upstairs.

The family was and still is devastated by what happened. The next day Vince was at school seeking the love from the

The Key to Stopping the Violence

brothers he knew would be there for him. Vince felt that we were the people he could find the most comfort with. That's when I saw Deke in the school hallway crying. My heart went out to Vince's family. Vince seemed to hold together well on the outside. We all packed in cars and went to Vince's house to share our feelings with his family. They seemed to appreciate our support. We sat in Bennie's empty bedroom and Vince told us what had happened to his older brother.

We went to where Bennies body was found and the store where he fought. I listened to the talking around me and felt like a hopeless 17 year old. We were fighting for our lives at Lindblom and Ray and Lamar were fighting over at the low end. I didn't know what the world would bring.

At Bennie's funeral, about 25 of Thee Family brothers came out to pay our last respects to the fallen prince. The Curringtons church was so packed that we decided to sit in shifts; 10 brothers sat down at one time as the other brothers lined the walls of the church standing proud and tall. Our standing was a sign of strength and unity to show this would not happen again to a brother of ours. We became very protective of each other.

Football Scouts Come to Lindblom

We had played our final game and lost in the playoffs to King High School. Now was the time that all the players on the team were waiting for a chance for the football scouts to come in and offer us scholarships. But as the months passed, that wasn't happening. Some of the players started giving up but I had my heart set on playing college ball.

One day a few scouts finally showed up and asked to see some of the players. They were from a few small Division III programs. Everything was going smooth until one of the men asked us what our G.P.A. was. We didn't know. The scout looked at us and said, "You are about to graduate next semester and don't even know what a G.P.A. is."

Then he explained that G.P.A. meant "Grade Point Average" and it accumulated over our four years of high school. We all said, "Yeah, I passed most of my classes," thinking that would satisfy these men. But they looked at us and asked to speak to our counselors.

A teacher walked by and said that all class rankings and G.P.A.s were posted on the board. We hurried the scouts over to the board to find that all of us were below the 2.0 minimum requirement to play college football. The scouts explained that it was very unlikely we would play unless we had a tremendous last semester to pull our grade point averages up to 2.0. Mine was 1.92, which meant I had averaged D+ work all four years at Lindblom. I was happy with that to this point because I had thought as long as I passed that was good enough. Now, these men were telling me all my dreams could be finished.

Getting the Grade

I wanted to play ball in college as much as anyone on our team I would talk to Coach Mette about it everyday and what it would take to get me on a campus. At the same time I had to get some pretty high grades in order to bring my G.P.A. up to 2.0. I had one semester left and practically had to get all A's and B's that last semester. I anxiously waited to find out who would be my teachers for the last semester. I figured if I got some easy teachers, I could put some effort into it and come out a winner.

I never will forget getting my class schedule and standing next to Andre Hughes, a friend on the football team. Andre had earned straight A's all four years as well as being ranked in the top 10 in our class. I showed Andre my schedule and he shouted that I had been given the two hardest teachers in the school: Ms. Leonard, a black studies teacher, and Ms. Ekhart, a literature teacher. I had heard of their reputations and I listened to Andre tell me how his parents had to come up and fight for him to get an A in Ms. Leonard's class because she was the first teacher who tried to give him a B in his life.

Everybody at Lindblom knew Ms. Ekhart, a white lady. She and her sister were two of the most intense teachers in the school. Andre had put the fear of God in me because I was a D+ student and he was a A+ student. He actually studied after school. How was I going to get out of these classes? My last semester. Damn! I thought maybe I'll go get the classes changed or maybe Coach Mette can get me out of them.

Then Andre gave me all the incentive I needed. He said, "E.J., you'll never make it past these teachers. Even if you struggle to do your best, you won't pass."

That was just what I needed, because I didn't study a lot but I was not anyone's idiot. So I looked Andre in the face and said, "I won't only pass these classes but I'll get A's."

Well I studied my butt off for both classes and got an A in Ms. Leonard class and a C+ in Ms. Ekhart's.

The Key to Stopping the Violence

I didn't know what my G.P.A. was at that point but I swore I would never put myself in that academic situation again.

Recruited

I continued to talk to Coach Mette about college. Lamar had been recruited by a college in South Dakota and Coach Mette said he had received a call from a coach at one of the Division II schools with a excellent football programs. He said the coach there was extremely concerned about bringing black athletes up to a campus without any blacks at the school or in the area. The college needed black players who could play well and adjust to the all-white environment.

Dad wasn't too happy when I told him about my choosing South Dakota. The coach there was calling me every week and planning for me to come up and visit. But what turned me off was when the coach called from South Dakota with a track member on the phone who had attended Lindblom the year before. The coach started telling me how excited he was for me to be coming and that he had someone he wanted me to talk to.

The former Lindblom student got on the line and said it was an experience of a lifetime. He said that the white people did everything he wanted done.

"E.J.," he said, "you don't have to study or nothing. These white girls will take your tests, write your papers and treat you like a king. The coach got on the phone and said that he felt I was making the right decision.

I felt stupid because I wasn't fired up for what I had teased the sisters about all the time: A chance to be an idiot jock. I made my decision from that conversation that I wouldn't be going to South Dakota.

Out of Control

Whenever there was a basketball game at Lindblom, there was an opportunity for a fight. The Lettermen's Club's job was to keep the students from both schools off the gym floor. The Lettermen's Club was comprised of athletes who maintained an outstanding grade point average and displayed leadership skills. Sometimes the young men got into power trips and one night when that happened some brothers from a rival High School, started fighting with a Lindblom student. During the pushing and shoving words were exchanged as Big D, a member of Thee

97

SILENT CRY

Family, helped clear up the action on the floor. Big D, like me, was raised on the low end and could easily be mistaken for a thug. However, he was extremely intelligent and a good guy -- but not a punk.

The shit again hit the fan once me, Deke, Vince, Big D, Rob Cooke and a few others left the school. When we got to the bus stop on 63rd Street, we ran into the group from the game and the words continued. They lived near Big D and me, so we rode the same bus, repeating their plan to follow Big D until he was alone. Deke decided to stay on the bus with us but the bus driver kicked us all off for fighting. After we got off the bus, the leader of the group said he wanted to fight Big D head-to-head. Deke said no because that wasn't the way we operated. Before we could react one of the dudes pulled out a gun. "Which one of you niggers is going to stop us now?" he asked. They grabbed Big D and started beating on him, as somebody drew another gun on us. We stood there helplessly on the side of 63rd up under the train track, watching as they kicked and stomped on Big `D. Blood rushed down his clothes. Deke lunged toward one of the brothers with a gun, when they took off running, I held him back.

We took Big D home and again discussed bringing guns to school. Big D's older brother got involved as we pointed out his chief attackers. Word came back a week later that a few of the guys were "taken care of" by the Big D's posse in the hood. Big D eventually went on to the University of Wisconsin and entered their pharmaceutical program. He and his wife now enjoy a successful life in Wisconsin.

The Shadow of Death

Even though football was over in my senior season, I wanted to go to college, but I still wasn't sure where. I knew Deke was going to a college called WIU in Macomb, Ill. T.D. said Deke had talked him into filling out an application and he was accepted. All I could think about was getting out of high school and out of the city without getting shot or killed. The area thugs were still robbing students, but so far, we had survived.

One night after a basketball game, I felt anxious as I got my books together. I walked over to Deke's locker and told him to hurry up. Deke, Vince and Rick Lee were joking around and taking their time. Julius Mays, a guy from the low end near 36th

The Key to Stopping the Violence

Street, was waiting for me so we could ride the bus together. I usually never left without Thee Family, but that day I told Deke I would meet him and the rest of the brothers at a small corner store on 63rd and Wolcott. Students bought candy and pop at the store before the bus came. Julius and me walked two blocks to the store where there was a handful of students, including Darryl Roberts (Film Director) Darryl was about 6'3" and not a fighter. Julius was about 5'5" and more of a pretty boy than a fighter. I usually tried to surround myself with people like me, people who would be ready to fight at any time. That's why Ray and Deke were my homies. They were able to "throw down" and watch your back, if necessary.

I stood at the counter after putting my books on a wooden shelf. You could leave your books there while you ate. Toward the back of the store was the cash register. The people behind the glass would hand you whatever you asked for, then you put your money through a small opening in the glass. All of a sudden about four of five gangbangers came in, led by the smallest of their group. They walked through the crowded store bumping into students while hollering that somebody was "going to get fucked up today." A chill ran through my body as I leaned over toward Julius and said, "Lay low and pretend you don't see them." Then I took my watch off and slid it into my blue jeans. There were probably 30 students in the store. None were my Thee Family Brothers and none would have fought with me. The short leader hollered, "Whose books are these?" Everyone in the store looked around. Darryl Roberts said they were his books and ran over and asked for his books. The thugs asked for five bucks to give the books back and Darryl said he didn't have that kind of money. The thug told him to give him his bus money. That's when Darryl turned around and shouted, "E.J., help me!" The thugs looked at me as if to ask, "Who the fuck are you?" I ran over and grabbed Darryl and told him to lay low, that Thee Family Brothers would be coming any moment.

But Darryl wouldn't listen. He was pleading for his books. The thugs took his books outside and Darryl followed. I knew I would defend Darryl but I had to be smart about it. I didn't want him to panic and I didn't want us to get our asses beat over some books. I leaned over to Julius and said I wanted him to go back to the school and get Thee Family Brothers. When I got out outside, to my surprise there were 14 or 15 gang members. They were harassing women, Darryl and other students who had walked to the store. The gangsters were throwing

SILENT CRY

Darryl's books back and forth, trying to make a fool out of him. Suddenly I looked up and saw Deke, Rob , Vince and about 10 other Thee Family Brothers walking with their ladies. The only brother that wasn't there was T.D., because he had gone home earlier. I walked to the middle of the street as I felt the gangbangers watching me. I stopped Thee Family on the other side of the street. "Today is thee day," I told Deke. We had anticipated this day for some time. These gangbangers had robbed teachers, students and even parents. We always said when they ran into us they would meet their makers.

The girls with us started to panic and cry because they knew we would fight. We told them (cheerleaders and pom pom girls) to walk toward the Ashland Street train station. Thee Family Brothers formed a straight line with Deke first, and me second. We walked across the street and Deke opened the door and walked into the store. At that instant one thug was coming out and his shoulder collided with Deke's. Deke gave him a forearm and knocked him back. From there we went in and leaned on the bookshelf. Deke looked at me and said to pass the word not to say anything yet because one of them would fuck up and then we would jump them. There was about 13 of us and 20 of them, but I still felt more than confident.

Deke said, "Let's go outside to see if the bus is coming." When Deke got to the door, their leader was standing there. He threw a fist into Deke's chest and said he would kick Deke's ass. That's when Deke's eyes lit up as he shouted to the gangbanger, "Do you know who I am? I'm the motherfuckin' Deke Dog." Deke threw a vicious left hook that made the thugs' head go sideways. The thug fell backward into some ice. From nowhere, Rick Lee came in. He had just walked up with about eight more of Thee Family Brothers. He hit the gangbanger, who was trying to recover from Deke's punch. Rick gave him a forearm to the face and knocked the MF out. We ran out of the store ready to fight. I stood face to face with one of them in the middle of the street. I told him this was the day he was going to go home with an ass kicking. The bangers were caught off guard. We were evenly matched, 20 to 20.

Suddenly, a big 6'6", 250 pound brother with pink lips came walking from across the street. He had to be at least 30 years old and wore a long, fake black fur coat. He had that look that said, "I just got my black ass out of prison." He screamed, "Who in the fuck is messing with my boys." We were a bunch of intelligent high school teenagers, but this was a gangbanger

The Key to Stopping the Violence

who was a lot older. He looked like a supreme gangster. We all froze. Then Robert Cook shouted, "We are all black brothers. All we want to do is go to school."

As Rob continued to plead with this big black asshole, I heard him say, "Fuck you and your school. We're gonna kick some ass." I thought, "Oh shit, I better get in position to hit this big lump of shit." I moved away from the gangbanger I had shaded and slowly moved up a snow bank, near a lightpole. I was positioned right behind him. He cocked his arm to hit Rob when a fist slammed into my face and my head smashed against the lightpole. My feet flew from under me and I saw stars. Fortunately, I had seen enough stars from hitting running backs and receivers so I didn't stay down long. I heard fighting so I got up cursing and swinging. The first thing I saw was Deke picking this motherfucker up off the sidewalk, hoisting him over his head and walking to the street, then body slamming him to the ground as if to break his back. One thug pulled out a knife and swung at Rick Lee. Rick said, "Okay. Now you're going to try to cut me. Ha." He hit the thug with an upper cut and smacked the dude to the ground. I went over and punched him in the face, all the while talking and swinging.

I began to tire out with all this fighting. As we continued, the thugs began running one at a time. I saw Vince, standing on the snow hill, with a milk crate in his hand. He never swung it, but was doing plenty of talking. We still joke about Vince and the fact that he never threw a punch the entire fight. Finally, even the big S.O.B. with the fur coat was running as we chased them a half of block in the opposite direction of the school. I started laughing as they ran off.

Deke hollered, "Brothers, it's too many of them. Fellows, get the hell out of here and make it back to the school." He had noticed a new crop of gangsters were popping out of their houses, the original gangster, were coming back with more support. We were two blocks from school when Deke turned around and said, "We left C.C. there. We have to go back." Thee Family Brothers were all out of breath, scared and tired.

Vince said, "I'll go to the school and get some help. Deke, get your scary ass back here." Deke sent one of the younger guys back to the school. Before I knew it we were running back to the very scene we were trying to escape. We couldn't leave a brother alone. Running toward the scene, I saw a a group circled around C.C. One person fell, then another, then the circle opened and C.C. walked out with his school jacket on his shoulder. In that instant, the Chicago Police Department arrived and the gangbangers started running in different directions. The police eventually caught the big black M.F. and they found the little punk who started the whole thing by taking Darryl's books. Those two thugs were 27 and 23, respectively. I never knew if Darryl got his books back.

The next day at school, we decided to have a walkout. We wanted more police protection and better bus service. The word got back to Dr. Ahern, the principal, and he called a meeting with Thee Family. I remember Deke, Vince, myself and the other brothers sitting at the big conference table with Dr. Ahern, who gave the standard line that the school was doing all it could. The entire school was buzzing. Dr. Ahern said he was in charge of the school and that the students only listened to him. I looked him in the eyes and said the students will listen to Thee Family and we would prove it with a walkout.

We sat at that big conference room table and argued with this white man who didn't live in our community. For the second year in a row, I pulled the fire alarm that started the walkout. The students were afraid to leave the area to go home. When it was time to go home, nearly 400 students were waiting at the front of the school for Thee Family. All the brothers formed a straight line and walked the students south to the 63rd Street bus stop. Then we walked students to the west a mile to 63rd and Ashland station. People from the neighborhood looked out of their windows, knowing we were the ones who had fought their sons and friends. Among other things, they shouted at us that we would die. We were 17-year-old heroes to the students; and Deke was our leader, he was proving to people he was willing to die for other students we really didn't know. We were young men ready to do battle for what we believed in. I was proud to be a part of this elite organization of black, intelligent men. Together we could accomplish anything.

That night, for the second time I went back to the low end and asked Ray for a gun. Ray wanted to help me out, but this time said no because he didn't want me to go to jail. I never pushed it, because I knew he was right. So instead I approached my dad with the idea of fixing the '65 J. mobile's muffler so I could drive to school. At first he refused, saying I didn't have insurance. I knew it was a matter of life and death because we were marked men in that community. We still had three months left. Dad didn't understand what I was going through. I said I wouldn't go back to Lindblom anymore and he fell for my bluff.

The Key to Stopping the Violence

Sunday night, he walked in my room and put the car keys on my dresser. He was a softie, once I got to understand his quiet side. So I started driving to school everyday, dropping the fellows off at different bus stops. I picked Deke up in the morning to make sure we got to school safely.

To keep the proud tradition of Thee Family going strong, Deke, me and the rest, decided to keep adding new young men into the organization, while we were getting ready for college. Deke had dreams of taking the organization to a national level. As the years went on over 300 young black men joined Thee Family. Unfortunately the problem around Lindblom High School continued to escalate, forcing parents to send their kids to other schools. Today Lindblom, although still an excellent academic school; has dropped from a once high of 3,000 students to less than 800. This is a serious message, that needed to be told.

Graduation was coming and we were all happy that we would be going to college and finally making it out of the inner city. Around the end of the year the senior class met in the auditorium to go over the graduation procedure. T.D., Deke and me sat together talking shit when a white lady came over and asked us to go to our proper seats. Somebody hollered out "Fuck you!" she told another student to get the principal. This happened three days before finals. Dr. Ahern called us in the office and said our parents would have to come up to school. Deke's mom came up with my sister. Dr. Ahern made a big deal about the statement. The white teacher said she wanted an apology as we sat in the same office where we had met with the principal when we fought to get police protection.

Dr. Ahern decided he would make an example of Deke and me by suspending us. The white teacher said she didn't want us suspended because that would be too cruel. Deke sat there and fell asleep; he had to go to summer school anyway to graduate. I told them that we had fought for the school. I was the captain of the football team and trying to go to college. I explained to Dr. Ahern that if I didn't take my finals I wouldn't go to college and the only thing left for me would be the projects. He looked at me and said, "Then that's the lesson you'll have to learn." I said, "Well the only problem is that if my life is going to be fucked up then I'm taking your ass with me," as I dove across the table, reaching for his neck. My poor sister and Deke's mom were holding my ankles as Deke woke up and tried to restrain me. I had nothing to loose.

After things settled down, Dr. Ahern gave me a long speech about how disappointed he was in me. But miraculously he decided to let me take my finals and graduate. I knew I was half street and half books , what we called a controlled thug. You can't threaten a man who has nothing to lose. Deke called the move crazy. I said, "Sucker, you slept through the shit anyway."

We avoided death that year. But it was a hell of a way to attend one of the best academic high schools in Chicago.

PART III
College Life: The Killing Ground

College Football: The Dirty 8

In the summer of 1979, after high school and before college, T.D., his mother, his sister, Evon, and myself drove down to Western Illinois University to register for the fall semester. Deke had encouraged T.D. to apply to be his roommate. Before high school graduation, T.D. and I were standing at the lockers and he showed me his acceptance letter. I still wasn't sure what college I wanted to attend. T.D. convinced me that Western would be a lot of fun. He and Deke had already visited the campus. So I decided to send an application in for acceptance. At the same time the coach at Western IL. visited one inner city school that year to recruit a football player from. The coach later said he had never been to Chicago before and didn't know what made him come to Lindblom. Coach Mette told him about me and we sent some football films to WIU. During the summer Coach Thornton called and invited me to a two-week football mini-camp. He let me know that I didn't have

The Key to Stopping the Violence

a scholarship but I did have a chance to walk on and prove myself. I jumped through the apartment like I had just won a million dollars. Because my dream Ray, Lamar and me talked about was coming true.

WIU is about 4 1/2 hours southwest of Chicago. Once we arrived, I saw the football field in the middle of the campus. Next, I wanted to go straight to the football office. I had talked to Coach Bob Thornton several times over the phone, but now we were going to meet in person for the first time. He thought I was much bigger than I was. On film I looked to be a 6'2", 185-190 pound defensive back. But in person, I was a 6', 160 pound scrappy defensive back/wide receiver. Coach Thornton talked to me about the season and complimented me on the high school game films.

I later met with T.D. He wanted to see a guy named Michael Bey, who he had gone to Thornridge High School in the suburbs with. From the day T.D. arrived at Lindblom in his junior year, he had always talked about his friends from Thornridge High School. He always told Deke and me about Bean (Michael Bey), Tookie and Dino, all ballplayers from the suburbs.

T.D. and I went up to the 5th floor dorm room and there he was, a 5'9", 170-pound running back named Michael Bey. Michael was very animated and instantly I got the notion he loved to have fun. I realized he was one of the prized pupils of the new coaching staff. Michael had broken all of Thornridge's rushing records, most of which were set by his older brother, Jerry, then the star running back at WIU and Mike (Jip), the second-team sophomore full back at the university. So WIU had the best three running backs in the history of Thornridge High, all on the same college team. Even though I didn't know Michael, I felt familiar with him. T.D. had talked about him while I always talked about my boys from the low end, Mitchell Brookins, Lamar Lewis and Chris Hinton.

Michael told us we just missed a girl he had in the room. He had just scored some action from her, the best, he said, he had ever had. He said that in the middle of making out he fell asleep because it was so soft. I sat back and listened as he described the whole scene. Yes, Michael loved to have fun. He told T.D. that he had to see this fine girl.

Michael decided to take us to the football field, which was toward the middle of the campus. He started bending down as if he didn't want to be seen. He said football practice had just started and he was supposed to be there, but he was pretending to have a tutor for his classes. He start pointing out players on the football track with the coaches running the hell out of them in the hot sun. He was laughing and telling us that his brother, Jerry, and the rest of the ball players had also missed workout sessions earlier in the week, so they were all in trouble. That was my first knowledge of what eventually became the Dirty 8.

By then it was time for T.D. and me to go to pre-registration at the university union. We went to the business section and the counselor walked us through the class curriculum. We decided to major in business and promised to take all the same classes from beginning to end.

Making the Team

A few months later, football camp started and word got back to me that Michael didn't make the team. Because of his poor summer grades, he would have to sit out a semester of football and redshirt until next year. Once camp started I met T.D.'s other friend, Tookie. He had been switched over to free safety for college.

I'll never forget the night before I left for the two-week mini-camp. Deke, Rick and T.D. and me spent most of the night on the Lake Michigan rocks talking about life. We talked about the gangs that were coming back more organized and vicious in the inner city. Deke talked about all of the old gangbangers from the 60's who were getting out of jail now and reorganizing. We knew Deke was right because we were on the front line of the problem all through high school. That night Deke gave me a present: a hand in the form of a peace sign. He said he was proud of me for playing college football and that I was going to be playing for him. I was the only one on my high school team that was going on to play college football.

As I prepared to leave Chicago the next day, Ray called me to his porch and handed me a box and said not to open it until I got on the train. As I boarded the train, I knew I was going to a unfamiliar place. As the train pulled away, I watched my Dad get smaller until he was out of sight. I sat alone on the train and opened Ray's gift (a pair of shoes) and cried for the next hour because I knew I was going out and away from the people I loved. I knew T.D. and Deke would be at Western in two weeks but that was not the issue. I was leaving Dad and friends and going to the unknown. During the summer T.D. and I had

The Key to Stopping the Violence

decided to room together.   T.D. later told Deke that the campus made a mistake and they didn't end up as roommates.

I got in to the train station about 9:30 and saw Coach Thornton with a white player who had just gotten off the train. The guy was about 6'3" and 195 pounds and Coach Thornton introduced him as a sophomore.   "Damn, this is a big ass white boy," I thought.   "What in the hell are they feeding him?" I looked like a water boy next to him. Coach Thornton drove us to a dorm and said the other players wouldn't arrive until the next day, then we would check in the dorm for the mini-camp.

I had a physical that next morning and met my mini-camp roommate, Tookie, and his family. This was the same Tookie that T.D. had always talked about. Tookie was the first suburban black I had been around. He was very excited about being in camp, but also seemed resigned about what he could and could not do.   Tookie gave me the scoop on who was going to be in camp. I wasn't on scholarship so I wasn't a "privileged recruit." I came down as a "walk on" and had to show that I deserved to be there. I had to earn my worth.

The coaches told Tookie what was expected of him and what he was recruited for. I had to make a name for myself, but it was no different from any other time in my life. All Tookie talked about was ballplayers like Jerry Bey, Reggie Johnson, Bump Jelly, Dace Richardson, Ham, Randy Shepherd, Herb Simpson, "Slick" Macomb and Steve Carpenter.

Tookie described how big these guys were and how Jerry and several more could play professional football. He also described how much drinking he did on his visit the weekend he was recruited. Jerry and Reggie (defensive Back) lived in a trailer home on the outskirts of town where all the black ballplayers hung out. To get into the trailer some of them made young football recruits drink and smoke reefer as part of their initiation. Tookie seemed to almost worship them. He quickly became my football eyes and ears, including giving me the scoop about the blacks on the team.

We had our physical exams and first equipment check. At a team dinner all the players were introduced and I got my introduction to the Dirty 8. As the dinner started there were more than 100 players there but Tookie didn't see any sign of the top players. Some of the star black athletes didn't come as the new coaching staff was taking a head count. Tookie knew some of the missing athletes. Finally, they all came in laughing. The coaching staff met with them in the hallway.   The veteran white players were whispering -- as were the blacks -- when the star players came in they sat down as though it wasn't a big deal.

As practice started, I was far down on the depth chart, unrecognized among the 100 players in camp, including 20 defensive backs. But I had three things going for me: enthusiasm, attitude and athleticism -- just like in high school.

My first opportunity came when we put on helmets, shoulder pads and shorts, which separated the men from the boys. I knew I had to take the advice of my high school coach, Coach Mette and knock the hell out of someone.

One of the starting wide receivers was a white guy who also doubled as the punter. The first one-on-one coverage drill involved defensive backs covering receivers. You either loved it or hated it. Defensive backs are very cocky, especially cornerbacks, so if you got beat even in a drill you heard about it.

I was fired up because I was going up against one of the starting wide receivers. I forgot that it was not a full-contact drill so as he ran his pattern and jumped for the ball I came up and ran right through him, knocking him five yards in the air. The offensive coaches went crazy. Who hit a wide receivers like that? I didn't try to hurt him. I was just doing what came naturally to try to make something happen. Coach Thornton explained that the receiver was a key player and that I should refrain from hitting, especially without equipment. But that was the kind of enthusiasm he liked to see. The season opener was two weeks away. I had been relegated to the eighth team. The first two teams traveled to away games and the other players only dressed for home games. I made it my mission to make the traveling team.

It was a long first week with three practices a day, often starting at seven in the morning. My second opportunity to showcase my talents came in the second week of camp on what they called the scout rag team, which comprised everybody not on the first or second teams, and extra players the coaches were grooming. If you were on the third team or lower, you stood as the next opponent's starting offense. It was embarrassing to be someone's punching bag.

The coaches wanted me to practice the full contact goal line drill. The drill meant the starting offense went against the rag team defense from the five yard line. The first play Jerry Bey, an all conference player, walked into the end zone and the coaches applauded. That's when I started to foam at the mouth and talk to myself. "Come on baby, run to the dog's territory." I read the

The Key to Stopping the Violence

next play perfectly and met Jerry Bey in the hole at about the two yard line. I put my helmet in his chest and drove him into the ground. The offensive players stopped and looked, including offensive lineman Don Greco (Greenbay Packers). As the impact of our pads hit, sounding like two trains colliding. Jerry got up shocked as his coach ran over to me and shouted, "Don't hit the star running back like that." I shouted back, "Then tell him not to run this way." That's when all hell started because the coaches designed the next play to come my way. This time with the receiver and fullback double teaming me, I again threw wide out to the side and sidestepped the fullback and met Jerry in the hole, this time picking him up and driving him into the ground. By this time Coach Thornton heard the commotion and came down. The offensive coaches were shouting at him and the black players started telling me I would pay for making them look bad.

It was a war of words as we went back and forth cursing each other. The coaches sat back and fed off the intensity. I hollered, "I'm the dog from the low end and my boys will be down in a week and all hell will break out." I was a walk on who earned my respect on the field from the older players. I was moved up on the depth chart after that.

Toward the end of mini-camp, a few of the of the Dirty 8 players found themselves in another scandal. There were rumors that some of the players had left camp one night during curfew. The coaches had some names but no one had been caught. They had even pulled a few of the black players out of practice but nothing materialized. During lunch the next afternoon six black girls walked in the cafeteria, headed to the coaches' table and started accusing certain players of coming to their campus, bringing them back to Macomb, having sex with them and not taking them back.

They pointed to some of the eight brothers in the cafeteria -- The Dirty 8. They all were on scholarship and contributors to the team, either as a starter or part-time players. So what could the coaches do? If they kicked them off the team we would lose. So they let the players off the hook. Tookie and I were impressed at how those players did what they wanted when they wanted. They were so talented the coaches couldn't do anything to them. They were our new role models.

The craziest of the Dirty 8 was Ham, a solid 6'6", 260 pounds. Ham couldn't remember the plays so the coaches would tell him what to do on every play. Ham wanted two things: football and sex. He once said, "all I want to know about is every girl on campus and how she fucks in bed." Girls were very uncomfortable with him because of his bold approach. If he saw a women he liked he would follow her for days. We all laughed; it was hilarious. The Dirty 8 was showing us what college football was all about. Some said if a girl came to your room she deserved to be fucked. And all the younger players believed it.

Coach Thornton came to me during the second week of camp and pulled me off the practice field. He said my high school transcript had just come in. He said I only had a 1.99 grade point average, which meant I wouldn't be eligible to play that year. He said a high school counselor was going back up to the school to recalculate my grades by hand. This would mess up everything I had going for me.

The next day Coach Thornton said, "Today is your lucky day. Your counselor recalculated your grades by hand and they came out to 2.0. Then he told me to put on my shoulder pads.

Roommates

Once school started we moved out of the football camp into our dorm rooms. By that time I had moved up to third team on the depth chart.

T.D. and I became roommates with Michael Bey on the top floor of Lincoln Dorm. Michael and T.D. were jealous of how well me and Tookie were performing in football. They didn't want to talk much about football. At one point me and Michael almost got into a fight because I asked him not to borrow my things without me knowing. It was tough for ex-athletes to give up something they loved.

During the season, I made the second team and traveled to all of the away games. We had played Eastern Illinois University, the college my brother Eric attended. I hadn't seen him in a couple of years and he had never seen me play football. I was excited because I had made the team and we were playing the National Division II Champs who had a 13- game winning streak. Eric learned I would be on his campus and went home to Chicago so he wouldn't see his little brother play. During the game I recovered a fumble that gave us the winning score. Eric never did see me play.

My friendship with Michael remained distant. One night, later in the season, on the way to see Deke in the north quadrant dorms, I saw Michael walking up a hill. He didn't see me behind him when out of nowhere a big 6'3" white boy walked

The Key to Stopping the Violence

toward Michael and yelled, "Fuuuuuck yooou!" Then he walked up in Michael's face and said, "Niggers ain't shit" and swung at Michael. My instincts took over and I hit him with a solid punch to the jaw that sent him to one knee. I started landing combinations like I was back on 35th Street, telling this white boy he didn't know who he had just run into. He fell on his back. I told Michael we had to get out of there. We started running up the hill. White boys, who heard the fighting, started hollering out the dorm room windows, calling us niggers and spooks. By then the white boy had gotten up and started hollering at the top of his lungs, "Niggers, niggers. Come back fucking' niggers."

We ran into a brother we called Big Nasty from the South Side of Chicago. Big Nasty was about 6'3", 215 pounds. We told him what happened and he wanted to know where the white boy was. Michael pointed to him down the hill and as the white boy saw us coming he tried to run to the dorm. He couldn't get in because the doors had been locked at 10 o'clock. So he turned around and started pleading, "Hey guy, I was just joking."

Big Nasty said "Kiss my ass," and started throwing punches. I urged Big Nasty to stop. And as we walked away the campus police drove up and Michael started telling them how he was jumped by some white boys. The police said they had gotten calls that some blacks were causing problems. Luckily the white boy had already run off. All this happened right after several black girls had almost been raped at night while walking across campus. So the races were at odds.

From that point on Michael and I had a tremendously close relationship. He understood I was the kind of brother who would defend someone. He talked about that fight with his brother and the older football players. I soon received respect as a person who would back my words with action. My reputation as the "Dog" grew on the field as well because of the hits I delivered playing special teams.

That semester I would visit the Dirty 8. They would tell jokes about women, your mama, daddy, sisters, brothers, cousins, friends and girlfriends. All were the butt of their jokes. Some of the ball players would claim to try to fuck anything that moved. They would tell the younger brothers about screwing ladies and how they did it. These sport stars on campus, knew how to take advantage of women, black and white. Tookie and me would sit around and listen to the stories of how much sex they got the night before. They were the funniest guys I ever heard talk about anything. They would tell us how they could screw a girl until she started bleeding and the blood would shoot out like water. Tookie and I were believing a lot of this stuff because we were just 18. They once told me how they tried to hit on the previous coach's wife and daughters because they hated the Head coach. Pretty soon in the locker room the motto became " I'll fuck anything that moves from 8 to 80, blind cripple or crazy." Things where no better with the regular students because one guy told me he was aware he had a venereal disease, but he was going to give it to every girl he could." It's their fault for giving up the ass." He said.

Separated in the Lunch Room

There were fewer black players on the football team than white players. The black players always sat together during meals. It was nothing more than birds of a feather flocking together. We all enjoyed joking and hanging out together. Most of our jokes went right over the white players' heads because of the language we used. The coaching staff would always come over to the black players and try to make us sit with the white players. The older players would get mad because they would argue that the whites should come to us. It wasn't like the white players were spending a lot of time coming to the blacks on the team.

Cafeteria

On the predominantly white campus the same thing went on in the dorms and all elements of campus life. All the black students sat in certain sections in the lunch room, and the white students had their sections. Occasionally we would see a black student sitting with the whites. That person would be considered an outcast or Uncle Tom, trying to be something he wasn't.

All our parties were black, all of our entertainment was black. The whites didn't have any interest in knowing us under most normal circumstances.

Abandoned

After the football season in my freshman year of college, I felt good about the situation as far as football was concerned. I had proven to the coaches that I had a burning desire to learn and work as hard as necessary to better my game.

The Key to Stopping the Violence

A lot had happened in one semester. I made the college team as a special team player. My grades came out excellent, getting a 2.99 GPA. However, on the personal side, I was still trying to adjust to campus life. One of the two people who had talked me into going to WIU had totally abandoned me. T.D. had moved out and was living with his girlfriend in her dorm. Deke was hanging with other brothers who talked about pledging fraternities. College was totally different from anything I had ever known. I was away from home living in a small room by myself. I was 18 years old and nobody told me to go to class. I was sick and lonely because the two people that I thought I would see most were not around. T.D. and I had always talked about the things we would do in college. He brought the stereo and I brought the TV. He brought the ironing board and I brought the iron. We talked about how much fun we would have and how it was going to be the time of our lives.

I didn't know T.D.'s girlfriend well but she seemed to dislike me and T.D's other friends. Deke hated the fact that T.D. had abandoned us. Every time I would see him, he would talk about doing something to the "T-mobile." T.D. never offered to take us home from school so Deke said we should cut his tires or break his car windows. I would laugh and tell Deke I didn't think that was necessary. Things became more stressed when T.D. and me enrolled in the same classes. I saw him daily but he would barely speak. It got so bad that his girlfriend would meet him after class so he didn't spend a lot of time with me or other friends.

Deke wasn't going for this love feast T.D. seemed to be having with his girlfriend. Deke didn't have a girlfriend and neither did I. One night I ran into Deke and he had a bag in his hand. He said he had staged one of his operation paybacks. He pulled out a the side view mirror from a car and held it over his head and said it belonged to T.D. He said the tires would be next. Deke talked about how T.D. was not an original brother and he should be beat for his actions against us. He then left into the campus night.

One of the meanest things T.D. did to me happened around Thanksgiving when he and his girlfriend prepared to leave for home during our first major holiday. Everyone was trying to get home for the first time. T.D. had been taking his things out of the room little by little. Since he still had the key to the room it was still his room.

SILENT CRY

During the holiday the dorm was almost empty as Thanksgiving was the next day. I had a late test so I couldn't leave until late that night. I didn't have a ride home so I had to wait until the next day to take Amtrak. T.D. was leaving that night around 6 p.m. I remember him and his girlfriend coming in the room, seeing me sitting there packed and ready to go. They acted as though I wasn't there, picked up the things T.D. wanted to take back and then left, leaving me in an empty dorm. I had a tear in my eye as I wondered what I had done to this brother and his woman to be treated like this. Deke was frantic when I told him about it. When we got back to campus between Thanksgiving and Christmas Deke continued to call T.D. a traitor. Deke could never get over how T.D. had betrayed Thee Family. But Deke, T.D and me made up as they eventually became fraternity brothers.

Pledging

After Thanksgiving, there was one month until the end of the semester. I decided to hit the last party before the Christmas holiday. All of the fraternities had started giving their "smokers," which was a gathering to allow interested students to check out which fraternities they might be interested in. The Omega Psi Phi fraternity (the "Q Dogs") appealed to Deke and me. Deke had always talked about going "Dog," but I didn't know when. To my surprise when I walked into the party I saw 12 guys in line. They all had on dark coats with skull caps and their heads down. I saw one of the older Q Dogs giving them orders. Each time an order was given they would all do the same thing in sequence. I looked closer and saw my boy Deke in the line. I was surprised and felt pride that my boy was on line. Then I wondered how when he was pledging as a first semester freshman.

I stood in the corner staring, trying not to be obvious. The Q's hurried the pledges out of the party and I couldn't talk to Deke until Christmas break when we got back to Chicago. Once at home around the holidays, all the Thee Family members got together at Deke's house for the first time since college started. It was like old times, with Thee Family brothers sitting in the living room talking shit about college and sports. Deke always had fun with his grandma and Grizzly (Deke's dog), which walked around with his belly about to hit the ground. We told the young brothers what college was all about. Deke showed them the Q's

The Key to Stopping the Violence

steps, breaking down and pumping on the floor like a dog. Deke told us what it was like to pledge a fraternity. He said all the homies on line are called "lamps" and to become an Omega you had to cross the burning sands. Deke leaned over and said he wanted to "make me" under him. We talked about how I would probably pledge during football season to assure I would not be beaten a lot.

During the night, Vince told us how he was getting along at a small all white college called Upper Iowa. We did our usual talking about how we kicked ass back at Lindblom in football and on the streets. The younger brothers shared with us how they were still fighting the gangbangers around the school. We said that while we were home we would go to the school and beat some ass.

Our conversation was interrupted when one of our brothers ran to the door said somebody was outside messing up. We ran outside to see a man frantically jumping in his car being chased by some other Thee Family brothers who were beating on his windows and doors to get to him. We knew we were back in Chicago. We went back in the house as it began to snow. Thee Family celebrated Christmas by tackling and body slamming each other. I stopped and froze that moment in time because I wanted it to last forever. I thought, "These are my friends for life."

Later I called all the girlfriends I had left behind. Because I wanted to tell them how well I had played football during my first season of college. One girl was very quiet on the phone, and I swore she was crying. I finally asked her what was wrong. She said before I left for school I had got her pregnant. I was in shock and asked why wasn't I contacted. She said she tried but couldn't locate me and had an abortion. She hung up, saying she never wanted to speak to me again. I was 18 and she was 17. I never heard from her again.

Taking A Beating

Ray was still in his senior year at Wendell Phillips High School Lamar had gone to South Dakota and gotten homesick, so he left after the first game, giving up a four- year scholarship. During the Christmas break I talked Lamar into enrolling at WIU and trying out for the football team. He did, right before the second semester of our freshman year. Once the second semester started, Deke also started pledging hard to become a Q Dog. I

SILENT CRY

would see the pledgees running around on campus in a straight line doing things. Their heads were shaven and they were always dressed in black, carrying food or something else to please their big brothers. I was training for football, which had become a year-round activity. The senior cornerback who played in front of me was gone as was strong safety Steve Carpenter, who tried out for the St. Louis Cardinals football team. I was ready to do whatever was necessary to win that spot. I had gained 15 pounds and weighed 175.

During Deke's second or third week of pledging I went to in a campus party one night and some of the oldest, biggest Q Dogs I had ever seen walked in shouting, Roof, roof, motherfuckers, we gone turn this motherfucker out." There must have been about 20 of them visiting from other campuses. When these Que's walked in I instantly thought about the hell Deke had gotten himself into. Like me, Deke was not going to stand still and let somebody beat the hell out of him in the name of "brotherhood."

I left the party and went back to my dorm room. Later that night after I had fallen asleep. The phone rang and Deke was on the other end whispering, "Ersk, I just got my ass beaten by the Big brothers. I need to hide out." I told Deke to come over but he was already downstairs on the first floor phone. I went to the elevator and waited as he got off dressed in black clothes and boots. He could hardly walk. He told me what happened and how the Q Dogs were beating the living shit out of him and the other lamps. Deke put his hand in his pants and said they had beat him so bad he couldn't even shit.

"Ersk, there's something I gotta show you," Deke said. He pulled down his pants and then tried to pull down his underwear but couldn't because they seemed to be too small. He got them down and showed me his butt. My eyes popped open and Deke saw the look in my eyes. "Look at the size of my ass," he lamented. "It's swollen about three times the normal size." I looked with disgust. Deke had hips like a woman.

Deke explained what they had done to him and his Line. He told about how his dean didn't really want them make to it in the fraternity and how they had beat them repeatedly with paddles. As Deke laid on the bed he told me about Big Dog, his dean, who had been around the campus for what seemed like 100 years. Deke explain that Big Dog had been all over him about talking too much in the sessions. Deke always said something back to the Que's who were pledging him and that irritated Big

The Key to Stopping the Violence

Dog. So earlier that night Big Dog ordered the pledges to get in a straight line. Deke knew they were going to go through more ass beating so he questioned what Big Dog and the other dogs were doing. Big Dog told the pledgees to get in "the cut." That meant putting one hand over their private parts, bending over and grabbing their ankle with their other hand. They would get hit with "the sweet wood of Omega."

Deke was captain of the line and his job was to take up for some of the weaker brothers who couldn't handle the beatings. Big Dog called on Quincy to step up in the cut. That night Quincy had been beat so much he didn't have anything left in him. Deke spoke out saying brother No. 2 had enough. Big Dog went crazy and called Deke up front to get in the cut. Deke explained to me that he knew Big Dog had bad knees from an old sports injury. When Deke got in the cut, he pretended to fall forward and threw two forearms blows into Big Dog's knees. His face filled with pain as the other Que's came to Big Dog's rescue.

Deke shouted for the line to make a run for it. They all went different ways, and Deke looked for me because he wanted to be where they wouldn't find him or fuck with him. He asked me for a clean pair of underwear. He also asked me to take a picture of his ass. He bent over as I took several pictures, then he jumped in the shower. He talked more about pledging and then wanted to call some females to describe to them what he was going through. He called Iris a high-school classmate on the phone. She lived in the next dorm and asked her to come over and massage his wounds. I sat there and we continued to talk until we went to sleep. Later in the week he returned my underwear marked with shit stains. He said I gave them to him like that. I told him that was the shit they beat out of him. I threw the underwear away.

That week the entire Q line dropped from pledging and Deke was the last to stay on. Eventually the chapter was closed because of their abusive actions. I wanted to pledge after Deke, but never had the opportunity. Deke's cousin Al later talked him and T.D. into pledging Phi Beta Sigma. I said if I couldn't be an Omega I wouldn't be anything. As the years passed I developed an appreciation and friendship with all the fraternities and sororities.

SILENT CRY

The Few, The Proud, The Marines

Every boy wants to wear a uniform and pretend to be in the Marines or Army. Deke had joined the Marine Corps Reserve and was going through training. He would leave every month on weekends while we were in college, and was often seen walking across campus in military pants and combat boots.

After college, he had four years to do. Anybody who knows anything about the Marines understands the discipline and respect they command. Deke fit that image perfectly. He was 6'2" and walked proud and tall. His demeanor was precise. Even when he joked, people knew he had something to say. Most of his jokes were replete with multi-syllable words that would send the average person to the thesaurus. Deke loved to talk about literature and history. He was a big fan of Plato and Aristotle. Deke would always tell tales about what the Marines was like. Once, he told me about the time they put him and his Marine comrades in a giant chamber filled with some sort of gas, then had them take off their gas masks. "Ersk, people were falling out," he said. The chamber was jam packed with soldiers. We had to state our name, rank and serial number before they would let us out." He joked that he was so mentally tough that he was able to tell them his name was Garry Dean Rashamond Bearwolf Kennedy before stating his rank and serial number, then asked if he could stay in the chamber a little while longer. Of course other Marines were throwing up before they could finish saying their first names. Deke said it was just one of the things to get them ready for war, in case they were caught behind enemy lines.

Summer Madness

There was another stumbling block in front of me during the summer after my first year of college. The coaches used the bait-and-switch tactic on the football team. At the end of the regular season coach showed Tookie, Reggie and me the depth chart. At that time Reggie and I were the starting cornerbacks and Tookie was the starting free safety. But as soon as spring football started they put a white guy in Tookie's position and moved him against me. They tried to make the white boy out to be a good player even though he was awful. The coaches were

118

The Key to Stopping the Violence

not ready for an all-black defensive secondary and there was very little we could do.

Then an element that I hadn't figured came into the picture. The coaching staff went out and got some junior college transfer players. I couldn't believe it; all this work I had done! This taught me that the coaches could not be trusted. It was obvious who the favorites were. I could tell from the coaches' practice conversations that the white players had a relationship that the blacks could never have.

I had an excellent spring practice while I was competing for a starting cornerback spot. I had knocked the shit out of everyone who came my way on the field. My nickname was the "The Dog" because, like a doberman, I could not be controlled.

After the spring semester I talked to the coaches about staying on campus for the summer to find a job. I moved in with Jerry Bey, Randy and Walter from New Orleans. Jerry was nice enough to let us stay until we found jobs. Tookie, Lamar, Deke, T.D. and the rest of the crew went home for the summer. The coaches had already let us know that it was a matter of time before the jobs came in. Keeping us at school allowed them a chance to work us out. That was exactly what I wanted and needed because starting the first game of the season was what I was aiming for. The coaches finally called Walter and me in the office to let us know about the jobs they got us. We would be working at a hog-killing plant in Monmouth, Ill. The coaches also got jobs for two white boys, Rod and Chris, at the same plant. Rod, our starting free safety, would pick us up at 5:30 a.m. and drive the four of us 45 minutes to the small midwestern town. Walter and me had already picked out all the stuff we would buy with all the cash we would make. I called Dad to tell him I would be making more than him. I don't think he appreciated that.

The hog plant was paying $9 an hour and time and a half for overtime. This was more money than I had ever expected to see in my life. The first thing we noticed was the terrible smell of death that hit your nose and stomach. The foreman showed us around the plant and he described what they did there. He took us to where the process started. Some of the men would run the pigs up a ramp wide enough to hold one pig at a time. The pigs at the bottom were pushing from the rear. At the next stage we watched in disbelief as a man with huge stun gun delivered an electric shock to the top of each pig's head. Then a lady standing next to the man was waiting with the largest butcher knife I'd ever seen in my life. She took the knife and slit the pig's throat. At the same time a third person put a chain on the pigs' rear back ankle. Sometimes the shock wouldn't be enough to knock out the pig, so they would shock him again while the conveyor belt and chain lifted the pig off the ramp. Then it would hang upside down, kicking while blood flowed.

This procedure continued every 10 seconds. Then the pigs were dipped in a pool of water and drowned before going through a fire that burned off hair. Next it was down the line where a man waited with a large gas saw to sever each pig in half as the animals' innards began to fall out. In each section on the line, people were pulling off different parts the pig. The terrible smell was something I never got used to, but had to deal with.

The foreman took us all to our positions with a smirk on his face. We all wanted to throw up by this time. I had to pull the guts out, which was perversely appropriate since black people eat chitlins. I had to use my hands and it became so repetitively nasty that after an hour I got sick and wanted to leave. I couldn't see the other ballplayers. That first day made all of us want to quit but I kept remembering that $9 an hour. It left me wondering how did these people do that shit everyday.

The next day I didn't have to quit because the foreman called us into the office and said the plant was going on strike. He informed us there might be trouble because some workers would be crossing the picket lines. So we spent the next few days around some union workers who weren't too happy and very uneasy. The following day they laid us off.

The coaches reacted quickly and signed us up as alternates at the physical plant on campus. I got a job the next week and started painting doors. Walter worked in groundskeeping and Randy, the starting linebacker from the South, worked at a grocery store. Walter was from New Orleans and always talked about New Orleans women and how fine they were. He felt a lot of hatred for the women on campus and sometimes acted like all women were bitches to be fucked. After work we would argue about who was going to be doing what once the season started. Randy and Walter always gave me a hard time about being a walk-on. You had to have tough skin to be around these brothers. The egos in the house were big. We lived and breathed football.

That summer, the subject of sex and identifying the big freaks on campus was second most important conversation after football. However, because summer school had not started there were few people on campus. Walter kept saying summer school was when the freaks came out to play. And I heard there was plenty to go around.

After work we hit the weight room for a scheduled training and running program. We would work out for hours. They were the perfect homies if you wanted to get better and stronger.

Sometimes after practice I would tell them I was going to catch up with them later. I remember just laying back on the grassy football field at the 50 yard line, looking up at the clear sky, I would think that I had made it out of the projects. Things down here were so peaceful and quiet. There was no falling asleep to gunfire or the sound of breaking glass. I felt everything was going to work out. I realized there was a different way for kids to grow up. It also reminded me of when Ray, Lamar and me would lay on the concrete project playground and look up at the sky and daydream.

Back at the house Walter cooked what he called Popeye's chicken, which he said was big in New Orleans. We would fight over how much food each person got. We always had a brother or two coming by around dinnertime, especially Herb Simpson, who had been kicked out with the Dirty 8. Herb would come over and the next thing we knew he would be sleeping on the floor. One day I didn't go to work and heard someone singing and cooking. I came out to see Herb, who had been waiting for us to leave everyday so he could eat and take a shower. He didn't have a place to stay. Herb would fix giant pots of gumbo and tell stories about how his uncle owned a company in California that he wanted Herb to take over. Herb told jokes like Richard Pryor and always kept us in stitches.

Nights were full of fun but there was one thing missing: the women. The weeks were getting longer with a house full of horny ass ballplayers, until one day after work Walter said he had seen some nice looking chunes(women) off campus and had gotten their address. We rushed over to their apartment but before we knocked on the door, Walter gave me the plan. He said they weren't the best looking women but they did have asses. I agreed it had been a long time since I had seen some bootie. He figured we could get some play if we got them high. Out of Walter's pocket came some reefer he had gotten from some one else. "We'll let them smoke our weed for some sex," he said, as I shook my head in agreement. Once we got in the apartment I realized that these two were dog ugly.

SILENT CRY

Walter whispered that they will look a lot better with no clothes on. One was tall with brown teeth -- at least the ones she had were brown. The other one was charcoal black and fat with a voice as deep as Barry White's. We sat in the living room and watched these two girls smoke up all the weed. Then to make things worse, Walter leaned over and said he was going to take the skinny one back to the house so they could be alone. He wanted me to stay behind and freak the fat one. He threatened to tell the Dirty 8 if I didn't, and he'd say I was afraid of the ass.

I had been sold on the "fuck anything that moves" theory. Like a young fool I sat there as Walter got up and left with his Olive Oil look-a-like. These girls had been around campus for several years so they were no puppies. Once alone, the big one started telling me how fine I was. My skin began to crawl, but even with crawling skin I still had a dick that was hard as a brick, as they say an 18- or 19-year-old man will put his pipe in anything. Within five minutes she was talking about taking a shower and asked me to wash her back. She showered and I was right there washing the back of the elephant. Before I knew it we were in her bed doing the nasty. She smelled as bad as she looked but I went back for more anyway. Hell, I didn't know when I was going to get another piece of action.

After the second time she started bragging on how good her stuff must be because I kept coming back. That's when she tried to kiss me. I thought, "A man will put his pipe anywhere, but not his mouth." I tried to pull away, saying I didn't know how to kiss. So she grabbed my head as her tongue shot out of her mouth like a lizard. She said she would teach me. I fought for my life and got away.

After that I felt pretty good going back to the apartment because it was mission accomplished. Walter didn't sleep with his girl; he said she was still in love with her boyfriend. Then I proudly broke the news that I tore the ass up. When he heard that he laughed and said I was crazy put my pipe in that butt-ugly bitch. He told me he'd never intended to freak her friend; he set me up. I avoided her the rest of the summer.

A few weeks later, summer school brought out the women. I realized that it was not just the guys on campus going buckwild, it was the girls too. They were chasing us just as much as we were chasing them. In one incident, a sorority girl slept with me and then announced to all her sorority friends the details of our encounter. After getting several stares and giggles from them, I asked her had she told them about the night we

The Key to Stopping the Violence

spent together. She said, "Yes. I'm not your woman, so what I say is my business. Besides, it wasn't all that good anyway." I walked away feeling cheap and used.

Whenever we drove to Chicago, it was a four-hour party. One of the ballplayers could drive with his knees on the steering wheel while rolling a joint in his lap. When he inhaled, his eyes would close while he drove blind at 90 miles an hour.

The summer continued, Randy, Walter and me were sitting around after a workout, watching a track meet when I noticed a black man walking toward us with an African robe and bald head. He introduced himself as Dr. Ahmad, an African studies professor. He said I was a pretty good ballplayer with a lot of intensity and that I showed good leadership abilities. He was polite and very well spoken. I had heard of him on campus but this was my first time meeting him. It was good to see a black professor on campus.

There were very few black professors, so the black athletes relied on the help of the white booster club members for support. Booster club members were financial sponsors of the athletic programs. We were like their little show toys. We were different from the regular black students because of our athletic skills. The boosters paid for their season tickets and made sure they knew the star players firsthand.

There was one white booster, who was a lively character with female tendencies. Jerry, Reggie and other players would go over to cut his grass and work around the house. They would wear tank tops to get bigger meals and tips. They would take younger players there and joke about how they would unbutton their shirts and the booster would fix larger and larger meals. This man acted like a women, but our attitude was as long as he fed us, nobody cared. Jerry, who was 5'11" and 205 pounds of muscle, would always flex his chest muscles to get him to cook or to pay Jerry for mowing his lawn. He would cook steaks, cornish hens and rice, the kind of meals we weren't going to get on a college campus.

This man let it be known that he liked having young black athletes around. Guys would be seen driving his car and working in his yard. Jerry would say if you're not a fag there is nothing a fag can do to you but give you his money. This man always squealed with delight to see us and I laughed until tears flowed while eating his food. One day he even stopped by the weight room and almost had a heart attack watching the sweat pop off of us. One of the players let him touch his arm and he let out a huge scream of joy as though he'd had an orgasm.

Campus Crime

During the summer, Ray graduated from Wendell Philips the year their baseball team made the playoffs. Lamar and me talked Ray into coming down to W.I.U. the next semester to hook up with the Low end boys. Ray wanted to play baseball, but once on campus, he found out it was an all-white team.

The semester was starting back and Ray, Deke and Lamar were all back for the time of our lives. Sometimes old behavior and experiences can travel with you, even in a new environment. That's exactly what happened during the first semester of my sophomore year at Western Illinois.

For Ray, Lamar and me, our entire lives we had viewed whites as threatening and that feeling manifested itself in aggressive behavior. Ray and Lamar felt it necessary to defend themselves even after the smallest offenses. Once Ray said a white boy stepped on his foot and wanted me and Lamar to go with him to kick his ass. I disagreed because I was on scholarship and might stand a chance of losing it. Ray and Lamar felt I had bought into the white man's system. They also saw the differences between Macomb and the mean streets of Chicago, particularly the low end.

Macomb was like being in Mayberry with Andy Griffith. You could either respect it and use it to your advantage or you could hate the slowness and whiteness of the town and become negative. They decided to use the latter. When I practiced, Ray and Lamar would go to the uptown shopping area. They noticed that were no surveillance cameras, nothing to separate them from the products in the store. Ray once said that the uptown stores made him feel like a kid in a candy store, and they started bringing home "candy" everyday. It started with track suits, then watches, gold chains, rings. You name it, they got it. Everyday they brought back stolen goods; it was a way to get the white man back, they argued.

In the dorm, we all lived on different floors. Ray would always be in Lamar's room or he would come down to my room. Ray started the school year with a white roommate, but that soon ended because the white guy found a reason to move. Lamar and Ray both had single rooms. After football practice, usually

The Key to Stopping the Violence

around 7:30 p.m., they would kick back, smoke a joint and listen to music.

There were community bathrooms on each floor. Most white boys had a habit of going to the bathroom to take showers without locking their doors. They felt safe and sometimes left the door wide open. To us that was the wrong thing to do. Where we grew up only fools left their doors open to invite a would-be robber or murderer. One day a white boy on Ray's floor left his door open while he went to shower. He also left his stereo blasting hard rock music. Ray figured he would convince Lamar to go into the white guy's room with him to check out the speakers.

It didn't make a difference that the room was next door to Ray's room. It only mattered that they saw what they wanted and the way to get it was to take it. They took the stereo and hooked everything up in Ray's room. In the low end, it wasn't a matter of not knowing who stole from you, but whether or not you were bad enough to take it back. That was the same approach they used with the white boy. When he got out of the shower, not only didn't he hear his hard rock, but he heard some black soul music blasting out of the room next door. He knocked on the door, all red in the face and panicky and said, "Excuse me, but my stereo system seems to be gone and I don't remember you having one."

Ray responded, "You better get your white ass out of here. What the hell is your problem? And if you knock on the door again, your ass won't be knocking on another door for a long time."

Afraid for his life, the white boy went to his room. Ray and Lamar figured he would call the police, so they disconnected the stereo and took it to Lamar's room. I was not aware of this until the next morning. I woke up and happened to look out of my 6th floor window and saw Ray and Lamar carrying the speakers and turntable to the train station at 6 a.m. I didn't see them again for two weeks They decided to go home in the middle of the semester. I was in and out of town playing football games, wondering what happened to my boys.

Finally when they got back, they said they got homesick and wanted to see their families. They said they also wanted to watch a couple of high school city football games involving Wendell Phillips High School I never heard anything else about the white boy and his stereo. I know he never came to the Low end to pick it up.

SILENT CRY

I constantly battled with them not to blow an opportunity for an education, but it was like pulling teeth. At the same time, along with a lot of other people, I was losing ground. Sex, fun and football had become the things to do. My study habits faded and all I was banking on was making it to the pros. People were flunking out, women were getting pregnant and we were beating up brothers in parties ... and white boys, too, when necessary.

Lamar and Ray later stole term papers off professors' desks and put their names on the papers. And of course, everyone used other people's phone card numbers to call home and talk for hours.

Fighting on Campus

Ray and I were coming from my dorm room on a Sunday afternoon we were headed up to Ray's room to hang out when we saw a former high school football teammate, Brian, on the elevator with his left hand over his eye. He was on the way up to his room. I asked him about the eye. He said a guy punched him at the gym. I wanted to know who and why the person had punched him. Brian said it was because of a basketball game, in which he hit the winning shot.

I asked, "Where's ol' boy at?"

Brian responded, "He's in the lunchroom downstairs with four of his boys."

I could not let some motherfucker come up on "The Dog's" campus and beat up a friend, but first I wanted to get Lamar so it would be four against four. Brian said the guy who hit him was about 6'3", 210 pounds and the others were average height. That wasn't a problem because I knew with Ray and Lamar we would whip anybody's ass, especially when he came into our territory.

Lamar met us at the front door of lunchroom on the second floor. We headed straight over to the black section to find these brothers. To my surprise, they were with some other brothers who attended our school. Actually, they were with some guys who lived on my floor.

We walked up to them and I spoke to the brother I knew. "My boy Brian here said that somebody over here smashed him in the eye."

This big brother said, "He got hit, what about it? The sissy motherfucker got what he deserved."

"Well, I'd like to talk about it outside the lunchroom."

The Key to Stopping the Violence

So we headed out in the main floor area. The big brother looked at Brian and said, "Now I'm gonna really fuck you up since you went and got your boys."

I stepped in. "I don't think you're going to kick anybody else's ass today."

The brother sidestepped me and went straight to Brian and began threatening him again. I stepped in between them again. By then, brothers were pairing off and pushing each other. We were clearly outnumbered. I looked up and saw Ray and one brother on the ground fighting. From that point, the fighting escalated. Lamar had been caught off guard and was being hit by three different people. I came from the back and hit a guy with four hard blows to the mouth and jaw. He dropped to the ground as blood flowed from his mouth. Then me and Ray pulled a move from a movie. We double teamed one brother and hit him at the same time, knocking him into the wall.

What was amazing was that the big brother doing all the talking didn't throw one punch. He talked big shit and did a lot of jumping around. I was beginning to wear out. My arms and body were exhausted. I looked at Ray and drew strength. He looked at me and continued to fight. I was in supreme condition, so I knew if I was tired the other guys had to be exhausted, too. I never saw Brian throw a punch either. Students were standing all around when the campus police finally came. The Macomb police knew me by name from football. The big brother continued to talk shit to Brian, but he never spoke to me directly. Finally, after a lot of arguing, the police got the other boys on the elevator. The big brother, now on the elevator, said I was going to get my ass kicked later. I broke away from the policeman's grasp and jumped in his face and told him that he would see whose ass would get kicked. I heard one of the guys from Western Illinois telling him, "Oh shit. You shouldn't have fucked with 'The dog'. That MF's going to go crazy."

I had held back on calling my boys, but after that comment, I sent a guy to get my homies, the football players. Then I sent a second brother to get C.C., Rock, Deke and Thee Family Brothers. In about 10 minutes, Randy, a linebacker, Big Carl (nose tackle), Walter and all other ballplayers came running to the dorm, yelling, "I heard somebody's fucking with 'The Dog'." I took them football players to the sixth floor. Deke and Thee Family Brothers hadn't arrived yet. My cousin, Rennie, joined in as 20 to 25 more brothers came to my defense. We went to his room and this big MF found out just how crazy I was. I was the man and made no bones about it. His big ass started apologizing and pleading for his life. He even knew Ray's older brother, Ivory, and Deke's older brother, "K", who ran the campus at Illinois State.

Through all the forgiving on the sixth floor, someone still found a way to hit Brian in the other eye. I laughed to myself and thought Brian had to throw a punch if he wanted to be respected. For Ray, Lamar and me, this was one more of the adventures we later talked and laughed about.

2d S. Side black found slain in north suburb

[redacted]

By Jerry DeMuth and Lawrence Dillard

A 20-year-old South Side man was found murdered Tuesday on a street in Wilmette, where he apparently had been dumped from a car.

The victim, Lawrence C. Green, of 3653 S. King Drive, was the second South Sider in a week whose body has been found in a North Shore suburb.

Rodney Harris, 14, was found last Thursday a mile and a half away in neighboring Evanston, his body stuffed into a canvas bag and dumped into a trash container. Green's body had a black plastic bag tied around the head.

Green, an assembly line worker for the Ford Motor Co., was found in the 700 block of Michigan Av., just north of the intersection with Sheridan Rd.

Wilmette Police Sgt. Philip Cangelosi said Green's head was bleeding. But because Green wore his hair in a thick Afro, police said they could not tell if he had been shot or beaten, Cangelosi said.

The Cook County coroner's office reported that the cause of death was a blow to the head from a blunt instrument. It reported that asphyxiation from the hood around Green's head may have contributed to his death.

Police were called to the scene at about 2:40 a.m. A policeman had patrolled Michigan Av. 20 minutes earlier but had not seen Green's body.

Black plastic bag over head

Cangelosi said the body was lying face down in the southbound lane, about 3 feet from the curb. His feet were bare, Cangelosi said, and he was wearing brown pants and a blue sleeveless shirt. A black plastic hood was tied over Green's head with a strip of cloth. A green Army jacket lay across Green's back, and a pair of leather sandals were at his side.

"It looked like they threw him out head first," Cangelosi said. He said it appeared that the sandals and jacket had been tossed out of a car after Green's body was deposited on the street.

Cangelosi said Green's wallet was in his pocket, but it contained no money.

Seek ties with Harris murder

Lt. Tom Joyce, chief of detectives in Evanston, said he was studying Green's case to see if it had any connection with Harris' murder. "At this time I don't connect the two," Joyce said.

He explained that the only similarities were that both victims were black and both had been dumped in the North Shore suburbs.

Green apparently had been shot or beaten, while Harris had been strangled, Joyce said. Harris was naked but Green was dressed. Harris was a school boy but Green was a working man.

Green had been married last March, and his wife, [redacted], 20, said she last saw her husband at about 10:50 p.m. Monday.

She said Green told her he'd be right back as he left their apartment. She reminded him that he had to get up at 4 a.m. the next day to go to work at the Ford plant at 12600 S. Torrence.

How wife was told of murder

Mrs. Green said she learned of the murder when Chicago police arrived at her apartment early Tuesday. She said the police handed her a piece of paper instructing her to call an investigator. She called and the investigator told her that her husband was dead.

Mrs. Green said her husband attended Doolittle Elementary School and Dunbar Vocational High School before taking a job at Michael Reese Hospital in 1968.

He joined the Army in 1970 and served in the infantry in Germany, Mrs. Green said. She added that he took his job at the Ford plant on July 31.

1972 news story covering Lawrence Green's death

Ben Wilson's Mom Sees No End to Crime Problem

High Schools
Taylor Bell

Like most people of my generation, I'll never forget where I was and what I was doing when I heard President Kennedy had been shot.

I also remember where I was and what I was doing when I learned Ben Wilson had been shot.

The Simeon basketball star, acknowledged as the No. 1 player in the nation, was shot twice by two gang members on a sidewalk near the school at 1:15 p.m. on Tuesday, Nov. 20, 1984. He died the next morning.

It was almost 10 years ago.

I was reminded the other day when Mary Wilson, Ben's mother, called to say not much has changed since her son was killed.

"I see the escalation of crime all over," she said. "I'm here to tell you there is no place where it is quiet."

Four years after Ben's death, she moved to Columbus, Miss., with her sons, Jeffrey and Anthony. "I thought my sons would have a chance to grow into maturity in a quiet country neighborhood," she said.

JOHN BOOZ/FOR THE SUN-TIMES

Mary Wilson and two of her sons—Anthony (left) and Jeff—pose in front of a picture of Ben Wilson, who was shot and killed nearly 10 years ago.

Mary Wilson, mother of the late high school basketball star, Ben Wilson, with her sons, Anthony and Jeff

Ivory Grandberry, Ray's older brother

Ray and me, 8th grade graduation

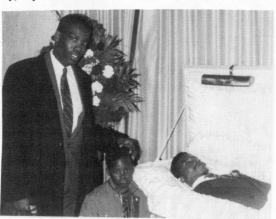

Me and Ray Jr. viewing Ray's body in 1989

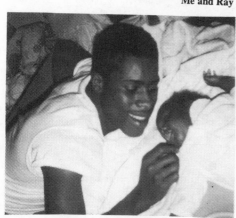

Ray and his son, Ray Jr.

Mrs. Grandberry and her sons, Ray (left) and Ivory

A pictorial memorial to my late friend Garry "Deke" Kennedy

Rites for Kennedy

Visitation and funeral services for Garry Dean Kennedy, a student at Western Illinois University, will be held tonight at 7 p.m. at Unity Missionary Baptist Church, 5129 S. Indiana Ave. Interment will be Tuesday at 10:30 a.m. at Washington Memorial Cemetery, 183rd & Halsted St.

Kennedy died Tuesday, Sept. 20, on the school's campus. He was 22.

A member of Phi Beta Sigma Fraternity, Kennedy was a senior majoring in Criminal Justice, and had been a student since 1979. He was a graduate of Lindblom Technical High School where he reportedly was an honor student. He also served in the U.S. Marine Corps Reserves where he held the rank of corporal.

Survivors include his

mother, Ruth Kennedy; his father, Charles Kennedy; two brothers, Kevin and Dwayne; and other relatives.

Manslaughter charge filed in student death

A 23-year-old Chicago man has been charged with involuntary manslaughter in the stabbing death Tuesday night of a 22-year-old Western Illinois University student.

Dead is Garry Dean Kennedy of Chicago. Kennedy's body was found at 10:09 p.m. Tuesday on the sidewalk outside 602 W. Jefferson St. The resident there, ▓▓▓▓▓, 22, flagged down police officers who happened to be driving by the scene, according to Macomb police reports. ▓▓▓▓▓▓▓▓ was placed in the McDonough County Jail on the manslaughter charge. He was taken into custody at the scene, authorities reported.

Kennedy was pronounced dead at the scene of a single stab wound to

the chest by McDonough County Coroner Larry Jameson at 10:28 p.m.. Kennedy's body was taken to Springfield Memorial Hospital early today for an autopsy.

Kennedy and ▓▓▓▓ apparently had argued before the stabbing, according to police reports.

▓▓▓▓ had been staying at ▓▓▓ residence since Sunday when he had come to Macomb from Chicago, police said.

Kennedy had been dating ▓▓▓▓, according to authorities.

Kennedy was a junior law enforcement administration major at WIU. ▓▓▓▓ graduated from WIU in May with a political science major. ▓▓▓▓ is a sophomore at WIU, studying law enforcement.

(From left to right)

Kevin, Deke's brother, Mrs. Kennedy, Deke's mother,

me and my wife, Donna, and Deke's college roommate, Biscuit

What's up EJ

How are thing coming alone up there in Macomb, good I know. Well things here are pretty fairly O.K. EJ you know I bet you wonder HEY he's writing finally. EJ I would have been writing but I just found the letters that I have receive from you. How good is your chance of going pro I know you're good. I hope you go so I can remember one of my best pals playing and watching you on T.V EJ it reminds me of Ghetto to Glory. EJ I know you're coming home soon for Thanksgiving. I be glad to see you man because I think life is slipping away. I been having so many problems but you no how I am. I'm Ray and that makes me hang in there because I'm young and strong. When this letter reaches you I hope you be in the best of health. EJ it's hard being away from you because you the kind of Bro that keeps me up. When started writing I was tried so you can understand my errors. Gertie said take care and to you stay up young fellow your the best. I respec you alot for what you have done for yourself.   , this have been a long year without a Mama I know you the only one who can understand. I have a phone and the number is 285-1026 I tried to call up you a couple of days a go but know answer your phone call when you get this letter. Everybody trying hard to keep me in the mud and filt of this white's man world. Allah hAs beEN tAlKing to ME. Your thE bEst. I LOVE yOu BROthER   STAY uP

News reports of the bizarre deaths of Marie Hudson and her

daughter Danielle "Nookie" Hudson

Her mother slain, then she's killed

By Phillip J. O'Connor
and Jim Casey

As Danielle Hudson, 20, stood talking with friends and relatives on a South Side street, she got devastating news—her mother was dead. A short time later, she was fatally stabbed.

Her ex-boyfriend. ████ ████, 23, came up and began talking to her Tuesday night shortly after she arrived at the home of a friend at 611 E. 37th, where she had been summoned to be told of her mother's death. As Hudson, accompanied by her new boyfriend, turned to walk away from ████ he pulled out a butcher knife and stabbed her three times in the chest, detectives said. ████, of ████ S. Vincennes, was charged with murder.

The deaths of Hudson, the mother of two young children, and of her mother, Marie Hudson, 43, whose body was found Monday in a vacant building at 6855 S. Merrill, rocked their family.

Relatives said they expect to schedule a joint wake and funeral for the two women, both of whom lived at 2140 E. 69th.

Detectives said the slayings of the two women do not appear to be related.

Detectives said ████ ████ was the father of Danielle Hudson's two children, Randy, 2, and Kittrick, 4.

Mother, daughter died one day apart

by Pat Jamison

A 20-year-old South Side woman, on her way to a relative's home where news of her mother's death one day earlier awaited, was fatally stabbed by her former boyfriend Tuesday night as she walked with a new friend.

Danielle Hudson, of 2140 E. 69th St., was pronounced dead at Michael Reese Hospital with three

(continued on page 26)

Mom, daughter dead

(continued from page 1)
stab wounds in the left side of her chest at 1:50 a.m. yesterday, a spokesman for the institution said.

Charged with Hudson's murder is ████ ████, 23, of ████ S. Vincennes Ave., who is slated to appear in Violence Court Branch 66 today.

According to police, Hudson had been summoned to her mother's home on E. 69th St. by family members, who were waiting to inform the young woman that her mother had been found dead Monday morning.

As Hudson and her current boyfriend, whose name police withheld, walked down the street near the CHA's Ida B. Wells Housing Complex at 611 E. 37th St. around 11:30 p.m. Tuesday, ████ confronted the couple, police said.

Det. Daisy Martin of Area 1 Violent Crimes added that Hudson attempted to turn and walk away from ████, and at that point, he allegedly pulled out a butcher knife, stabbed the woman three times in the chest and then fled from the scene.

████ was arrested at his home soon after the alleged stabbing and the murder weapon was recovered, police said.

Hudson and ████ are the parents of two children, according to police reports.

Hudson's 43-year-old mother, Marie, was found dead in the basement of a vacant 17-unit apartment building at 6855 S. Merrill on Monday at approximately 9:30 a.m. by the building's janitor.

Police said elder woman, who was pronounced dead on the scene, was last seen by her son on Sunday at 11 p.m.

Bey sparks Gladiators

By Jeff Danowski
Journal Times

RACINE — Halfback Jerry Bey has provided the spark to the rushing attack for the Gladiators of Racine so far this season.

Bey was named the Northern States Football League's first Player of the Week, and after two games, he leads the NFSL in rushing.

In 32 carries, Bey has rushed for 228 yards, a 7.1 average, and has scored one touchdown.

Bey, who is 5-foot-10 and 200 pounds, said he is motivated by a spiritual fire that burns deep within him.

"My brother Michael was a big spark in my life," said Bey. "We worked out together, lifted weights together, he was my best friend."

Michael, who rushed seven times for 11 yards and caught one touchdown pass in the Gladiators' 1983 championship game, died four months ago from carbon monoxide poisoning.

"We were very close," said Bey "I felt like I lost something inside when he passed away. It was like I lost half of myself."

Bey played for the Chicago Blitz of the United States Football League in 1983, but was released after eight games.

He then joined Gary, Ind., of the

"I really miss Michael and I want to dedicate this season to him. If it was the other way around I know he'd do the same for me."

— Jerry Bey

NSFL, and competed against the Gladiators and his brother.

"It was the first time we played against each other," said Bey. "We complimented each other throughout the game, and admired what the other was doing.

"The Gladiators won, but the game between those two teams was the best one of the season.

"He (Michael) was two years younger than me," said Bey. "In high school (at Thornridge in Dalton, Ill.) I set the records, and he broke them."

Bey has seven brothers and four sisters. One brother and one sister from his family are deceased.

"We're a real close family," said Bey. "I really miss Michael and I want to dedicate this season to him.

If it was the other way around I know he'd do the same for me.

"It's going to be a lot of hard work, and I'll give all my glory to God and my brother."

North Chicago man die of fumes; woman hurt

My God. Bean I am going to miss y

By TOM OSRAN
Staff Writer

A 25-year-old North Chicago man died Sunday and a Waukegan woman was hospitalized after breathing carbon monoxide leaking from a furnace.

Michael Bey, 25, of 507 10th St., North Chicago, was pronounced dead at St. Therese Hospital, Waukegan, at 6:31 p.m. Sunday, after his brother Greg discovered him lying in the basement, apparently overcome by furnace fumes.

Lynn Gray, 19, of 930 N. Jackson St., Waukegan, also found in the basement, was in good condition today at Lutheran General Hospital in Park Ridge.

Fire investigators said the basement of the two-story house was the scene of a party Saturday night. Apparently someone had accidentally knocked the flue pipe off the furnace without noticing it, said North Chicago Fire Lt. Bruno Bobrowski.

"Every time the furnace went on, it blew carbon monoxide directly into the house — primarily into the basement," he said.

When Greg Bey, 26, of 902 Bishop St., Chicago, went to the house at 5:30 p.m. Sunday, he found 11 members of his family sick, "nauseous, tired, drowsy, sleepy and sick to their

I Love you Bean, I Love

stomachs," Lake County ... Barbara Richardson said. B to the basement, where he fe brother and Gray unconscie mattress next to the furnace Chicago police Detective Holderbaum said.

After carrying his brother to the kitchen, Greg B outdoors and spotted a sq parked nearby with two W Waukegan officers Ozzie Ge L. Tessmann went to the he began cardiopul resuscitation on Bey. Told ti was still in the baseme carried her upstairs.

"It's a good thing he (G came home when he did. many people in the house, have had a lot more t Holderbaum said.

Richardson said the c death appears to be monoxide poisoning.

Other than North Chica officer Randall Price, who w oxygen on the scene, no one treated, Holderbaum said.

Articles and photograph of the late Michael Bey

Wes Chamberlain, Starting outfielder for the Boston Red Sox

The late Rick Thornton, pictured in uniform

sports

Brookins leads Illini chosen in pro draft

by Renny Zentz

Mitchell Brookins had no idea when or where he would go in Tuesday's National Football League draft and he wasn't about to make any predictions.

But when the Buffalo Bills made him the 95th pick in the annual event, Brookins said his lifelong dream of becoming a pro had come true.

"I'm really happy about it," the former Illini wide receiver said. "I was just sitting here watching the draft. It didn't really matter what round it was."

For the record, it was the fourth round, as the Bills apparently sought a younger receiver to back up veterans Jerry Butler and Frank Lewis.

Brookins said he isn't sure where he fits in the Bills' plans.

"I don't know, I really haven't talked to them about it," he said. "I hope they're good plans."

The Bills, who missed the playoffs with an 8-8 record last season under head coach Kay Stephenson, may give a younger player like Brookins more of a chance to play than would a proven contender.

"They had a disappointing season," he said. "But they picked some good players in the first couple rounds (Notre Dame running back Greg Bell was their first-round pick). And they still have some good players—veterans who are looking for a good season. I just hope I can contribute as much as I can."

Brookins' credentials indicate he'll be able to do that. He caught 22 passes last season in a non-starting role for the 10-2 Illini and scored five touchdowns despite his limited playing time.

MITCH CAN RUN THE HITCH — Mitchell Brookins (5-11, 190) can just plain run. He has been timed at 4.3 seconds in the 40-yard dash. "Mitch will be one of the 10 fastest receivers in the United States," says assistant coach Brad Childress. The Iowa secondary will support the claim.

Last week, Brookins caught only four passes, but they covered 131 yards. He scored once (54 yards) and he now has nine catches and four touchdowns. Not bad for a converted running back who accounted for 10 TDs in 1982.

Mitchell Brookins

Illinois wide receiver Mitchell Brookins was selected by the Buffalo Bills in the fourth round of Tuesday's National Football League draft. Brookins was the 11th player taken in the round, 95th overall. (photo by John Konstantaras)

Football Conference championship game.

"I just talked to him today," Thorp said. "He's a good coach. He just told me a little about the team and that they're glad to have me."

Brookins said he was glad to be with the Bills, even though he doesn't know too much about the area.

"I'm not too familiar with Buffalo," he said. "All I know is that I'm going to play for the Bills and I'm going to try to make the best of it."

The late Mitchell Brookins,

former player for the Buffalo Bills

Ameritech executive was a proud role model

BY ROBERT MUSIAL
Free Press Staff Writer

Robert Hurst

Growing up in a modest home on Stanford Street on Detroit's near west side, Robert Hurst learned about responsibility and the habit of hard work.

Both ideals served him well as he rose to become the president of Michigan Bell in 1992 and then, in 1993, president of Ameritech Network Services, the largest unit of the Chicago-based telephone company.

Mr. Hurst, 51, the first black person to head a local company with the size and visibility of Michigan Bell, died of a heart attack Monday in a Chicago hospital. He lived in the Chicago suburb of South Barrington, Ill., where he moved in 1993 after taking the Ameritech post.

Active in numerous community organizations while he was in Detroit, Mr. Hurst was proud to serve as a positive role model for young black people — and for corporations looking to make similar appointments.

Born in Magnolia, Miss., Mr. Hurst moved with his parents to Detroit at an early age.

His mother, a nurse's aide, and his stepfather, a mechanic, insisted he work hard in school. But, as Mr. Hurst once recalled, he was "not a brilliant student by any stretch of the imagination."

After graduating from Northwest-ern High School in 1960, he entered South Carolina State College.

In Detroit, he said, he had felt equal to everyone he knew, but in South Carolina, he felt racism for the first time.

Mr. Hurst became active in the civil rights movement and once was arrested in a demonstration. Years later, he still had an old copy of Jet magazine featuring a photo of himself being marched off to jail.

After earning a degree in chemistry, Mr. Hurst spent four years as a salesman and regional manager with Sterling Drug in New York before taking a sales position with Michigan Bell in 1969.

He held key posts in the company's personnel, marketing and business development departments and served as an Ameritech vice president before taking the helm of Michigan Bell.

When he had time for hobbies, they included travel, photography and cooking spicy dishes.

He also loved music and once took a spontaneous road trip with his wife Joyce to see their son, Robert III, a musician with Branford Marsalis' "Tonight Show" band, perform with the Chicago Symphony.

While living in Detroit, Mr. Hurst served as a board member of the Museum of African American History and of Help Against Violent Encounters Now, a shelter for victims of domestic violence.

In addition, he served as a board member for Henry Ford Hospital, the Metropolitan Detroit Convention and Visitors Bureau and the Michigan Opera Theatre.

Services will be at 11 a.m. Friday at St. Paul AME Zion Church, 11359 Dexter, Detroit.

The late Robert Hurst, former president of Ameritech

and my mentor

(left to right) John, Eddie, me, Ralph, Nate, Vince, Lamar

Tookie, T.D., Eric, Grady, (front) little Chucky

(left to right) T.D., Ray, me, and Lamar

My late high school/college friend, Buzzy (right),

with his son Morris Ellis III and Buzzy's dad Morris Ellis

The Bassette family: E.J. and Donna; and children
(left to right) Dominique, DeMario, and Deanna

Momma

(left to right) My six sisters, Eldora, Elouise, Evette,

Elleana, Earina, and Elaine

(left to right) Eddie, me, and Dad

My in-laws, Donald and Johnnie Mae

Annette and Eric Bassette

SILENT CRY

Black Women -- Nowhere to Hide

Race relations on campus was always a concern. At one point a lot of black women where being harassed and sometimes threatened with rape by white males. It got so bad that at night many of the sisters where afraid to walk across the campus. The Black Student Association held a meeting addressing the problems. I sat there, just a sophomore, knowing that I had six older sisters back in Chicago that I would kill for. However, most of the black girls on campus wouldn't want me to walk them home because they were afraid of me. I, like a lot of brothers, had developed a reputation of intimidation and fear. How could I help my own women when in a lot of ways I was as big a problem to them as the white boys were?

The Bold Dr. Ahmad

During my sophomore year, a number of black students kept telling me I needed to take Dr. Ahmad's African American history class because he was a trip. They said he would talk about white people like a dog and he was down for the brothers. I had decided to give it a shot. My cousin, Rennie, also enrolled in the class.

"Dr. A," as we called him, always wore African garb with dark glasses and a clean shaven head. He spoke with grace and intelligence and was educated in African and African American history.

The first day of class was full of black students as Dr. Ahmad talked about that "white peckerwood." I was shocked at first by his boldness, then we would laugh at his comments. I heard what Dr. Ahmad was saying but I didn't get into it too much. I felt different than the others because I had a way out in the form of football. I was going to play pro football and that was the end of it. Anything he said didn't apply to me. And it didn't apply to Rennie either because he could never make it to class.

As the semester passed, Dr. Ahmad would ask me where Rennie was and why he didn't come to class. I told him I would do my best to get him there. We lived together and had the same class at the same time, but Rennie would not get up to answer the bell. Most times he hung out with Ray, Lamar, C.C., Grady and Paul. They would all get up for 7:00 breakfast and then go back

The Key to Stopping the Violence

to sleep before their 8 a.m. class. I tried to talk to them, but I had my own problems. I was close to flunking a few classes.

Too Much Party Time

Deke and me were sophomores. One weekend, Marty decided to visit our campus. He attended a small, predominantly white school of 500 students in Iowa. I left Friday afternoon for Chicago and Marty got to WIU Friday night. I told the younger Thee Family Brothers to make sure Marty was taken care and stayed out of trouble. I knew that Marty would come on campus and play big man. That wasn't the problem. The concern was that Marty wasn't used to our campus and I didn't want him to have any run-ins. We normally got pretty drunk before we headed to the parties, and I knew this weekend would be no different. After I left, Thee Family Brothers did the usual drinking of Barcardi 151 and beer, Then got ready to go to the Corbin Hall party. Once intoxicated, the fellows would usually need supervision. With Marty as ring leader, they headed to Corbin Hall all ready to party. Deke was already there waiting inside for them. Unfortunately because of their drinking, it was like the blind leading the blind. Marty, C.C., Pope and Grady, were all stumbling to the party. Marty accidently walked into a white student about half way to the party and the student said, "Hey fuck man", and walked toward Marty. Before Marty could react, C.C. hit the white boy with a cane. Marty, C.C., Grady and Pope kept walking, not giving what just happened another thought. They were carefree and being ex-jocks, they decided to stand outside the party and play football. The police drove up and put the lights on the brothers right in front of Corbin Hall. Marty walked up to the police and said, "C.C. had a little too much to drink and shouldn't be taken in." As he offered his advice, the cops said, "he's not the one we're looking for, you are." Then the white boy came out of the police car with blood all over him and confirmed that Marty was the one who hit him. Marty begins to cry and say it wasn't him. He even looks at C.C. and asks him to tell the truth. C.C. tells the cops, but they don't want to hear it. Marty cried all the way to the police station and repeating "God help me, please don't lock me up."

Deke found out his main man was in jail and became furious. The next morning he got the guys together and they went up to the police station. Before they went in, Deke said, "Let me handle this." The younger guys thought Deke had a master plan. Deke walked into the police station with a briefcase and demanded to see Marty Jackson. The officer at the front desk said that he is not allowed any visitors. So Deke walked away, put on dark glasses, returned to the front desk and said "I would like to see the honorable Marty Jackson." The police repeated, "Look, boy, don't you hear? I said no visitors." So Deke and the boys left the jailhouse and stood outside. Deke put his briefcase on a car hood and said, " I think I got the right shit for those officers." The young brothers thought Deke was going to pull out a gun, bomb or maybe even legal documents. But he opens up his briefcase and revealed a jock strape, shorts and t-shirt. "There's nothing we can do for Marty now. He shouldn't have gotten his ass in this mess. Fellows, let's hit the gym and play some basketball," said Deke. This was typical Deke-always funny and unpredictable. Marty did get out because his father wired some money to him.

Happy New Year

Back in 1980 I had a successful football campaign in my sophomore year, with more than 33 solo tackles and several big plays. I went home to see Dad and celebrate Christmas and New Year's. The city looked so much different now that I had been away at school. The atmosphere was scary with all the abandoned buildings and vacant apartments. Ray, Lamar and me would sit in the washroom of the Almtrack train to ride home free and save our tickets so we could cash them in. On the train Ray sold me a gold chain for $25; it retailed for $300 but he'd stolen it from a store in uptown Macomb. I gave it to my woman for Christmas.

Ray and Lamar had flunked out and knew they wouldn't be back at Western. Every Christmas Eve, Ray and I went shopping downtown and this year wouldn't be any different. On New Year's Eve I visited my homeboys in the next building and knocked on Frankie's bedroom window. I told him to come out. We knocked on Aaron's door and we three talked about what was going on in the 'hood and about what we all did in this strange place called college.

Frankie and Aaron had never been on a college campus so I kept them intrigued with stories of football, women, fraternities, the whole thing. They had also met Deke, T.D. and Vince, so I also talked about them. About 4 p.m., I told the homies I had go before it got dark because the shooting would

The Key to Stopping the Violence

start and I wanted to make it to my woman's house. Just before I could say my last goodbye, three men came walking through the backyard. They were dressed in knee-length dark winter coats. As they walked by we nodded to show respect and said, "What's up." One of them stopped in front of us about 4 feet away and pulled a sawed off shotgun from under his coat. He looked us straight in the eye. We didn't have time to run or react. All we could do was stand there. In a deep voice he said, "Happy New Year motherfuckers." My heart raced knowing I was at the wrong place at the wrong time. A smirk creased his face as he and his boys walked off.

I told my boys I was out of there. We all went our separate ways. I caught my breath and headed upstairs. I had just dodged another bullet. How fast all of my dreams could have left at that moment.

Slow Road to Nowhere

Starting the spring semester in my sophomore year, my grades began to drop. Lamar and Ray had flunked out, Rennie had flunked, and C.C. was also back in Chicago. All four major fraternities were fighting one another. Sometimes the fighting would get so vicious, you would think we were back in Chicago on the streets. Deke, and T.D. pledged Phi Beta Sigma. Reggie had been kicked off the team just when he was making his run for the pros. Michael Bey was about to play semi pro ball and Jerry Bey had been cut from the Greenbay Packers. I was running wild and out of control like everyone else and I didn't know how to stop. Football was the only thing I went all out for, but the politics of the game had taken away from it. I wanted to fight anyone for anything and when I did try to hit the books, my white tutor wouldn't show up so I thought he wanted me to fail. Most of the black students weren't serious about their to studies. If it had to do with studying, I had another reason to fall asleep in class. Even when I put in the effort, the football team was always on a bus, plane or practice. So during the season I would fall asleep in class. Most of the time I didn't pick up a book until it was time to cram. So as fun as everything was that first semester, it was all changing. There were hundreds of people flunking out. My grade point average was okay, but I was not putting in the effort I should and could have. When it came to tests, a lot of us thought cheat first, cheat second and cram third.

SILENT CRY

During the same semester, the Phi Beta Sigma's (Deke's and T.D.'s frat) were having a step down show. During practice, the brothers decided to use a broken starter pistol to kick off their show. Deke had been given the pistol to bring to practice. On the way there, one of his frat brothers got into an argument with another fraternity member. Things escalated and they began fighting. Other members of the opposing frat joined in the fight. Deke wasn't going to let one of his frat boys get beat up without doing something. To stop the commotion, Deke pulled out the old broken starter pistol, held it up in the air and shouted, "Stop this shit now!" Then he told his boy to make a break for it and they ran across the open field toward an apartment complex. Unfortunately, the campus police saw Deke pull out the gun. Being black at Western wasn't the best position to be in when pulling out a gun of any kind, broken or not.

Deke was suspended from school for the remainder of the semester and had to go back to the city. This story was blown out of proportion and added even more fuel to Deke's bad boy image around the campus. It was T.D. who payed $250 to get a crying Deke out of jail.

During the summer before my junior year, I lived off campus with Renee, a childhood friend, and her two roommates. I weight trained and didn't date anyone. At my yearly summer job painting the dorms, I'd talk to Gwen, who had painted with me the year before. Gwen was from Keokuk, Iowa. A black girl who had grown up in a small town. She acted more like she was white. She couldn't relate to the black experience and didn't know how to interact with other blacks on campus. I told her she didn't have the street smarts to deal with big city blacks. She was enraged by all the words I used to describe things and the fact that I had experienced most of the things she had only read about her own people.

Gwen and had been on the campus for six years, but was only a sophomore because of her grades. I would talk to her about my problems with women. We painted rooms eight hours a day and talked about the differences we had as black people. Gwen was in two worlds, but she wasn't accepted by either, so she spent a lot of time complaining. She was so naive to everything. I had a ball with her, teasing her about the way she talked, walked and looked but it was all in fun. In my heart I knew Gwen was as sweet as pie. I talked her into being my roommate off campus that next semester. Gwen had found a great

The Key to Stopping the Violence

apartment near the football stadium. And even better she knew how to cook.

My junior year was going to be a fantastic year. Randy Sheppard and I practiced in combat boots the entire summer as I was lifting more and more weight and producing faster times in the 40-yeard dash. Randy, our starting linebacker, was fired up for his last season. During the summer Randy and I started spending more time with Dr. Ahmad, who continued to compliment me on my potential. At the end of the summer I went home and Ray and I would run from 35th Street north to downtown Chicago. We would visit Eric's job, at a ladies shoe store, where they called him preacher because he had a huge cross around his neck. He never flirted with any of the female customers. He was 6'1" and 140 pounds and appeared physically and mentally weak. We knew he would barely speak to us but we went by anyway. He was still my big brother and I loved him.

Ray would tell me he had seen my mom at the grocery store. She didn't recognize me anymore as I had changed a lot between the ages of 15 and 20. Ray was always with me when I went to her apartment where we stood and waited until she came out just so I could to see what she looked like. Every Christmas I would go to her and Eric's apartment, knowing she would close the door on me after she found out who it was. I would go the door pretending to be my brother Eric but when she saw it was me she would say, "I'm sorry, but you're not my son" and close the door in my face. The same happened with my older sister Eraina, who lived next door. Eraina never wanted to let me in, but Sam her husband would sit down an talk to Ray and me. That treatment hurt but and I took it out on other people by fighting or causing hell. I used sports as my way of dealing with it the best way I could.

But something started changing during my junior year football season. Carrie, my off and on girl friend from high school, was coming back around. I really didn't want to get back into a relationship with her, but for a short while I did. One incident stands out. The coaches didn't play Randy in the opening game against Illinois State, which we lost. Randy went to the coaches after the game and asked why he didn't play. I went with him and we stood there and listened to the coaches double-talk about how they forgot to put him in. It really made me think that if this could happen to Randy, a team captain, then it could happen to me.

143

SILENT CRY

During an argument with Carrie she told me that football was the only thing I knew and if I didn't go pro I would end up a bum because I was nothing but a jock. Everytime we argued she said she couldn't wait until I got bullshitted in football because she was tired of dealing with a spoiled athlete who only thought of himself. She always used Randy as an example of what would happen to me.

As the football season was winding down I thought back to all the things in my life that seemed to be out of control. I wasn't doing my best in school. I couldn't declare a major because I wasn't accepted into the accounting program. I had a solid season with 44 solo tackles and two interceptions, but I dropped nine potential interceptions. I also became an MCC all conference player. I knew I had to have a great individual effort my last year to make the professional level because I didn't think the coaches would look out for my best interest.

Also during the season a doctor came to practice to talk about the lifelong physical damage that football was going to cause. He explained that because of all the physical contact we were killing brain cells with every hit to the head. Those cells would never be reproduced so we were cutting short our life span by years. I thought about all the contact I had endured over the last seven years and how long it took to recover from the pain. After explaining the consequences to us, we had to sign a release form that said we knew the risk involved. Every person signed without even a slight thought to what the man was saying. I seemed to be the only one concerned.

Coach Smith the new defensive back coach, said there was no way I wouldn't go pro, what with my physical stature -- 6' 1 1/2", 185 pounds and 4.4 speed -- and a knack for knocking the hell out of anything close to me. But inside I was empty because I knew there was something wrong with my personality. I had a cold spirit. I would curse at a black woman before I would speak. I was ready to beat a brother or a white boy up before I would help them. I hated the fact that other students hated me. Others were as mean as me but I didn't like the fact that so many people avoided me.

As the season ended the Head Coach had his regular meeting with all the players. He said that in the NFL I would probably be moved to one of the safety positions instead of playing cornerback. "Fine with me," I thought. Carrie was wrong. I'm going to make it because I can't be stopped. After the season, there was a whole crop of ball players who dropped

The Key to Stopping the Violence

out of school to wait for the professional draft. They thought they would make a pro team. During the year some of them were taking classes on how to use the library and numerous gym classes.

I still had not declared a major. On campus "The Dog" was still going strong with parties and the women. During the second semester of my junior year I decided to take my first level 300 business course. On the first day of class I didn't see a black person in the room. I was so intimidated that I dropped the course. I knew at that point I needed help because I was afraid and had no direction. But as I turned to some of the black students, I realized they were just as confused as I was. I decided to take another African studies course with Dr. Ahmad. Carrie also decided to take the course. It had been a year since Ray and Lamar went home and Deke was back on campus with T.D. The fraternities were still fighting each other. Fights were breaking out all over campus and the dropout rate among the black students was probably 80 percent each semester. There were more black men in prison in Macomb, Ill., than in Chicago, or so it seemed.

I decided to take a semester and figure out what I wanted to do with my life. I needed to buy some time because I was failing on the inside. I was only a football player, big, bad and tall. I wasn't contributing anything else. I thought about what Carrie said and wondered what would happen if I didn't go pro. I wasn't going back to the projects and I couldn't go home without a degree. I wanted to be involved with people but only a handful of people really understood me. Most thought I was wild, crazy and intimidating and would speak to me and laugh in my face but talk about me behind my back.

The same thing was going on with Deke and the fraternities. We all got away from Chicago and went buckwild. There were brothers on campus walking around who didn't even go to the school. They pretended to be students because they didn't want to go back to the city. Many actually attended Spoon River Junior College but acted like a W.I. U. student. A number of girls were getting pregnant and leaving campus. I was even guilty of getting another girl pregnant back in my sophomore year. She decided to have an abortion against her mother's wishes. I borrowed money from a professor to help pay for it.

There was a department that brought underachieving minority students to WIU, most of whom started in summer school. However, the classes they often took included zoology, chemistry and physics -- all in the same semester. Therefore, the failure rate was high. Many of the students thought they were being rail roaded by the white-controlled university to bring black students in to meet quotas, then failing them so they would fall through the cracks.

The Nation: A Search for Truth

I figured there wasn't a better place to find myself than in Dr. Admad's class. In his class, Dr. Ahmad talked about how blacks were once great people and our condition before slavery. I had never heard that before. After class I would ask questions and he would patiently offer answers. Wayne Foster, a former high school, classmate and all-state basketball player, also took the class. One day after class I followed Dr. Ahmad to his office and there was a poster of a man who spoke about the Honorable Elijah Muhammad's teachings. I asked Dr. Ahmad what it was all about and he handed me a cassette to listen to. In my apartment, I heard the voice of a man I had never heard before. He was speaking in front of Stevie Wonder, James Brown, Jim Brown and thousands of others in Hollywood. He spoke about what Black people needed to do to gain respect for self and why the Black man in America had no respect for himself or anyone else. He talked about his relationship with Malcolm X and why he left the Nation of Islam. He discussed what we as black men needed to do with respect to our women and how the Nation had family values.

I sat there on my bed and cried because I felt this voice was talking to me. I felt fear and anger from growing up in the projects, witnessing black-on-black crime, and racism on the football field. My question of why there were so few black people willing to help other black people was being answered. The man called himself the National Representative of the Nation of Islam. His name was Louis Farrakhan. I had to hear more of what he was saying.

Dr. Ahmad told us students that because we were from Western Illinois University and not an Ivy League school like Princeton or Yale, there was no way we could work for a major corporation. I was scared shitless. He said that Africa was the only way to go. Dr. Ahmad always talked about his travels through Africa and our brain power was needed to build up the motherland. So I decided to take Dr. Ahmad's advice. I got a passport and started talking to other brothers about Africa. I

The Key to Stopping the Violence

talked to Nigerian exchange students. Black Americans on campus didn't speak to the Blacks from Africa and we knew very little about their people and their culture. We said they smelled. The Blacks from Africa were told not to trust Blacks from America. They were also told that American Black men were thieves and that our black women were no good freaks.

By talking to them I began to appreciate their country. I started wearing African clothes. Carrie was 100 percent behind me. I came home to visit the projects and Dad almost had a heart attack. I came in wearing an African robe and told him that I could not find a job in America and that I had to go to Africa. My father was extremely upset and wanted to know who was teaching me. He said there was good and evil in every race and I had to search for each element in people. I told him after college I would be moving to Africa. Dr. Ahmad even introduced Ray, Wayne, and Randy to a man living in Africa who had started a trading business with various African nations.

I started becoming more pleasant to black people on campus. I started understanding that what I was looking for was inside of me. I learned how to look for the good in my people and other people. I started to study and look for ways to make a difference in my life. I had to manifest the God-like character in me. I got more tapes from Dr. Ahmad and heard Minister Farrakhan talk about how the government was against the rise of "dark nations" around the world. Knowledge is the key, I learned, and once it's turned on, you can see and you will never walk in darkness again.

I started sharing the teachings of Minister Farrakhan with all the brothers on campus, but most of them would run. For the first time in my life, my commitment to football was taking a back seat. Dr. Ahmad decided to have his students invite Minister Farrakhan to Western, although most had never heard of him. I realized a lot of our own people didn't want to hear anything positive about ourselves. We were content with white people taking care of us. Even as bad as we were doing on campus. Most of us didn't want change in our lives. We were happy with blaming other people, and afraid to change ourselves.

On visits home to Ida B. Wells projects I again shared "The teachings" with Ray and Lamar. I told them how we could make a difference. This new-found knowledge was actually changing my life. I had a business law 400 level class and as usual was sitting in the back of the class calculating my football statistics. Whenever the white professor called on me, I looked at

147

him with eyes of death, never answering or even smiling. He came to me one day and said that he knew how I was and just wanted to help me become successful. With his encouragement, my outlook changed. I started being part of the class and by the end of the semester, I had earned a "B" in his class.

When I was with Wayne and Dr. Ahmad, Wayne would tell Dr. Ahmad about how he was going to use certain knowledge he gained from the Minister tapes to show women how articulate he was. He used it as rap lines to get more involved. I had problems with that because it now bothered me to use knowledge to manipulate people. It reminded me of what had happened to Momma in pastor's church. Dr. Ahmad would talk about black people and a minute later he was talking about women. I continued to move closer to the ideals of the Nation and move further away from Dr. Ahmad, and Wayne's views.

When Minister Farrakhan came to campus to speak I had a chance to meet him after he spoke. I had the poster that Dr. Ahmad had given me. I worked my way through his bodyguards as the minister sat in a chair shaking students' hands with a warm, friendly smile. He was polite and humble. I asked him to autograph my poster and looked him in the eyes and said, "Minister Farrakhan, I'm for the liberation of black people all over the world."

He replied, "Brother, you don't have to tell me. I can see the struggle in your eyes." That moment will always be locked in my mind.

Ray started going to the temple with me. Other football players like Thomas and Kevin would also listen to the tapes but the others friends, including Deke, T.D., Tookie and most of my homies back in Chicago, would run from me. They said I was talking that "black talk." But I knew in my heart that all of us had things going on in our lives that needed clear direction and thought.

Finally I talked Deke, Ray, Rennie, Carrie and Gertie, Ray's girlfriend, into going to see Minister Farrakhan speak in Chicago. These were the closest people to me and I wanted to save them from the mud and filt of this world. Deke enjoyed it but said he didn't like people touching him (the FOI guards patted us down at the door). Ray continued to go. Rennie and the ladies liked it but wouldn't go on a regular basis.

No one had answers for the black student high dropout rate on campus. I still hadn't declared a major. I wasn't going to

The Key to Stopping the Violence

graduate on time. I knew what happened to Gwen, who finally graduated after seven years.

Now I still had to find a major in order to eventually graduate. In the locker room I heard star white players saying they weren't going to graduate. One said he was going to get a two-year certificate and I decided I would do the same thing. I went to the admissions office and picked up all the graduate books and started looking for information on the liberal arts program. As I read, I remembered that the Minister Farrakhan taught that, land is the basis of all nations. Without it you can't build and produce. That's when I selected agriculture as my major, with finance as my discipline. I went to the agriculture department and there were no Black Americans there. I talked with the dean of the department and told him I wanted to transfer. We agreed that I had taken the necessary courses and I started taking classes before the start of my fourth season. I mapped out my courses and with summer school factored in, it appeared that I needed 85 hours of credit, or four semesters -- with summer school. I realized that if I was going to graduate, I would have to graduate in five years instead of four. It was better than the other alternative, facing my father without a degree, trying to make excuses to a man who made no excuses and didn't except any. So, I mentally geared up for it, happy I had found a way out.

As I changed, my friends started changing. But sometimes when you hear a new message you interpret it based on your old attitude. Back in Chicago I had a female friend, who lived alone with her grandmother. I worried about her because she lived in a bad neighborhood. Beatrice was the kind of person who wouldn't hurt a fly. I called home once and she told me a man tried to rape her. I instantly called Ray and said we had some business to take care of. She told me where this creep worked and Ray and me planned to break his hands in front of his employees. I was operating on pure anger and rage. We walked into his business wearing long coats and armed with hidden baseball bats. Ray was carrying a pistol. We asked for him by name. The plan was to go upside his head and not say a word. He knew what he had done. The place was tense when we walked. One of the owners said he had just left. I knew after I grew more in knowledge that God spared me because we probably would have landed in jail.

SILENT CRY

Momma, Don't Go

By Spring 1981 Ray found a job, in the computer department. He started school at Triton Community College and had just purchased a new car to get to the school in the west suburb of Melrose Park. He had completely settled down and was enjoying his new opportunities his new career. All Ray would talk about was programs on computers and becomimg a programmer. On a visit to Chicago I noticed that Mrs. Grandberry was really worried about how many of her friends were dying. She was frustrated as she spoke of some of her friends who had died. Then one of her friends was robbed on the way to church and that caused her more panic. A few times Ray and me walked her to church and to the bus stop because of her fear of the neighborhood.

Then Mr. J., her close friend, died and Mrs. Grandberry seemed to be even more depressed as she continued to talk about how things had changed. Ray and Ivory would always laugh and say, "Momma's just tripping." They didn't seem to worry as much as I did. One day when I went to their apartment Mrs. Grandberry called to Ray to answer the door although it sounded like she was closer to it. Ray answered the door and I saw Mrs. Grandberry lying on the kitchen floor with a pillow and blanket. I walked in and Ray walked around her and headed upstairs. I stopped and asked Mrs. Grandberry if something was wrong. She said that by lying on the floor in the kitchen she could breath better because of the cool air coming in from under the door. I asked her if there was anything she needed. She said she didn't and she was tired. I went upstairs and questioned Ray about what I had seen. He didn't seem concerned, so I left it alone, but I wasn't comfortable with what I saw.

Now that Ray worked in the computer department at Triton. Each morning he would get up for school and then wake Mrs. Grandberry to start the day. One morning Ray called for Mrs. Grandberry to wake up, but he didn't hear anything. He went in the room and she appeared to be awake because her eyes were open. But when he shook his mother, she didn't move. Ray hysterically called emergency for an ambulance. As she lied there Ray watched his mother take her last breath. She had suffered a heart attack.

Mrs. Grandberry's funeral was held at West Point Church. I wondered what Ray would do and about the support

The Key to Stopping the Violence

Mr. Grandberry would give Ray. Ray never did get along with his father, who he always called cheap. Mr. Grandberry often had been Ray's secret disappointment. Ray had always been angry about the way his father treated his mother, leaving her and the family, and beating them when they were smaller. Ray blamed a lot of his childhood illnesses on him. In addition, Mr. Grandberry never wanted to part with any money. Case in point: Ray needed some shoes for his mother's funeral. I'll never forget what Mr. Grandberry did. Ray approached his father with a boyish look and asked for some money. Mr. Grandberry pulled out a $100 bill, put it back in his wallet and pulled out a $50 bill. He looked at it and pulled out a $20 and looked at Ray and asked, "Don't your brother Ivory have some old shoes you can wear?" Ray looked at him with disgust and later told me he hated him for the way he treated him.

I would always get Mr. Grandberry on the subject of white people. Because he was born in the early 1900's. He would always start whispering as though white people would hear him and kill him. There we were in the middle of the ghetto where there were no white people even if you tried to make one. I would ask Mr. Grandberry to tell me how those white people were when he was growing up. He would look around as if checking the room for white ears, then he'd lower his voice to a whisper and say, "Those people are the meanest people you want to ever deal with. They will get you if they can." It was only later that I understood some blacks had been through so much with white people that they couldn't talk about the trauma and shock they experienced when living in the south.

At Mrs. Grandberry's funeral I felt for Ray, Ivory and Vail because their mother was the best. I wanted my best friend to know I was going to help him get through it. Gertie, Ray's girlfriend, said she was moving in with Ray about the same time Ivory went back to Illinois State. I struggled when I returned to Western because I knew I had to find a way to keep Ray motivated, because he was trying to stay on the right path.

Losing the Will to Live

After Mrs. Grandberry died Ivory and I tried to keep Ray's spirits up. All of Ray's life his mother made sure he was happy. I would always come by to see Mrs. Grandberry when I was in Chicago because she had been like a mother to me and helped ease the pain of Momma leaving home five years earlier.

SILENT CRY

I often visited her just like her own sons, Ray and Ivory. They would come in the apartment and I would be there with her eating dinner. She always worried because Ray hadn't made it at Western. She knew Ivory would be alright at Illinois State.

She knew her youngest son had two sides to him. One side was a young man with unlimited talent and the ability to rally people around him to do good things. Then there was a destructive force, like me, he had an alter ego, that hated just for the sake of hating. She knew it was partially caused by Ray and his fathers relationship. But she was the person he lived for and they both cared for each other unconditionally.

After her death Ray couldn't even articulate his reasons for doing these things. Other friends would tell me that I never saw the Ray they saw -- a brother who could terrorize a person with his nonstop approach to fighting. Then you had to add in his growing anger over seeing his mother's death, which set Ray up for destruction.

I was in constant contact with Ray back in Chicago. I was also taking him to see Minister Farrakhan speak because he had helped so many of us in the ghetto stay out of the mud of this world. But Ray had another influence in his life -- drugs -- that made him do things for a quick buck. I was really worried about Ray because I knew he had been struggling with some of the no-good friends he and I had in the 'hood. I would tell Ray they were no longer his friends and that he had to make new ones to improve his relationships with people.

Within a month after Mrs. Grandberry died, Ray and another homie were selling drugs in the park across from Frankie's building. They had made a number of drug sales that still-young Friday night. They sold drugs to some dudes from the 39th and Lake street projects. About 20 minutes later these dudes drove back and asked Ray why he tried to beat them out of some of their merchandise. Ray told the dudes that they got what he paid for. It was dark so Ray and M.C. didn't see the other dudes coming up on them from the other side. Suddenly Ray noticed them and hollered out to run. They both broke out running back south toward 36th Street and Vincennes. They heard a rash of pops from the gun shots being fired. Ray and ol' boy thought they had escaped until they got in front of Frankie's house and Ray felt a tingle in the back of his leg. He told Frankie that he had been shot. They put Ray in Frankie's car and drove him to the hospital. When I received the messages from Gertie, I rushed home to Chicago see Ray in the hospital.

The Key to Stopping the Violence

Ray was difficult to talk to; he was not afraid of what happened to him, despite being shot in the back. On the other hand, I was concerned about him because this was the first time he had shown me he didn't care. At the same time I thought he was acting like an asshole. They had to take out his bladder and he wore it next to him in a bag. I tried to look on the bright side. The doctors said that he was fortunate to not suffer any permanent damage. Ray kept saying he knew who shot him and he was going to get back at the MF. I tried to get him to understand that it was what he was doing that put him in the situation to get shot, but he wouldn't listen. I talked to Gertie and she felt Ray was hanging with the wrong crowd ever since his mother had died. She planned to move back from Texas for good and live with Ray.

I found it very difficult seeing Ray shot. After Mrs. Grandberry died. He seemed to almost not care anymore. He later told me he robbed a fag in front of my apartment the night before he got shot. He saw him sitting in the car kissing another man. The fag was somebody we had known for years. Ray just never liked what he was doing. Ray said, "E.J., me and another friend slapped these two sissies around like a couple of bitches. Then we made them kiss while kicking them up the ass and taking their money."

An Eye for an Eye, A Tooth for a Tooth

Ray had recovered from the shooting and I spent a lot of time calling home and giving him tapes from the Nation of Islam. If we weren't on the phone we were writing letters. I encouraged him to go to hear Minister Farrakhan speak at 79th at Halsted, which he did. Then I'd call to see what the minister had spoken about. I figured if we stayed strong and learned the knowledge of self, there was nothing a person could do to someone who had strength and purpose. Ray was still struggling to stay away from the bad influences in the 'hood.

One spring Sunday, Ray came from the temple wearing his suit and bow tie when he saw one of the regular 16" softball games going on in Ellis Park. As Ray stopped and looked around he saw that one of the dudes playing looked familiar. He went a little closer and saw it was the dude who had shot him a few months earlier. Ray thought of what I would do. Then he thought about what would Minister Farrakhan do. Then he decided to do his own thing and get back at the dude who tried to take him out.

Ray calmly left, went upstairs to his apartment and changed into a jogging suit and baseball cap. He went back to the park and watched as the dude played third base. Ray remembered the hospital bed and the pain of having his bladder hanging out of his side. He couldn't stand the fact that this MF could be back in his neighborhood playing softball, not knowing whether the brother he shot was dead or alive this irked Ray.

Ray walked through the crowd and picked up a baseball bat and started swinging it as though he was part of the game. Like a man on a mission, he walked down the third base line toward the dude who had shot him. The guy on third base was puzzled, like most of the crowd. He didn't recognize Ray until Ray got close. Ray cocked the bat just as the guy realized who he was. Ray swung straight at the dude's head, intending to kill him with one blast. The guy lowered his head at that very second and hollered to his boys, "This MF is crazy" and took off running.

Many of the people watching the game took off running in different directions. And the shooter/third baseman took off south toward 39th Street and the lakefront with Ray in pursuit. Ray chased him from 36th and Vincennes to Cottage Grove, to 39th Street, past the Darrow Homes projects and across 39th Street and back toward the lake. By the time they got to 39th and the lakefront they could barely run. But the dude tried to make one last push to run to the safety of his building. Ray swung and struck the dude in the back of the head, knocking him to the ground. With blood rushing from his head, Ray kicked him in the side and face. Ray turned and walked away as a crowd gathered and looked. Later Ray found out he had put him in a coma for eight weeks.

Ray felt, "An eye for an eye, a tooth for a tooth." I came home from school trying to make sense out of what happened. I argued with Ray that MF probably would have died at the hands of someone else anyway. But Ray had never let anyone get away with anything.

Love at First Sight

Back at school I had gotten engaged as I tried desperately to keep myself together. Dr. Ahmad was still having a big influence on me and I knew I had to make a change. Carrie I

The Key to Stopping the Violence

had been dating off and on for five years and I really thought I loved her.

We were young when we started dating. I was 16 years old and she was only 14. She had to deal with all of my moods and ways. Before the semester I never thought about too much other than football. Now my mind was expanding with knowledge that helped improve my personality, attitude and behavior, as well as relationships.

At the beginning of the semester, I entered Dr. Ahmad's class and Carrie sat next to me. Shortly after that a young lady walked in who I had never seen on campus before. I gazed at her and thought to myself, "That's the girl I'm going to marry." Then I looked at Carrie, wondering if she somehow had overheard my thoughts, but I didn't care.

I found out her name was Donna and I just knew that she was the one I wanted, but I never approached her. As a matter of fact, throughout the semester, I avoided her as much as possible. I didn't want her to ever think that I was disrespectful. While there were some sisters I had been known to sleep with and never give it a second thought, I wanted to meet Donna under the right circumstances.

We ended up joining the same black student organization, which meant that we would talk occasionally, but I kept my old "dog collar" tight around my neck. I knew that when I really got to know this sister, I would marry her.

Leaving the Team

Going into that last football season was really a stress because the coaches were in the last year of their contracts. During my senior year, the blacks on the team still complained because the coaches continued playing the white players. Just like the older players had complained my freshman year. I saw brothers sitting on the sidelines. It seemed the coaches would rather lose with less-skilled white players than win with the best black players. I told my teammates that we had to stand for our principles and do what was right. If that meant another protest, then we had to walk off. I was all-conference player, could have had an All-American year, and a professional career. The coaches thought me and Tookie could play professional ball. I was willing to stand up for an athlete who wasn't on scholarship before he was willing to stand up for himself. I equated this to a slave who was afraid to escape even though he would surely die

155

in the end for being a slave. Fear was, and still is, the most powerful tool used against people.

After not being able to get the black players to walk off for their rights. I continued to play but the joy had finally been taken out of football. I was on track to break the all-time tackling record set by Mike Wagner, former All-Pro from the Pittsburgh Steelers. I was disappointed, but I continued to play until the last two weeks of the season. Then two things happened. The football secretary, a white lady, came to me and said, "E.J., the coaches are not even talking about you to the pro scouts despite all the hard work you put in. I think you need to be aware of it." After hearing that, and knowing all the black players who were kicked off the team, over the years. I owed it to myself to finish school. I told the players on the squad that it was worth giving up something you've loved all your life to save your life. I contended, I would make more money as a businessman in the real
world than I could make in the pros.

During next game, I told Tookie on the field that I didn't think I would make it through the game. And this would be my last game. While the game was in progress, I walked to my coach and thanked him for the years of football, walked passed the fans watching the game into the locker room, said a prayer and cleaned out my locker. Then I went in the stands where T.D. and some of the fellows were. T.D. couldn't believe what I had done. But I promised myself again. I would make more money in business than a lot of guys make in football. I left the game and went to my apartment, opened a book, cried and studied. After that move I called Ray and told him we had to fight together with our minds because we could be the shining stars of our community. Ray said he still thought we should write that book about this from Ghetto to Glory.

I continued to get more involved with the Black Student Organization and became vice president. Thomas , one of the other ballplayers decided to join the Nation of Islam. My confidence grew in other areas and I decided to join the Nation also because it seemed to be the best outlet for meeting me and Rays needs. I started going to the library every day studying and reading for five or six hours minimum a day. When Thomas and I periodically came to Chicago, we would go to the temple. I became a member of the Fruit of Islam and sold newspapers for the Nation. It was difficult trying to keep a schedule that included school and homework. Most of my family thought I was crazy or

The Key to Stopping the Violence

becoming a racist. But they didn't understand I was not just fighting for myself. I was fighting for Ray, Deke and T.D. I, like the people in the Nation, wanted to see better for black people. The Nation taught me to respect all man kind, but to respect myself first. Only then could I respect others. As I learned more, I became more understanding. I tried to get Ray to join the Nation as I studied my lesson plan. I was constantly driving back and forth from Macomb to Chicago, trying to look out for Ray's best interest. Ray would always tell me that the brothers back in the low end were trying to keep him occupied with negative things.

Ray confided in me that he could read items in the paper or magazine but had a difficult time comprehending what he read. He said that was the main reason he hated school. I asked him why he had never told me this before. He said, he was too embarrassed. We started to cry because we understood that the school system had miseducated him all of his life. Education and sports were our only way out of the low end, now I realized, Ray knew he had neither. With tears in my eyes, I promised Ray we would sit and relearn how to do everything even if it took going back to the first grade level.

James Currington and Grandpa Kennedy

Back on the campus Deke had become almost paranoid about people who were dying. He had always lived with Grandma and Grandpa, his father's parents. They loved and spoiled Deke because he was their youngest grandson. Even though Grandpa and Grandma were getting old, they had a hip youthfulness about them.

After living with an illness, Grandpa Kennedy passed away, and that really hurt Deke. After that told me he couldn't go to another funeral. He was very concerned about Grandma because she and her husband had been together close to 50 years.

Back home on the West Side of Chicago Vince had started working as an insurance salesman. He and the Currington family never fully recovered from Bennies tragic death. Vince and his younger brother James, who was an honorary member of Thee Family, had picked up the mantle to carry on. Mother Currington and Pastor Currington prayed hard and long for God to guide and protect their two remaining sons. However, one night at the Currington residence, Mother Currington heard James snoring unusually loud so she told Vince to go in James' room to turn

SILENT CRY

him on his stomach or wake him up. Vince went in and realized James was not snoring but gasping for air. Vince let out a holler that woke up the entire Currington house. Their father rushed in the room and gave James CPR. Vince got on his knees and begged God to save his remaining brother. But before the ambulance could get there James Currington died.

Vince had lost his last brother, Rev. and Mrs. Currington had lost their second son in five years. Ever since James' death, I've felt guilty because Deke and I didn't go home to support Vince and his family. I know for a fact these two deaths made Deke panic and talk about death more than ever.

Struggle for the Mind

Deke and I had started arguing because I was changing and I knew he was still doing the things we used to do. He walked around campus always clowning or tripping people out. Although he was nice to alot of women on campus the ones who didn't know him still heard he was wild.

In spring 1983 I asked Deke to reconsider some of the friends he had been hanging around. Deke was getting high and partying regularly, always surrounded by 10 or 15 people. I was constantly in his face telling him he needed to be more productive and to respect the women on campus. "Ersk, you're the only person that can do this to me," he'd say whenever I got close in his face. "Just because your tripping on the righteous tip, that don't mean I have to" "But I'm the 'Deke Dog' and that's my tip."

Deke himself sensed that something wasn't right. He went to T.D's. apartment and told Von, T.D.'s. roommate, that he wasn't happy with his life. Deke knew Von was a very stable, religious person. Deke said he felt he was going to die and didn't know what to do. As Deke sat there with tears in his eyes, Von offered to pray for him. Von went to another room to get his bible. And when he came back, Deke was gone. Later at Von's wedding, I saw Deke holding Doris's hand. I turned toward Carrie and told her to look. I had never seen Deke hold a girl's hand in public before.

The next time I saw Deke he was with some of the football players, as they were standing outside of Deke's apartment. I knew those players were in to drugs and I was furious because I saw my brother Deke, being led into a black hole. Deke was my friend; he had come to me when I needed

158

The Key to Stopping the Violence

him years ago in high school, now it was time for me to help him. He looked at me and turned back toward his get-high friends. I knew some thing was wrong. So I continued coming down hard on Deke.

One night I received a phone call and heard that Deke and T.D. had been in a fight and Deke's head was busted. Deke had stopped a fight and the dudes fighting turned on him. I put my clothes on, then stopped to wonder how much longer the madness on the campus could last. I prayed for the brothers, but I got back in the bed. I had fought too many nonsense fights in my life.

T.D. was graduating on time and Deke and me had one year to go. I knew T.D. had made it over the hump and with a lot of hard work, a good attitude and perseverance I, too, would make it out of school. I decided to devote all of my time to studies, which meant leaving the Nation of Islam. I realized I had joined for the wrong reasons. But at the same time I had developed the right attitude.

A Mate for Life

In the summer of 1983, I saw Donna walking down the street with one of her roommates. Carrie had just initiated one of our routine breakups with me two weeks earlier. Donna was the same sister I had met in Dr. Ahmad class a year and a half ago. We had spoken occasionally from time to time, but I didn't know which E.J. she had seen, the football player, the dog, the womanizer, the fighter, Africa-bound man or a member of the Nation.

They were heading home, so I asked her if I could walk her and her roommate to their apartment. Donna lived off campus with two other girls. We began to talk and Donna said she had just gotten out of a relationship. I knew I wanted to marry her from the first time I saw her, and now was my chance. But I had to make sure that her roommates didn't mess things up because they knew of my past. So instead of going to see Donna, I just made general visits. I got her roommates to do things with me as friends, first, to get them on my side, and second, I knew Donna would be there anyway so we would invite her sometimes.

I started making regular visits. One day I was sitting in the chair reading a book. For some reason, they thought I had fallen asleep. They started talking about who I was really coming over to see. All three girls started pointing to the other person. Actually, that was what I wanted because it kept them off balance and guessing.

I later found out that Donna had some time in the afternoon alone when her roommates were at work or class. That's when I made my move. I started coming over every afternoon at that time, saying I just happened to be on the block. We would have fun just talking and I loved her personality. After about a week or so, I stopped coming by, knowing she would miss me knocking on her door everyday.

Donna started coming around my apartment looking for me. That's when I knew she liked me, too. Then she broke the news to me that her friends had warned her to stay away from me because I was supposed to be one of the wildest brothers on campus. Donna knew I had changed because she was in class with me, but her friends had known the old E.J. I assured her that although I was a "Dogg" at one time, things had indeed changed. We became close that summer and I asked her to marry me after two weeks of dating steady. She said no, but I eventually got my wish and we've been together ever since.

Deadly Love Triangle

I had a new painting partner named Monica who was a roommate of Doris, the girl I saw Deke holding hands with the previous semester. All Monica talked about was the problems between Deke, Doris and Wayne. Doris and Wayne had been a couple, but I didn't know that Doris had caught Wayne sleeping around with other women on campus. Wayne and Doris had a baby boy together so that was the one thing that forced them to deal with each other. Monica said many of their conversations ended in arguments and physical confrontations.

Doris's anger drove her to figure out a way to get Wayne back for fucking over her. Monica said that since Wayne was sleeping with other women, Doris decided that two could play that game. But Doris was not going to freak just anybody; she wanted somebody who was popular, good looking and not intimidated by Wayne. As we painted the dorms, Monica added that Doris also wanted someone Wayne considered his friend. That candidate became Deke, one of the most popular dudes at Western.

Wayne became aware that Doris and Deke were freaking each other. Doris had Wayne where she wanted him: begging

The Key to Stopping the Violence

her to stop and to try to work out their problems. Doris recognized the power she had and put Wayne on his knees, crawling to come back. Wayne 's offer of reconciliation turned to anger. Monica said," Wayne would curse out Doris for fucking around after Deke would leave their apartment." Doris would often come back with statements like, "Deke freaks like a real man, which is better than you ever could." Monica said Wayne sometimes would beat Doris up after Deke left. However, after all the fights and arguments, Wayne and Doris would end up in bed together.

Monica knew her roommate was playing with fire. Doris was sleeping with Wayne again and he told Monica and Doris what he was going to do to Deke if he ever had a chance. Monica said Wayne talked shit behind Deke's back but wouldn't say anything to Deke's face. Why? Deke being a marine would kick his ass.

Me and Monica talked about the Deke, Wayne and Doris triangle the entire month before summer school. Wayne had graduated and Deke would be back for summer school. Monica said Wayne often talked about hurting Deke or killing him, but Deke's attitude was as long as Wayne didn't say anything to him, fuck him.

I talked to T.D. about what Monica had told me. He confirmed that Wayne had been doing things to Deke's personal items. For instance, Deke drove his roommate's car to Doris's apartment and while there, someone scraped the side with a sharp object. However, all Deke knew was that Doris was a campus freak he could have fun with. As a matter of fact, T.D. said he named her "the black bitch" because of her dark complexion and nasty attitude that allowed her to be as cold as ice.

Deke still believed like I once did that if a girl was going to give up some ass, it was worth taking it. I was concerned about everything I heard but I knew Deke would attend summer school so we would have a chance to rap. But as school started. I started a new relationship with the girl of my dreams, Donna. So when I did see Deke, there wasn't time to discuss my concerns. Anyway, in the back of my mind I knew Wayne wasn't anywhere around the campus. Plus I had known Wayne for years. I couldn't see him being a fighter.

After summer school I drove home with Deke and a few other friends. Because there were other people in the car, it still wasn't a good time to talk. During that two-week break, Deke continued to see Doris while she was in Chicago. One day while Doris was sitting on Deke's front porch, a dark Volvo driven by Dr. Ahmad rolled up. Wayne , the passenger, started cursing at Doris and telling them both they were fucking up his life. Deke's Grandma heard all the profanity as Wayne and Dr. Ahmad drove away. Grandma had a good look at the two men threatening her grandson. She asked Deke to come in and explain the threats.

During those two weeks, for the first time Deke started treating Doris like his woman. He called T.D. and told him he had a surprise, which turned out to be a couple of hundred dollars he had borrowed. Deke took Doris to Great America with T.D. and his girl. He even took Doris to Vince's parents' church to get Vince's approval. Deke was falling in love with Doris. T.D. and Vince wanted to tell Deke that she was just a freak using him to get back at Wayne.

After the two week break, it was time to head back for the last year. Two more semesters and we were out. I called Deke to let him know that we would be the only two driving down in the J-mobile. It was a four and a half hour drive, so it gave us a perfect opportunity to talk. Deke started telling me about all the things Doris was doing for him sexually. I listened as he reasoned with me why he was in love with her. No one, he said, had ever freaked him enough to make his toes curl that much. He loved all the physical things she was doing. I asked Deke to understand that he could be in love with the sex but that love was more than a sexual attraction. As we talked our conversation took on many tones and moods, from fun to serious, to anger and even near tears. Like my other brother, Ray, I loved Deke and at that moment after knowing what was going on I wanted it to stop. I told Deke that it was time to give up the Deke Dog image.

"Ersk," he said, "I want to change but everybody wants to be around Deke Dog."

"People will always want you to be who they want, but we're in a new stage of our lives where we should go about the business of finishing school and moving on," I explained. "People are going to continue to challenge you because you're out there in front. I stopped everything that was negative," I continued explaining to him, "and pulled away from the drinking, partying, fighting, dogging women sexually and then talking about them." "All I want is for you to be Garry not Deke," I explained.

Deke got quiet for a moment because he knew I was right. Then he looked over at me as I drove through the farm land,

The Key to Stopping the Violence

away from the crime of inner city Chicago. Deke said he wanted to change. I reconfirmed that I still had his back because nobody was going to punk us. However, change was important if we were to grow. I asked him if he was going to do anything differently. He started joking to avoid my question. "I'm going to have my frat brothers build me a coffin to sleep in," he said, "because I'm not afraid to die. I'm not afraid of a coffin." He said when he died women would be crying, "The Dog is dead. The Deke Dog is dead."

"They're going to be kissing me all over with lipstick all over my face," he added. I told Deke not to play like that because God answers prayers. He smiled and gave me that look as if to say your right.

Deke told me about the first time Wayne found out he was the one sleeping with Doris. Wayne was let in by one of Doris's roommates and barged in the room. Deke threw the sheet over his head. Deke said Wayne walked in the bed room and pulled the sheet back and saw Deke's fraternity brand on his arm. Wayne asked Doris, "Is my boy freaking your ass?" Deke said he had protection in case Wayne tried something. Deke felt Wayne had no right to tell Doris who to fuck around with.

I still didn't understand why Doris was throwing Deke's name in Wayne 's face and still freaking Wayne at the same time. But Deke couldn't see that because the ass was so good. He told me he had nothing against Wayne and that they, along with T.D., were on the same intramural basketball team.

After our long drive back down to the farmlands of WIU. Deke decided to spend the night at my apartment. The next morning Deke and I met up with Donna to register for classes. They had met for the first time over the summer.

As the semester started Deke and I would meet in the student center. "One more semester and we're out of this camp." was Deke's favorite saying. I called him Malcolm X as he walked with a bright smile on his face. "I know I'm like Malcolm," he would say, "because I have the knowledge to save the world. But I'm going to die like Malcolm -- violent." Then Deke threw on some dark sunglasses and walked away laughing. He always left me with a big smile and thinking that he was the one who should be in front because Deke did have the gift.

I made a mental note to talk to Doris about all this information. About three weeks into the new semester, I ran into her in the student union. We had been pretty close over the years, and I had no problem with her. I asked, "What's up with Deke?

SILENT CRY

I've never seen him react to any female like this before. I'm seeing you and him holding hands and everything."

Doris responded, "Deke keeps wanting to get close, like he's falling in love, and because of the baby, Wayne 's parents are pressuring us to get married. "E.J., I don't want either one of them."

I was late for class, so I told Doris we would get back together later. Doris walked away, saying she wanted to talk to me also because I knew them both. " E.J., we need to sit down and I'll tell you the whole thing." Then we went different ways. That was Thursday and now the weekend had come and gone.

Too Young to Die

I could see myself finally getting out of school along with my roommate Nate, and Deke. Monday morning as I walked to class that I saw Deke quietly sitting on the cement bench in front of the student union. We had just had it out with each other during the past weekend. On that morning, I decided not to bother him or slap him on his bald head. I just spoke. I hesitated before hitting him, then decided to go on. I said" What's up Garry" as he said, "nothing what's up Ersk." Little did I know that this would be the last time he would speak to me. Later I found out Deke had in fact confided in the advice of several older males. One in particular a white professors said that Deke had come to him several times in fear that his life was being threaten by Wayne. The other was Deke's superior officer in the Marines who later said he was very confused about his personal life with a certain young lady.

On Tuesday, the morning of September 20, 1983, Deke woke up and said to his roommate, Biscuit, "Man, I need to see Doris today." Biscuit replied, "You know you can't go by there because Wayne is still in town."

Wayne had already graduated from Western in May , but because of the baby boy, he shared something with Doris. Deke had been with her for eight or nine months. Doris let Deke know that Wayne was coming that weekend and asked Deke not to visit until Tuesday night. So that morning he knew he couldn't go over to Doris's house until Wayne was gone. Deke even joked with Biscuit saying," I'd better to be careful with Wayne being down because he is crazy enough to try to kill me."

At 6 or 7 p.m. Thee Family brothers said Deke was in rare form. He talked about all the subjects you could imagine:

164

The Key to Stopping the Violence

war and the marines, peace, what it took to be a man, and the fact that he was not afraid to die. He called them all punks. They would never talk back because this was Deke, our leader and friend.

I was at the library and Dr. Mason, a professor who taught math, said she would come by later to talk, I didn't know what about. I was excited to talk to her because she was older, maybe 37, and seemed to take an interest in my career after college. We met in the front of the library. It was a nice night so we decided to walk and talk. Being a black woman, Dr. Mason was interested in seeing the brothers do their best. I met her through Carrie before we broke up.

I told her about my plans to go into commodities and trading, and how I wanted to go into business for myself. She thought these were admirable plans, but she felt I could do even more with my talent. She explained that I had the world at my feet and that there was so much to learn. I didn't doubt what she was saying. I talked about the need for me to go to graduate school like she did at the University of California at Berkeley.

By this time we had walked for an hour and the conversation was taking on a different twist. Dr. Mason started making statements about Donna, my new girlfriend, and how she felt since Carrie and I had split up I was too young to be with one person. She felt at 22 years of age I was still a baby and needed to experience more before I let someone stifle my ability. I'm from the Ida B. Wells projects in Chicago and I wasn't born yesterday. I knew where this conversation was going. I decided to play along.

She said I would do well to experience what it's like to be with older, more mature ladies. I said the young lady I was with was right for me and she would be getting her degree in computer science, and we would grow together. Dr. Mason became even more persistent. She said she knew if I tried what she was talking about I would go to Berkeley and get away from this nonsense about one girlfriend. But I kept to my guns with a pleasant tone.

While I talked to Dr. Mason, Deke was leading Thee Family brothers to the apartment complex where he and Biscuit lived. Once there, Deke had a couple of drinks and asked Biscuit what they were going to eat for dinner. Biscuit told Deke he had put some steaks on; he did most of the cooking. Deke was laughing and joking with all his homies and had another round of drinks then asked Biscuit, "Where is the bike?"

SILENT CRY

Biscuit said, "It's on the porch. What do you need it for?"

"I'm going to make a quick run. I'll be right back." Biscuit didn't think anything of it. He thought Deke was going to see one of the many friends he had.

Deke road the bike for a few miles to Doris' off campus house. When he knocked on the door, to his surprise, Wayne answered. Because of some earlier business, Wayne hadn't left Doris. He was supposed to head back to Chicago in the next half hour. Wayne opened the door and Deke spoke. Wayne spoke back. Deke had had enough of Doris's playing games. She was pitting two intelligent friends against each other.

Deke had fallen in love with Doris, a tall 5'7" sensuous woman. She had two powerful, athletic, bright young men in love with her at the same time. With Deke, she worked her freaky sex on his body. She would excite him with fishnet stockings, red lace panties and bras. He once told me of a time when she made him a steak dinner. While he ate, she danced for him in the fishnet stockings and then went under the table and put peanut butter on his penis and licked it off while he ate. That's why he used to call her the "Black Bitch": But now things had changed and Deke wanted to call her his woman.

When he came in, Doris and her roommate, Shelly, were in the living room. Kim, the third roommate was in the bed asleep. Deke looked at Wayne and said, "Hey man, we have been friends for a long time and this doesn't make any sense." Then he turned to Doris and said, "Doris, you're going to have to make a decision. Is it me or Wayne ?"

Wayne mumbled something and walked out of the room. Deke looked at Doris and said, "Well, what will it be?" Doris appeared dazed and confused and said she couldn't make a decision. Deke started talking loud and Wayne walked out of the kitchen. "You have to go because you're not wanted here," he told Deke. Deke said he had always been welcome and it wasn't Wayne 's house to put him out.

They decided to take it outside and settle it like men. Not being a fighter, Wayne didn't really want to go outside. He also knew that he couldn't handle Deke, who was knowledgeable in hand to hand combat training from the Marines. The girls tried to step between them but Deke grabbed Wayne by his collar and said, "I know and you know that I can fuck you up. But, I'm not."

166

The Key to Stopping the Violence

Deke realized neither Doris nor Wayne was worth it. Deke let Wayne go and started walking toward the bike. It seemed settled. He got on his bike and started to peddle away when Doris walked to the screen door and said something. Deke looked up and said, " What in the hell are you looking at?"

Doris said, "I'm looking at you, asshole." Deke stopped and got off the bike and went back to the door. At the same time Wayne was in the kitchen getting a butcher knife. He got past the girls and put it in the top drawer of a desk in the hallway by the front door. Wayne 's rage had finally given him the courage to act on his hatred for Deke. He had his chance to do what he'd wanted to do for an entire year. Doris told Deke not to come in. Then Wayne stepped in front of Doris and she moved back next to Shelly. Deke opened the screen door and he and Wayne stood face- to-face for the second time.

Shelly began to cry and asked the two not to fight. She and Doris pleaded with them, Kim was still in her room asleep. Wayne and Doris' 2 1/2-year-old son had been running around and playing. Deke stood with his back to the screen door. Wayne stood about a foot from him. The girls stood behind. The baby boy started to cry. Doris and Shelly looked down at the baby, and at that moment, Deke's attention was diverted. Wayne reached back in the top drawer, and without looking down, he felt for the knife. Still looking Deke in the eyes and continuing to talk, saying, "we're friends alright," Wayne lunged forward with an overhand thrust, bringing the 8" blade in one full swing over his head and downward into Deke's chest. The force of the blow pushed Deke backward off the porch, down the two stairs and onto the sidewalk. His head struck the sidewalk with a loud thud. Wayne 's momentum carried him onto the porch where he stopped and started screaming obscenities at Deke.

Kim woke to all the noise. Doris and Shelly still didn't know that Deke had been injured. Deke turned from his back to get up and bent over on one knee. He was able to push himself up on one knee with the knife still in his heart, but fell face first onto the knife, breaking off the steel portion into his chest. Then he rolled over onto his back. The girls ran out of the house frantically crying and screaming at the top of their lungs, while Wayne continued to holler at Deke like a maniac.

A neighbor, a white female, looked out of her window as the girls got close to Deke. Shelly cried out, "He's bleeding!" Doris ran in to get a blanket. At that moment a police car was driving through the residential neighborhood. Shelly flagged down the policeman, then ran back and held Deke's head in her arms, and continued crying, asking Deke if he was okay. Doris came back with the blanket and asked Deke if he wanted it on him. Deke looked at Doris and said, "Get the hell away from me."

The white police officer came on the scene after calling the paramedics. Deke was mumbling to himself and lapsing in and out of consciousness. The police officer got down on his knees and bent over Deke, begging him to hold on, and telling him everything would be okay. The police officer asked Deke how he was doing. Deke said, "I'm okay," then smiled and said once more, "I'm okay". No sooner than he had spoken those words, Deke took his last breath and died there on the sidewalk in Macomb, Illinois, a college town where black men supposedly escaped the widespread killing on the streets of Chicago. There, in the small town of Macomb was the first murder in quite some time. Less than 10 percent of the college kids were black. The killing never should have happened.

The police cuffed Wayne and took him into custody. He hadn't tried to escape. Then there was Deke, his lifeless body dressed in gym shoes, jeans, T-shirt and a red jacket. He was pronounced dead on arrival at the hospital.

Shortly after Deke was pronounced dead, rumors started to spread around the campus, particularly the black population. Because Deke was so popular and also a frat brother in the most popular fraternity, the news spread quickly. By this time, I had left the library. I remember not seeing Nate, my roommate, who was also one of the first friends I made at Lindblom High School, so I went to my room. The phone rang almost immediately after I got there. It was Carrie, my old girlfriend. She had not taken our breakup well and asked me if she could come over to talk. I broke down and picked her up, knowing that I wouldn't have a clue to explaining her presence if Donna were to come over unexpectedly. Carrie sat up doing homework in my room. I remember jumping in the bed, which in college -- at least for me -- was nothing more than a mattress on the floor with sheets and a bedspread. Just as I started to dose off, someone knocked on the door. I thought it was Donna, so I hollered out for Nate to get the door.

"I'm not here," I said as panic sat in. Then I hollered again, "I'll get it." I rushed to the door and to my surprise, there stood the two black girls who lived on the first floor below us. They had strange looks on their faces. I knew something was

The Key to Stopping the Violence

wrong because it was after 11 p.m. and they never knocked on our door, especially at that time of night. One of them said something that at the time seemed like a dream: "I think Deke is dead."

I felt my head get light and my knees weaken. I remember my mind racing, as I tried to think what I should do. I had just talked to Deke about staying out of trouble. What did they mean, my boy, Deke, is dead? I left them at the door and ran down the hall and beat on Nate's bedroom door. I knocked a hole in the door as I yelled for him to open it. We joked so much he thought I was kidding around. I screamed through the door, "Deke is dead."

Nate opened the door and we both got dressed, throwing on whatever we could find. We jumped in my red '74 Monte Carlo. The night air was cold and I was talking to myself. " This can't be true. This can't be true."

Since we lived right up the hill from the campus police station, we drove there first. I jumped out of the car and ran to the glass window at the front desk, and asked the officer if there had been an accident involving a student named Garry Kennedy. The officer said he could not give out any information, but if we went to the main Macomb police station we could get our questions answered. As we were rushing out of the door, the officer said that someone had been killed that night. I started to cry silently, as I drove frantically to the Macomb police department uptown.

When we got there, I walked in and saw dozens of black students. Some were hugging and others were crying. I'll never forget it. When I walked in, everyone stopped and looked up at me. I knew that they were looking because I was Deke's best friend. I shouted, "What in the fuck are you looking at!" Then I began to cry. I walked over to the counter and put my head down. I didn't know what to think or what to do. Then Jesse, the only African-American police officer on the force, walked over and began talking to me. He asked me to come to the back of the station where the officers' desks were. He explained to me that Deke had been murdered at 10:09 p.m. and was pronounced dead. He said the primary suspect was Wayne Foster and he had been placed in custody. He also explained to me that Doris, Shelly and Kim were being questioned.

SILENT CRY

The Call Home

"I know Deke was your homeboy, and we need to notify his next of kin," Jesse explained. I said that I knew his home number. I explained that Deke's family owned two houses on the same lot. We always referred to them as the front house and the back house. Deke lived in the front house with his Grandma and Grizzly, his dog. His mother, father and brothers lived in the back house. I always called the front house.

Grandma was Deke's heart and soul and he was hers, but she was getting up in age. Because of that, Jesse said it would be best if I spoke to her since I was close to the family. He nodded and assured me I was doing the right thing as I sat there fighting the tears and dialing the phone. After a few rings Grandma answered in her usual sweet voice. I apologized for calling so late.

"Grandma, it's me E.J."

She interrupted me. "What's wrong with my baby?"

I didn't answer her. My heart seemed to drop into my stomach. "Grandma, could I speak with Keith or Kevin (Deke's older brothers)?"

Then she said in a calm whisper, "I can take it. My heart can take it."

It was one of the most painful things I ever had to do in my life. I was trying to say the right things for God's sake! Deke was dead. I'm 22 years old, calling from a college campus to tell my best friend's family that he is dead. I asked Grandma once again to put Kevin or Keith on the phone.

She asked me again, "What's wrong with my baby?" I didn't know what to say. I was trying to keep it together. It's hard to imagine someone is dead when you haven't seen any evidence of it. All I knew was what the police were telling me. My mind was trying to make sense out of it.

Finally, Grandma asked me to wait a minute while she called to the back house. Sitting in the room with me were Jesse, a few white officers and my roommate, Nate. After what seemed like an eternity, Keith came to the phone. Keith knew me well enough to recognize my voice.

I said, "Keith, this is E.J. down at WIU with Deke. I have some bad news. All I know is that the police are saying Garry is dead."

The Key to Stopping the Violence

Keith asked me to repeat myself. "All I know is that the police are saying Garry is dead," I repeated as best I could.

Keith began speaking frantically on the phone, asking me if I was sure it wasn't a mistake. Then the phone dropped on his end and hit the floor. No one picked it up. Later I found out that Keith walked from 67th and Halsted to the lakefront with no shoes or shirt. Kevin, the older brother, came to the phone and I began to explain what happened. "K", as we called him, was 6'2" and 205 pounds of power and calmness. After speaking to "K" I handed the phone to Jesse, and Jesse, explained the details of the attack and death of his little brother. He confirmed that Deke was found by police murdered at 10:09 p.m. at 602 W. Jefferson St. Then Jesse gave the phone back to me. I told Kevin not to try to come down that night because it was so late. I said to wait until morning and I would call back with more information. I continued to try to do the right thing to make sure that Deke's family had someone to rely on until they could get to Macomb.

During the conversation, I could hear Deke's mother frantically asking questions in the background. I felt totally drained and still confused. Jesse looked at me very understandingly and confirmed that Wayne was in custody, and what a terrible tragedy this was because Deke had such a bright future. I walked back out to the main lobby with Nate and saw Artie, a graduate student and one of Deke's frat brothers. He was hysterical. Other students were trying to restrain him. He kept crying and shouting, "This can't be true!"

I felt like I was smothering. I told Nate that I had to get some air. An overweight white man walked in and told the officer at the front desk that he had completed his job and was on his way to Springfield. I walked out and made a left turn, walking about five or six feet, talking to myself and trying to make sense of the entire night. I saw a large van and leaned my head on it to say a silent prayer. Nate was still standing at the door. He was giving me enough room to be alone, and at the same time was making sure I was okay.

Eyes closed, I said to myself, "Deke, you can't be dead because you wouldn't leave me here like this." I opened my eyes and looked through the van's glass window. What I saw will be forever engraved in my mind. I saw a body laying on a hospital gurney. I walked around to the street side of the van, my eyes fixed on this image. I stared frantically. The body became familiar. It was Deke, with a blood-stained blanket partially

171

covering his face. His head was leaning toward his right side. His hands were visible because the blanket was folded to his waist. His hands were strapped to his side and he had on a red jacket, blue jeans and gym shoes.

This added to the nightmare that was getting worse as the night grew older. My first thought was to get him out because he looked so helpless. Then the sadness turned into rage, anger and grief. I began hollering Deke's name and trying to get in the van. There was a giant knot in the pit of my stomach. I didn't have any energy. I felt like I was moving in slow motion. There laid one of the best friends I've ever had in my life. I saw him, but there was nothing I could do. Nate rushed over. I don't think he ever looked in the van, but he knew. He grabbed me and put me in the car. The coroner heard the commotion, got in the van and drove away. I had never felt so physically helpless in my life. I bent over and laid my head on my knees. I was crying so hard that my insides felt as though they were coming up. Nate drove off as I cried, "Deke was in there!" We drove through the dark night. Three of my Thee Family Brothers were walking down a back street to the police station. I told Nate to stop and jumped out of the car, still in tears. I started hugging them, and confirmed the rumor. They had heard he was in the hospital, but I told them what I knew because I saw it with my own eyes.

We all began to cry as we went back to my house. When we got there the phone was ringing of the hook and students came by. I thought more about the way he was murdered than about the students. I became hostile toward the ladies who came over, particularly Carrie and Tory. I decided to find Deke's roommate, Biscuit. I drove to their apartment and Biscuit was sitting there with friends. I asked him what happened and he told me about Deke's love affair with Doris and how Wayne had come for the weekend. I knew I had to call Deke's family back the next day, so I wanted to get as much information as possible.

I told Biscuit that Deke's family would be coming and it might be good for us to clean up his room. Biscuit couldn't believe I said that and lashed out at me. We went in Deke's room, which was a typical, messy college student's room. Clothes and books were everywhere. Biscuit went into the closet and told me to come look. In the corner was a pair of red high heel shoes, red panties with lace and a pair of fishnet stockings. Doris had left the evidence, that in my mind, signified Deke's death. He died because of a woman. Not just any woman, but a freak.

The Key to Stopping the Violence

After talking to Biscuit and others in the apartment, I decided to make it home. Around 2 a.m. I called my dad and explained Deke's death. He told me not to get involved. As we ended our conversation I felt he couldn't relate. He always had a stay-away-from-trouble attitude, and all I was looking for was some support. Then I called T.D., who was at home in Chicago after having graduated in the spring and was selling encyclopedias door-to-door. I was thrown for a loop when upon hearing the news T.D. said call him back in the morning. Then I went to Tookie's apartment. He had recently married and his wife K.K., had a baby over the weekend. Tookie even seemed to be distant about what happened. I was hurt because all the people I confided in didn't have a reaction or answer.

I finally got an hour or so of sleep. The first thing in the morning, I felt like I had had a dream from hell. I had to continue to take things in my own hands. I jumped in my car about 7 a.m. and went to Doris's house, the site of the murder. On the way, I saw Monica, my painting partner and Doris's ex-roomate. I needed to talk to Doris to find out what had happened.

Outside of the house they had marked a chalk line around where Deke had died. There was blood on the stairs and I saw where Deke had hit the sidewalk. I knocked on the door and one of Doris's relatives answered. She said Doris wasn't there and closed the door. I thought Doris might be hiding at someone's house for fear of her life. I found her at a frat house. Because I knew them well they told me that Doris and her roommate, Shelly, were hiding out there, but they had stepped out for some McDonald's. When they returned Doris looked like a black zombie. Her hair was all over her head. She saw me as she was getting out of the car and looked like she was ready to run. As she walked slowly toward the house, I approached her and said I was only interested in letting Deke's family know exactly what happened. I told her that it wouldn't do me any good to harm her.

I got her to agree to go to my apartment. Shelly accompanied her. I called Deke's family and told them I had Doris on the phone and that she knew what happened. I gave her the phone. She didn't want to talk, but I insisted, then went to my room and listened on the other phone. Shelly listened on the phone in Nate's room.

As Doris explained what happened, she kept talking and crying about how she didn't think Wayne would kill Deke. Deke's mother tried to keep her composure. She spoke calmly, asking intelligent questions. Grandma, Keith and Kevin got on the phone at different times. Doris and Shelly explained the whole story, including Deke's last words. I kept asking myself why I hadn't figured out that this would happen, and found some way to prevent it.

I later suggested to Deke's brother Keith that they come to the school to move all of Deke's things. Then I called T.D. back at work. I told him that Deke's family would be coming down and that he should call them. After we got off the phone, T.D. sat there, numb. As the news sank in, he started to cry. T.D. explained to white his boss the circumstances of his friend's death. His boss told T.D. to forget about it because Deke wasn't a family member. He couldn't get Deke off his mind, so he called Deke's family and made arrangements to drive down to Western with them.

I didn't know what to do, so I decided to walk on campus. It was about 10:30 a.m. and word of Deke's death had reached the 1,000 or so black students and the majority of the white students. Most were in disbelief and many had misinformation about what happened. There were some sisters in the student union collecting money for Deke's funeral, so I went home to get Thee Family's picture out of my high school yearbook. That's when I heard people saying some of the cruelest things. Black students who had only heard of Deke or Wayne but didn't know them were saying that Deke got what he deserved. I realized then that Deke had been greatly misunderstood. He liked to shock people, but he was no killer. He was a college student. I couldn't deal with what I was seeing and hearing, so I went home.

I waited until Vince, T.D., Keith, Kevin, Dubb and Deke's cousin drove up. Finally I was around people who loved Deke as much as I did. Once the boys got there, we knew we had been through these battles before. Vince had lost both of his brothers. We hugged and greeted each other. I still felt awkward because I was the one there with Deke. To some extent, I will always feel responsible for not being on top of what was going on with him. I have played back that period in my mind over and over again, hundreds of times as the years have passed. Why wasn't I at that house to save Deke from his death? I wish I had been there to come between my two friends and stop what ultimately became another silent cry for help.

After T.D. and Deke's family arrived in the van, I told them what I had found out. I noticed that Kevin, Deke's older

The Key to Stopping the Violence

brother, seemed to have a quiet confidence. Perhaps he was just fighting off the obvious pressure that was on his shoulders. We decided to go to the house where Deke was murdered. We tried to picture what happened in our minds. We stood there staring as though it was a scene from a movie.

We left Doris's house and went to Biscuit and Deke's apartment. Deke's body had been taken to Springfield. We sat around at Deke's apartment and started to tell his brothers what a caring and fun person Deke was. We talked about Deke's life in a way he would have been proud. His brothers listened there in amazement at some of the things we said their brother did.

Deke's brothers and cousin stayed at my apartment for the night and then left for Chicago with Deke's belongings. I had missed school for two days, so I went to the football office to have a letter drafted for my professors. One white professor gave me the time I needed to go to the funeral. Another white professor wouldn't allow me to make up a test and eventually flunked me in his class. As I asked for a make up test he rolled his eyes in his head an walked away.

One of the things that continued to concern me was what students said about Deke's death. Even men and women who didn't know him well said he had it coming, that he was a wild person, out of control. Many of them, however, were younger students who had only heard about Deke's reputation. I knew we as black people had a lot to learn about respecting life. By this time, Donna had found out what happened. I pushed her away because I was hurt and confused. I constantly thought about Deke. His speech, his jokes, his walk, talk and body language. There wasn't a person I talked to who didn't mention something about Deke. Donna became concerned, and rightfully so.

Biscuit and I went home for the funeral. Back in Chicago, Vince organized a meeting of Thee Family on the rocks at Lake Michigan. More than 200 brothers showed up. As I explained what happened, I cried and called out to Ray. I told him I just lost one friend and I didn't want to lose him to violence, too. Ray promised me he wouldn't die. Deke and I had formed a powerful collection of black men.

The only thing that seemed to save my spirits at home was T.D., who was doing so bad at selling dictionaries that we could only laugh at his situation. The week before we were in Chicago for the funeral, he earned $8. His company would drop T.D. off on a street corner, preferably in a business district, and tell him they would pick him up at 5 p.m. on the next block. Because he was rejected so much, T.D. lost confidence, so he would find the nearest game room and play pinball machines all day.

The night of the wake., T.D. and me went to the funeral home on the South Side. As we entered we noticed the names on the board. One read "Garry Dean Kennedy." I couldn't believe it. T.D. had more of an upbeat, positive attitude. We entered the small room and I saw the body of our beloved brother for the first time since the night he was murdered. We stood there in amazement at how peaceful he looked. T.D. began reminiscing about how many good things Deke had done in his life. We talked about all of the women he had, including Doris, who had been responsible for his death. We laughed about the suit he had on; it was T.D's. He had let Deke wear it to a fraternity dinner. We joked about taking Deke out of the casket, driving all around town, and picking up women like the old days. That helped me laugh during one of the saddest times I'd ever faced.

We felt the coldness of his once-warm body that played football, basketball, studied, loved and cried. Deke was the cement that held people together. He was an emotional leader. I knew then that I had to live my life to make sure this never happened to me. I believe to this day that a lady can really get you killed if you're not aware of what's going on.

We felt his chest. We wanted to know what happens to your body after you die. We also wondered if Deke was over our heads, floating around, watching us. So we jokingly asked him if we could share some of the women he left behind.

People were coming in and out of the funeral home and we would simply move and let them view the body. Deke's family had already been in before us. Later Doris came in with three or four people. She saw me and T.D. and left in less than 30 seconds, pretending to cry hysterically.

We must have spent close to three hours in that funeral parlor, talking to Deke as though he was still living. Deke had done more for me than anybody I knew. For years people who didn't know we were friends would say, "You remind me of someone else I know."

I would say, "You know Deke?" and they'd say, "Yeah, that's who it is."

The funeral was scheduled for a Tuesday night. I talked Dad into letting me wear a blue tailor-made suit he had from the '60s that fit me perfectly. I picked up Biscuit and we went on to Unity Baptist Church, the Kennedy family's church at 5117 S. Indiana. I was totally overwhelmed by all the people outside the

The Key to Stopping the Violence

church. My mind went back to the conversation we had a month earlier in the car when Deke said all his ex-ladies at his funeral would be crying, "Deke is dead."

There were about 500 people seated in the church and another 300 who people couldn't get in. In the choir stands, Thee Family Brothers stood in rank with another 100 brothers behind us. Looking out into the church, many of the people had come from college and I hadn't seen a lot of them since high school. Teachers, former high school classmates, football teammates and other college friends. Deke was represented by the U.S. Marine Corps, his fraternity and Thee Family. Vince spoke on behalf of Thee Family. Public speaking never was my thing, but inside I had so much to say about my fallen brother. As people viewed Deke's body, I saw ladies and girls crying and hugging Deke. We were the next to last group to view the body before his family. Just like Deke predicted, there were hundreds of lipstick marks all over his face.

Deke's body was laid to rest the next morning. The U.S. Marines gave Garry Kennedy a hero's salute. Upon returning to WIU, I reminisced about the times I shared with Deke, and wrote this memoir of my friend and hero, Garry Dean Kennedy.

"To love a man is to pull the good from his soul. To love a man is to truly study his life, word and purpose."

I loved Deke with all my heart. I would often sit back and watch him with great admiration. He was proud, funny, shy, bold and forceful all rolled up into one. A wirery-legged yellow man, his vocabulary was outstanding. His charisma was unbelievable. At times, we would get angry with one another. But we would always make up. Through him, I learned how to express my emotions openly. When I saw him cry, I knew that it must have been all right. Deke will never reach the stage in development where his friends and family are now. He never had a chance to get married or have kids or buy a house. I would compare Deke's untapped ability to the likes of Malcolm X before his spiritual conversion. Malcolm X, a great man, a kind man, a man who, even in his last day was trying to find a new direction in an undirected world. Like Malcolm, Deke was killed in a process of finding that new direction. Malcolm died because of his love for his enemies as they disguised themselves as friends. He didn't have his bodyguards search the people entering the Audubon Ballroom the day of his last lecture. By not searching the crowd, it allowed the enemy to take advantage

177

SILENT CRY

of Malcolm's kindness. And because of this, Malcolm lies dead. Like Malcolm, Deke's love for his enemy (Wayne Foster) allowed his enemy to take advantage of his kindness. Wayne struck like the boys in the ballroom, rising up in a time when death or murder were the farthest things from Deke's mind. Like Malcolm, if Deke wanted to strike, he would have.

During Malcolm's day, many watched his life, but would admit to not understanding his motives. Today, I hate to admit, many of those watching Deke didn't understand him. They didn't understand the metamorphosis that was taking him from one phase of his life to the next. But there's one thing for sure, both Deke and Malcolm are dead. But their ideals and thoughts will live on in me because I understood Malcolm. And I sure as hell understood Deke. My love for them won't depreciate. As time goes on, my love for them gets greater and greater. For we shall always be part of each other until the end of time.

Graduation: Headed Back to Chicago

I had to make it through that last semester, without Deke, T.D. or Donna. After Graduation, my oldest brother, Eddie, strongly suggested that I not interview for a job. I didn't and he said he'd have a business set up for us. Eddie is an accountant by trade. He always wanted his two younger brothers to work with him. Back in the '70s, Eddie had worked as a comptroller for several hospitals in Chicago. He would always tell me about how vicious white people were in corporate America. Eddie had come up in the '60s and was part of the first generation of blacks to benefit from the March on Washington and the Civil rights movement. He always said he would never work for a white man again.

After leaving corporate America, Eddie opened a carpet store with some buddies, who began stealing from him so he decided to strike out on his own. He opened another carpet store and his business flourished. He invited a friend to join him. but soon thereafter more than $100,000 worth of carpet disappeared from a major hotel site they were working on. Then Eddie's wife asked him to leave and he was forced to file bankruptcy.

I never saw Eddie until close to graduation because he was always working. Then he would call me everyday to help get his car started because he was stranded somewhere in Chicago. His car was so old and rusty that everyday a part would fall off into the street while he was driving. Through all of this Eddie

178

always kept his spirits up. He was so poor he couldn't buy the hole in a doughnut. I knew he needed me and I needed him because I was intimidated with entering the real world. Eric had missed his opportunity because God had told him and Momma not to trust us. When Eddie needed family, we had let him down.

Graduation was on a Saturday and Ed had me out with him the following Monday. He said that with his knowledge and experience and my youth, we would be able to turn some of the small black businesses around. He took me all around Chicago and introduced me to all kinds of black businessmen. Eddie said that most of them didn't know how to expand, many didn't keep good records and a number of them didn't know how to market themselves.

During that time T.D. had stopped selling dictionaries. I was still in my last semester when T.D. came down to celebrate his new $18,500 a year job. We thought that was the most money a person could want to make. We celebrated and drank like fools for an entire weekend. We drank and then started crying about Deke and how he had died.

PART IV

CORPORATE AMERICA: A DUAL BURDEN

Welcome to Business

CBC foods Inc. on the South side of Chicago was on a block that was once a thriving business center. Eddie began carpeting the floor, which took two or three days. By the end of the week he was trying to figure out things to do for Chuck, the owner. Chuck had been in business for 14 years and was one of the few black food suppliers in Chicago. He was best known for suppling x-rated cakes. I had no training; Eddie had all the business sense and ideas. He decided to propose to Chuck that we work with him to expand his business all over the city. My father hated the fact that I had graduated from college and didn't have what he considered a real job. He was retired and was treating me like a 10-year-old instead of an adult.

CBC Foods was full of lively characters, but it wasn't earning up to its potential Even Chuck had no idea what he could make. We started by having me go around to all the major churches on the South Side to promote our products. We figured that most black folks ordered their services and food from the white companies in the white neighborhoods, so if we came up with a competitive price we could compete.

Eddie always talked about how we would be wealthy in a few years. He had already picked out the cars he would drive and the suits he would wear. All I knew was, at the time, I was making $50 a week and Dad and Donna were growing angrier at me by the minute. Eddie kept saying he and Chuck were "working on things." My car was falling apart, and as a matter of fact, one day I came home, and Dad had taken the phone. I think Dad was ready to throw me out of his house.

But, as we kept working, we made major strides. We did work for Operation PUSH and Jesse Jackson, whom I had a chance to meet, in his run in the presidential primary. We worked for celebrities like Doug Banks of WGCI radio, musician Ramsey Lewis and various professional basketball players. I had a chance to meet people all over Chicago. We did a number of banquets for Harold Washington, Chicago's first black mayor, Ed Gardner Chairman of Soft Sheen Products, and Jocelyn Robichaux who then owned the Baldwin Ice Cream Company. We even did work for Flukie Stokes, the drug king of Chicago. I delivered cakes for the El Rukns at their mosque on 39th Street. We began organizing ourselves to work with other businesses like florists, limousine companies, tuxedo shops and wedding gown makers. We became a one-stop service. I handled all the sales and Eddie did the books. We had a complete program with fast delivery and prompt service. It was all one happy family.

However, there was one problem: It wasn't growing fast enough to support all of us. CBC foods inc. wasn't a big corporation with a training program. But when Eddie and Chuck threw me out on the South Side, I learned how to deal with people. I did everything from making business cards and brochures to selling our food services to companies like Illinois Bell, the State of Illinois building on Randolph Street and to

The Key to Stopping the Violence

brides and grooms. I knew I needed things like medical and dental insurance. In our second year with CBC Foods Inc., Eddie landed an account with one of the city's black-owned construction companies, and the owner was one of Chicago's black millionaires. As Eddie's confidence grew, so did mine. In 1985 I decided to marry Donna, my college sweetheart. I wasn't making a lot of money, but I had learned how to deal with people. Anyway, Eddie would always tell me it didn't matter how much money I made, it mattered how much effort I put into it. He said the money would come. Despite Eddie's views, I promised Donna that I would start looking for other opportunities.

I would visit Ray at the fast food joint on 119th Street. He would tell me how he could steal $50 a day, plus they were paying him $250 a week. But by the end of the week, he and Gertie would be fighting because he had spent all of the money. I would always stop by Ray's apartment to talk about opening our own foodstand, but it was all talk.

Visiting From a Distance

The first time Donna laid eyes on my mother, I hadn't seen or spoke with her in years. She had denied me so long I had no feeling toward her. But I thought it was important to try to explain to Donna what had happened in my family life. I knew Momma would sit outside on the porch during the day. So, I drove by the alley where she lived and about 30 yards away I stopped the car, and told Donna that was my mother. Donna couldn't understand why a person we could practically touch, would deny her son who graduated from college and why she wouldn't speak or appreciate me. Donna didn't meet my mother face to face until awhile after we were married. Eric left the church as he and Mom went different religous ways. Eric, Eddie and I started hanging out together for the first time in our lives. Eric was also in my wedding.

The Pain Continues

They say the toughest thing to lose in your life is your kid. I know it's true because I watched Mr. Kennedy go downhill after Deke's murder. I watched him at the funeral as tears flowed down his face. Mr. Kennedy was a proud man. So was his son.

SILENT CRY

They were two stubborn people who were too much alike to get along. I loved what they had -- a love and respect for each other, even if it was tough to show. I knew Deke would never get in pop's face. Their conversations were abrupt, with one walking away with their feelings hurt.

In summer 1984, during the trials for Deke's murder, we all headed down to Macomb. Grandma, Mr. and Mrs. Kennedy, T.D., Vince, "K" and myself, all packed into the Kennedy family Cadillac. I drove all four and a half hours while we listened to Mr. Kennedy talk about the shamefulness of his son being killed. His emotions hit a fever pitch when Wayne was brought into the court room. I was sitting next to Mr. Kennedy and that was the first time I had seen Wayne since the murder.

Wayne strolled out in a dark suit. As he entered through the back of the court, he had a cockiness in his walk. His face didn't show any remorse; he seemed to have a smirk on his face. I turned my attention straight to Mr. Kennedy because I wanted to see if he was seeing what I was seeing. Before I could ask him anything, Mr. Kennedy started to mumble under his breath. Tears began streaming down Mr. Kennedy's face as he sat there, looking Wayne in the face. This was the first time any of Deke's family had seen the man who took their son's last breath.

I put my hand on Mr. Kennedy's arm as he rocked back and forth. Then Mr. Kennedy shouted, "He killed my son! He killed my son! How in the hell can he walk in here like that." The judge asked for quiet as Mr. Kennedy tried to get up. We held him down. Then I looked behind us toward Mrs. Kennedy. Her eyes had a look of disbelief. She was in the same room with the man who murdered her son.

After returning to Chicago, Mr. Kennedy still couldn't deal with the fact that his youngest had died. He started to drink heavily. He lost his vigor for life, so much so that his health started to deteriorate. One night while in the alley behind the house, a car backed up over Mr. Kennedy's foot. Because of his depressed state of mind, he refused to go to the hospital. His family couldn't get him to seek help. His foot was swollen and the pain became unbearable. By that time, gangrene had set in and the poison flowed through his body, causing him to suffer greatly. Mr. Kennedy died in the hospital never returning to his family.

Grandma had now lost her grandson, Deke; her husband, Grandpa; and her son, Mr. Kennedy, all within two years. I watched a family fall apart because of Deke's senseless murder.

The Key to Stopping the Violence

Mr. Kennedy was buried next to his son Garry Deke Kennedy. The death of Deke was killing an entire family.

Another Blow

Three weeks before Donna and I were married, Lamar married his college sweetheart, Loretta. After Ray beat up Gertie in the summer of 1985, I let him know that I couldn't ask him to be in my wedding. I was trying my best to be the disciplinarian he needed along with his brother Ivory's direction. Ray still blamed most of his behavior on his mother's death. I would always tell Ray we still had fathers who were trying to help as much as possible because they were from the old school. Mr. Grandberry wasn't going to show much compassion but he was going to straighten Ray out and talk to him when necessary. Mr. Grandberry was getting up in age. At my wedding he had a good time dancing and singing. He talked about wanting to see me and Ray together even more because I was a good influence on him. The wedding was at the same church Deke's funeral was held. Mrs. Kennedy was my mother that day as she sat in the front of the church.

During the wedding reception Mr. Grandberry stopped three or four times to let me know how happy he was and what a good time he was having. The strange thing was that I only briefly spoke to Ray that day. Gertie was in the wedding and Ray Raheem Jr., their 2-year-old son, was there. All of my friends from the low end, high school, college and work were there, too.

I promised Mr. Grandberry I would spend more time with Ray. After returning from my honeymoon Ivory called and said Mr. Grandberry was dead.

Here's what happened: Ivory explained that Mr. Grandberry would always go from Chicago to Indiana to play bingo. One Friday night he and a friend were traveling by car and Mr. Grandberry was on the passenger side. A semi-truck sideswiped the car on the passenger side, killing Mr. Grandberry and badly injuring his friend.

At the funeral I could see that Ray's eyes were glassy, and reflected death and misfortune. He felt that his family had fallen apart. Ray was never the same and didn't feel there was much left after his mother and father died. Ivory, Vail, Gertie and I tried to put the remaining family back together.

SILENT CRY

Endangered species

Because of my wishes, Gertie would always call me to say that Ray was in trouble and she needed me to come down to get him. So I would go from home just to find Ray drunk and ready to fight. This time, he was on his back porch. I asked him what happened. Ray said Psycho and his family had fucked him up. Ray wanted revenge and I sat there and tried to talk him out of doing anything stupid. Before I found Ray on the porch, I ran into a member of Psycho's family. They told me I better get control of Ray because he was not respecting anybody in the 'hood. He told me that Ray was walking around with a death warrant on him, and his enemies were standing in line.

I talked to Ray about these things as we sat on his second floor porch. Even though he was drunk, I saw the sadness in his eyes. I asked him why was he trying to kill himself. Ray said with a straight face that he wasn't afraid to die. I talked to him about all the things he had to live for. He reminded me that his mother was dead and he wanted to be with her. He told me that when he saw his mother coming from the grocery store with all her bags, he would drive right by her with his boys in his car and not pick her up. He said that he never told her that he loved her. I told him that his life was what she would have wanted and that living would give his son a chance to know him. Trying to shake him up, I asked him what suit did he want me to bury him in.

I took him to my house to get him out of the projects. The next day, Ray thanked me for saving his life because he said he would have killed someone that night or someone would have killed him. I took Ray out to a friends house in Joliet, a quiet city with ranch style houses. Ray and I talked about how nice it was there and how a change of scenery would probably be best for him.

Surviving the Odds

The next time Gertie called me she was hysterical. Ray had shot into Frankie's house. Again I drove down to the projects. When I got there, no one was around and I started looking for Ray. I went to Frankie's house and the windows of his bedroom had been shot out. Debbie, Frankie's younger sister, came to the door and told me how Ray and Frankie had a fight that started because Ray and Frankie had been drinking with

184

The Key to Stopping the Violence

some friends. When Frankie's mom asked Ray not to use strong language around her. Ray started going off on Frankie's mother. Frankie jumped in and whipped Ray's ass. Ray left and came back and fired a flurry of gun shots into Frankie's first floor windows. Debbie was in the bed with her baby son while the bullets sailed over their heads.

Frankie and Ray go back to when they were 6 years old. Martha, Frankie's mother, was like a mother to Ray. I found Ray that night and talked to him. He told me he had a little shortie shoot into the apartment for $20. The "little boy" was 13 years old. I couldn't believe the irresponsibility and stupidity of what Ray had done. But Frankie later told me it was Ray who did the shooting because he saw him. Eventually, Frankie and Ray became friends again and Ray was back over at Frankie's house drinking and hanging out like old times. That's the nature of the ghetto. Sometimes, shooting at your boy is not the worst thing that can happen.

The next time Gertie called was to tell me Ray had been jumped on by Psycho's family again. I remember being dressed in a suit and tie sitting on the coach, playing with my baby Deanna and jumping in my car, telling Donna that this would be the last time. She always feared that something would happen to me. But I felt as though nothing could happen. After all, those were the homeboys I grew up with.

Once I got there, I parked at 37th and Vincennes in front of Ray's building and walked two blocks toward Cottage Grove. At first I didn't see anyone. Once I got down there, there seemed to be hundreds of people crowded around Psycho's house. I worked my way through the crowd. I saw Lamar and Frankie and they gave me the scoop on what had happened. Lamar said Ray and Ivory were in the house with the police and that Ray and Psycho's family had had a fight. Ray had been on a fighting binge, kicking ass and taking names. I didn't know who Ray had fought and I surely didn't know that Psycho's family had been attacked. Psycho, who was high on cocaine, started to mumble that somebody was going to get their ass shot. Then he said, "Yeah, Ray's boy Ersk is down here. What the fuck you gonna do? 'Cause motherfucka, you're in the wrong place today."

I started thinking he can't be serious. I haven't fought down here since I was a kid. I looked around as people started backing away from me. Suddenly, about 15 feet away Psycho pulled his shirt back and I saw the handle to his .38 caliber pistol. I looked at his half-closed, drugged-out eyes as he put his hand on the handle and started pacing past me, getting more and more intense. He began talking louder and louder. He was saying things like how my ass was not going to make it out alive. I looked at Lamar and Frankie and thought, "I'm just a brother trying to make a living."

Ray and Ivory were still inside. I knew I had to get out of there or I was a dead man. I had no way of protecting myself, no gun, no iron pole, no bat, not even a rock. My next move would spell the difference between life and death. If I made the wrong move, Donna's worst nightmares would come true. I stepped back slowly and confidently and said as loud as I could in Psycho's direction, "Shoot me motherfucker! Shoot me motherfucker!" The crowd looked alarmed and continued to back away from me, forming a straight path line me and Psycho. "If you don't shoot me now," I yelled before turning to run, "If you don't shoot me now, you'll never see my ass again."

I ran through the crowd and jumped over a four-foot fence like an Olympic hurdler. Once over the fence I zigzagged as I ran just in case bullets were coming. I ran through the playground on 37th and Cottage Grove, complete with suit and tie, looking like O.J. Simpson in his car rental commercial, running through the airport, all the way back to my car. I jumped in the car and drove as fast as I could back out of the low end. I realized that my days of trying to save Ray were coming to an end. Ray had to want to save Ray.

But I was back down again and I saw Psycho two months later. He asked me to take him to the Alco Drug store to buy him a sandwich. When I refused, he looked at me as though I had done him wrong. That encounter epitomized the inconsistent rule on the low end. A brother could shoot at a man one day and play basketball with him the next day as though nothing happened.

Corporate America 101

T.D. always talked about the corporate structure and training. He had gotten married a year before me to his high school sweetheart and moved into a house in the south suburbs. Things were going well for T.D. and I was happy for him. After I had gotten married I knew I needed to go out to make ends meet. When I got married to Donna I was still making $50 a week. I was so broke and poor. She turned me down what seemed to be a hundred times. I had to get down on one knee and propose to her in front of a crowed grocery store in order for

The Key to Stopping the Violence

her to say yes. I had been out of college for two years and decided to go into the corporate job market for the first time. T.D. was a help because he got me an interview with his company to work in the telemarketing department. My car barely made it out to the North suburbs.

T.D. introduced me to a white woman who was the No. 1 sales representative, she made more than six figures a year. She told me to keep trying and I would do well. I told her I wanted to be No. 1 in a company like her. She assured me that if I worked hard enough and didn't give up I would get there.

I decided to start contacting all of the job search companies in the Yellow Pages, as well as looking in the Chicago *Tribune* and Chicago *Sun-Times* to try to get some job interviews. Just meeting the placement people became a job within itself. I never knew how disappointed I could get by people telling me I couldn't make it or I didn't have the experience. A headhunter finally got me an interview with a major consumer company, but you had to take a number of evaluation tests. I was sure that the tests were difficult but at the same time the recruiter said the company had a poor representation of minorities. This man was a special minority recruiter. He worked very hard to get good candidates in front of this company's management. I didn't pass the initial evaluation exam. He was livid because he told me none of the last 10, top-notch minorities he sent in made the initial grade. He assured me that I had talent and for me to keep the search up.

Donna had gotten a job and even though she made 100 times the amount of money I made and paid the bills, she never made negative references toward me. We added what little I made to what she made and developed a family budget. But there were still other things going wrong -- like my car,. It was the car I had in college and it was falling apart. Donna's car was starting to overheat all the time and stall on the expressway during her commute to and from work. During those times I had to control my frustrations. Eddie was making money and he and Dad took me to a clothing store and purchased a suit, tie and coat for me. That was the suit I eventually wore on every interview.

Job Search

Although disappointed I started to make the best of the job search by making a game of calling as many people as possible. I finally had two agencies call me in for an interview. The first company was a major job search firm in downtown Chicago. I went in and a young white guy met with me and immediately started telling me to be patient and to look in other areas besides sales. Based on our conversation he recommended that I go into pharmaceutical sales because I wouldn't make it in capital equipment sales. Then he gave me the old "Don't call me, I'll call you" line. I was disappointed because I knew he was blowing me off. I let it ruin my day.

I had a second appointment at 12 noon at another agency. I'd taken the train from 35th Street and when I got back to my car I decided I would just go home. As I headed back to the expressway, I thought, "No, I'm not going to cancel this next appointment. I'll go any way. What do I have to lose?"

I drove out west to Oak Park, and met with a young white lady. She was very polite and listened to my interests.

"I know something that sounds perfect for you," she said, flipping through her Roladex as I looked on. She flipped to a company called OBT Co. and said that this was a very aggressive position that sold office products and earned a high commission. I was familiar with office products from being around T.D. She told me it was a dynamic young company and that she would set up an interview for me with Paul Coleman, the district manager. She said I would like it because it was group of young go-getters.

I left the agency with a burst of energy. It dawned on me that this interview was possible because I made the effort to go to this second agency. I couldn't wait to get home to tell Donna. The young white lady had also told me the first-year reps made $50,000 a year. My heart almost hit the floor. The next phase was to get ready for the interview, which T.D. prepared me for.

In the company's office, I admired the plaques on the wall. When I saw those awards I knew I wanted to work there. Paul, who was only 27 or so, came out to meet me. I was 24 going on 25 at the time. I noticed that he wore a gold ring that read "OBT Co."

The first interview with Paul went very well. He asked me all kinds of questions then started talking about how much commission his salesmen were making. By this point I heard some of the salesmen coming in as Paul opened the door slightly and looked out. Then he told me to look at the black guy. Paul closed the door and pulled out some of the black guys monthly commission reports. One was $8,000; another $6,000. After he showed me those stubs I knew there was nothing that could keep me from that job.

The Key to Stopping the Violence

After the interview, I walked out and met Ron O'Toole, a white guy, and James Johnson, a black guy, and the other reps as they came in and displayed the enthusiasm of a locker room. These guys where literally bouncing off the walls. Paul had asked me if I would go out in the field with a sales rep so that I could see what the job was all about. I rode in the field at 7 a.m. and we made cold calls. We made more than 20 cold calls and brought the office products out of the van on carts about four times. John, another white guy, said he was he was right on track to make more than $40,000, which was alright with me because he was 23 years old.

Work-The Secret Ingredient

After a day in the field, the sales rep would let the manager know if the person is right for the job. I knew I asked him plenty of questions about how he did his job and how to be successful at it. John highly recommended me for the job so the next interview was very intense. Paul also made me sell him an ink pen by showing him its benefits. After the heart of the interview Paul asked me if I would have a problem getting a van. I was so fired up at that point I would have tried to buy a fire truck. I got the job and needed a van to carry all my equipment. I called my dad and we went shopping for a $15,000 minivan. Dad loaned me $3,000 for a down payment and I purchased a 1986 Ford Aerostar. The job was straight commission with a $1,000 monthly draw, which meant that you received a $500 advance every other week. However, at the end of the month you had to at least meet your quota or you would owe the company the difference. My philosophy was that if I was only concerned about just hitting my quota, I shouldn't be there anyway.

All of the salesmen started the day at 7 a.m. By 7:30, guys were full of coffee and buzzing off the wall. By 8 a.m. we were in Paul's office discussing how many office product sales we were going to make that day. Ron O'Toole had just become the new sales manager of the office. He had won a trip that qualified him to be one of the elite in the company. I was his guinea pig.

They put me through a training course called Fast Go, which was two weeks of intense training on how to sell with cold calls. We had to make 15 cold calls a day and show the office products to prospects. My first month was May 1986. I set in my mind that I wanted to win the Dirty Dozen Award and reach the President Club. I also wanted the company ring.

Ron worked with me the first day. He followed up on a lead from the West suburbs. I didn't know enough about the business to know what he did. But I knew he walked out the door with a sale. We came out with Ron jumping up and down giving me high fives and saying what a great job I had done. In the van Ron showed me where I had just made $600 in commission. When we got back to the office, he came in screaming to the veteran sales reps how I had closed this sale. After a sell, we'd come in and ring the bell, then add your sale and dollar amount to the board.

We had some good salesmen in our office. James Johnson drove this huge van. He was a heavy set guy with a large head and bulging eyes. He was not very good looking in a traditional way but what I first realized when he opened his mouth was that he talked like a white guy. Actually, he sounded like a black guy imitating a white guy, so upon meeting him, I didn't know if it was his real voice or him trying to poke fun. I went along with it. But James was the man and his destiny that year was to win the trip that he had just missed the year before.

We also had Mark, a white guy who smoked all the time. I learned very fast that he wasn't very good at the job. All his day consisted of was sitting around the office trying to figure out a way not to work. I worked my routine up to 30 to 40 cold calls a day. Instead of two presentations with our equipment I was making three or four. The first full month I sold eight office products and I made $4,000. I couldn't believe it. I also won my first "8 So Great" award.

The winners in the office had the nice plaques on the wall. These salesmen stood out like studs. The other veterans dismissed my successful first month as beginner's luck. June, they said, was one of the largest buying seasons of the year because most businesses would be closing their end of the year books. OBT co. had a "blitz" in June, bringing in managers from all over the Midwest. These managers were hard closers, guys who knew how to sell anything, anytime, anywhere. So the south Chicago office had to be ready with quality appointments and top-flight agendas so the managers would enjoy their stay. It was also a way to make a name for yourself. We wanted them to be aware of who we were so when it was time to get promoted, they would remember.

The Key to Stopping the Violence

To prepare, we spent two days straight on the phone setting appointments. Ron had us sit with mirrors in front of us to smile into while we were on the phone. We used the old customer files to find out who had old OBT Co. equipment.

Closing the Deals

As the blitz came around, managers started coming over. They identified themselves and stated where they were from. Each of them carried a badge of honor from their offices. Some were known for being funny and others were known for shooting from the hip. Their reputations were bigger than life.

The first day I worked with Bob from Indiana. He was known for his humorous style of selling. And oh, what a style it was! Our first call was to a bowling alley where he sold a office product that netted me $500 in commission. He was joking about how the owner had been waiting his whole life for us to come in to sell him that office product. It almost looked that easy. Then we made one of the funniest sales I'd ever seen. It was at a dentist office. We had picked up an old office product that was outdated from the bowling alley as a trade in. This was one of the first office products OBT Co. made. It was so obsolete that many of them didn't work or weren't used much. While Bob was trying to sell the dentist a office product, the dentist said he didn't want to spend much money and that he only used the product rarely.

Finally Bob asked how much money did he want to spend and the dentist responded that he didn't want to spend a penny over $500. Bob told him that he had just what he wanted in the van. We walked outside, opened the van door and took out this old broken office product that we picked up as a trade in. Bob asked me to take it out of the van under a tree across from the doctor's office. He said "Doctor, this is what you want. It can be used the way you want, and it costs $500. We'll have it refurbished but I need a check today." They stood under the tree and made the deal. Bob told the doctor that if he got it that day, he'd also throw in a spare part. Bob talked with the confidence of a true closer.

The more the managers could sell with you the better they looked that night at the manager's dinner meeting. Ron was always talking about the OBT. corporate power structure and how everyone was trying to make it up the ladder. James Johnson always gave me information on who was who and why it was so important to do well.

SILENT CRY

The June blitz also included wonderful prizes as well as money each rep would put up for a contest at the end of the day. Five bucks a rep or two bucks a rep. I came out of the blitz doing pretty well. Three sales in three days along with a whole new arsenal of closes to use in combat. There were three weeks left in the month and things seemed to slow down. I had gone for days without a sale and in office products, days seemed like months. I began getting depressed so I headed home. Once there, the negative bug told me to take a nap, so I turned on the Oprah Winfrey show. I put my head down, but before I fell asleep.

I decided to call this small company that I had tried to contact several times before but the owner was never in. I spoke to the secretary and surprisingly, she put me through to the owner. He said that he had planned to call me but he hadn't gotten around to it yet. He said, he did want the office product but he wanted to trade in his old one. I jumped out of the bed and I delivered the office product and ended the day with two sales. That started me on a roll that ended with 15 sales in 20 days and a commission check of $8,900. I also won the Dirty Dozen green beret. I had made almost $13,000 in my first two months. I had truly started living the high life. Donna and I went out and purchased things we needed with cash: a washer and dryer, clothes, etc. I couldn't believe that anyone would leave a job like this.

The next month, although only my third in the business, Paul had already told James and Ron he needed me to be one of the senior reps because of how well I was doing. The other reps told me I hit an unconscious competence stage, which meant I had done something, but I didn't know how I did it.

In July the talk was after a busy June, business dropped off in July. I went through a personal emotional let down. The board was clean and I had to start all over. Paul and Ron were asking me, "What are you going to sell today and this month?" There were guys who couldn't handle that kind of emotional and psychological pressure. I started desperately asking Ron and James what I did right the last few months because it certainly wasn't working now. James said he couldn't explain what made him successful; he just knew how to get the business. But I needed him to tell me how to get the business and he didn't know how. That month I was sucking wind with other reps in the office.

On the last day of the month in July, I walked into a real estate office. I had called on this office in June and the first thing

The Key to Stopping the Violence

I said to the owner when I went back was that I didn't want to talk about office products. I just stopped by to say hello. During the conversation, she asked me about the office product I had showed her the month before. She wanted to know what a trade in would get her. I closed the deal that day, and at month's end I cleared $2,000.

Race: Always Part of the Game

Before July, race had never entered any of my conversations with Paul. But one day he pulled me in his office and asked me if was having any racial encounters. I said, "Paul, if race is involved I wouldn't know because the white guys in the office are also getting rejection every day. It would be different if they were selling to everyone they came in contact with. But since they aren't, who really knows why someone rejects your business."

Paul called James into the office and he explained to me that a particular customer didn't want a black salesperson calling on him. He asked if I would have a problem with that. I said no. Paul said he would send a white salesman in to make the sales call. Within the office, I was earning a reputation of hard work and excellence. I had made up my mind that I wanted to win the trip. On the other end of the business, I quickly realized this was not a business for someone who could not work month to month making cold calls and take rejection. I was spending a lot of time, from 7 a.m. to sometimes as late as 9 p.m., around the office. Every month, there was some poor salesman who was on the brink of being fired. If a person didn't hit the minimum monthly quota, managers would look at them sideways. If this occurred in two consecutive months, the company would hold the draw check.

After that, it's out the door, stuck with a van payment. There was no expense account or a gas account. It was you against the world. I had become O'Toole's second horse behind James . To keep me fired up, he gave me a book called "The Art of Selling" by Tom Hopkins. The book put into perspective the questions I had bombarded Ron, Paul and James with. It gave excellent examples of closes to use. As time pass, I did become sensitive to my territory because the better you became, the less a manager works with you.

Before this job, I was like the majority of my black friends in the black community. My territory was 80 percent

SILENT CRY

white and 20 percent black. I was dealing with people who had never had exposure to blacks and if they did, it was very minimal. I tried not to make it an issue because I wanted to maintain my composure and keep a positive attitude. In the office was a different scene because it was apparent that some of the white guys had certain prejudices that would come out in different ways. For instance, when they told jokes, if the joke was inappropriate, because Blacks were the butt of the joke, the attitude was, "Oh don't take it personal." Or It's just a joke." I tried to get along as well as possible. But I was always consciously or subconsciously aware of what was going on. James Johnson was my eyes and ears for the first six months. He let me know right off that there were very few blacks in management positions. If I had a problem with my sales calls. I was would try to relate to owners by talking about sports. Ron O'Toole always used his Irish heritage. It was natural for him to relate because he usually had a lot in common with his prospects. I later found out we were in a heavily Irish community -- Oak Lawn and Evergreen. These areas had a very low black population.

From time to time, my contacts at certain white accounts had what they called "fun." One business owner said he didn't mind buying products from me as long as he didn't have to live next to me. I learned that there were some things I would have to swallow as a minority in a large company if I wanted to stay in the Corporate environment.

November rolled around and a lot of people who started with me were no longer employed. But there were some young superstars on the horizon. Bill Mann who was the perfect salesman. His dad was a salesman and he had the gift to make the business work. Mark Carl and Bill Mann, Ron O'Toole and James Johnson became the epitome of OBT Co. Paul became the symbol of what could be achieved at a young age. He was single, 27 years old and making an estimated $100,000 plus.

I started using some of the examples the young lady who worked with T.D. said I should use. Always judge yourself by the best, not the worst. And only look at the Top 10 percent on the President Club List. I had learned how to fight through the slumps. November was the month I hit another case of conscious competence. It happened with a real estate office I had been trying to sell since July. I had followed up, stayed on top of it, sat down and discussed many subjects with this real estate owner by the name of Peter O'Flaherty, who only bought from someone

The Key to Stopping the Violence

or bought something that he believed in. He shared with me how he had been stranded on the South Side of Chicago and a black man helped him to get out of what could have been a dangerous situation. He also told me about his mother and father and how they had come over to America with nothing and were able to build a business for their family. He introduced me to his top salesman, who was making more than $100,000 annually. I learned a lot from him. I was at a tough time again because sales were not coming. I stayed in there until finally the day came when I got him to say that he would put one of our office products in. He told me I had done all the right things by working with him. But he did let me know that because an ink pen is a status symbol, the Bic ink pen I'd offered him to sign the order form made my presentation look cheap. I talked Donna into buying me a $100 Mount Blac fountain pen. Learning about the subtle things in business was what I enjoyed about corporate America. What kind of pen to use, the right shoes to wear and the right suits; things that most people would take for granted.

November started slow, but ended well with me leading the district in sales. I was also in position to win the elite trip and company ring after just seven months on the job. James Johnson was also on track to win the trip to Hawaii and I had an outside chance, but everything had to work just right. There were young white guys who had come in and the trip had set them apart from others. My name was starting to be known because there were only two black sales reps in Chicago and we were both in the south office. The rep in my office had begun calling me "The Leading Edge" because I was making a reputation of being on top.

December was approaching and it was time for another blitz. I had established myself as the No. 2 man in the office behind James Johnson, who was nearing a promotion. I figured if I made the trip that would show that I deserved to move to the next level.

Winning the Prize

Bill and other young bucks were coming up on my heels. Everyone wants you when you're on top. We started preparing for another blitz. Three days of long appointments and top managers. Our office was at full staff with 20 reps. We were pumped to make the big money. I needed to sell a minimum of $40,000 worth of equipment to make the trip to Hawaii and get

SILENT CRY

the President Club ring. That meant two months of selling in one month. It was a long shot, but possible.

The first day of the blitz started with me and Jack, who was known for his wide body and confident sales and closing skills. He would get in a person's face and ask probing questions and turn them to his advantage. Jack would close everyone. The first call we went on, we closed on an accountant. Then we closed a school principal. Then at 7 p.m., we closed an 80-year-old man at his house. We ended the day with six sales and $18,000 in business. Jack had helped me stay on track by selling the most office products in a day from the south office. Everyone started saying I had a good chance to reach my goals. I went on a mission after the blitz, selling 17 office products. I could taste that trip to Hawaii.

But one thing interrupted my plans: Christmas. After Christmas, I only had a few days and needed two sales. A bank that I had worked on purchased a competitor's office product. People who had promised to purchase a office product from me ended up purchasing elsewhere. There's a rule in sales that says one-third of what you have worked on will close with you, another one-third will not buy anything and you'll lose the last third to the competition. Ron and I went out two days in a row trying to secure that last sell. I was $2,000 away. A trucking company had been putting me off for two months and they needed an office product. I called and the secretary (gatekeeper) there, went off about how the owner didn't want to be bothered and if he wanted a office product, he would call. So I called back again and asked to speak to the owner to apologize. I explained to him that I was trying to save him some money, but instead I hadn't done a good job because he was upset with me. He said that he wasn't upset and asked me to tell him about the special savings. I explained that we could bring the office product over immediately to show him. He agreed and we signed the order that day. The day of closeout, I sold a $3,000 office product, which took me over the quota by $1,000. I made the dream come true. I defeated all the odds and put myself on the elite level with other company superstars. I had won the much talked about trip. I was admired among my peers and I stole some of the spotlight from James Johnson. But he was going to be promoted and I began wondering where I would go. That month I made more than $9,000. I was at the top of my game. We needed another manager and everybody knew James would be the man. He had already picked out his white BMW 325i (Ron O'Toole had a

The Key to Stopping the Violence

black BMW 325i.) And it all came to pass. James became the second district manager. They split the teams in two between James and Ron . I became a lottery pick and Ron won. I was like an heir apparent. Paul would pull me in his office and say, " This is a company of young, hungry superstars and you're one of them; look how fast I moved up, it could happen to you too. "

A Cold Corporate Lesson

January was a slow month, but I still led the district in sales. In February, James and Paul asked me to come into the main office. Everyone thought they would be informing me of the next area in the country that would be opening up and what I would have to do to get it. But instead James and Paul had come up with an idea to move me to a more depressed area on the South Side of Chicago. They never asked me if this would be what was best nor did they talk to my sales manager about it. That meant several major things, including losing the territory I had developed by making hundreds of cold calls. A transfer would also mean that all the demonstrations I had given would be lost because I wouldn't be there to close the business. I knew that it takes start-up time to adjust to a new area and that selling on the South Side was totally different from selling in the suburbs. Finally, since we worked on straight commission, I was solely responsible for all the office products I sold in my territory. If a customer didn't pay, I would lose all the commission out of my next check. But they still moved me to the South Side. Major companies had always been known for trying to put a black rep on the south side and leaving the more lucrative territories for the whites.

Moving was a veteran sales rep's nightmare. I found out later that this practice was unheard of. Why mess with success? I was responsible for the food on my table. My 3-year-old daughter was there with Donna, who was pregnant and due in June. Then to top everything off, James Johnson did not give me one lead. He kept terrible records and his selling skills were adapted to his own unorthodox style. He knew where to go to get business, and I relied on follow ups and textbook methods.

As I made cold calls on the South Side, it became evident that the white business district and the black district were totally different. In the suburbs, I could get out of my car and cold call for hours straight. On the South Side the businesses were scattered. In the suburbs, you could walk in a business, go to the secretary and start your sales pitch. In the city, I had to ring a bell. If they don't know you, you might not get in. Once you did, there might be a security guard to get passed. That made the call very unsmooth and unnatural to me. In the past, I worked on repetition and adrenaline, knowing I was going into each call with an opportunity to get to see the decision-maker. Now I was selling through bulletproof windows and to businesses that didn't have any money or didn't want to admit to having any money. Every business I saw had a good chance of already owning a office product. I would come back to the office wondering why I was chosen to be fucked with, considering the job was hard enough to do right the first time. Talking to James Johnson was even worse because all he would do was talk about how he came to the South Side of Chicago when the company wouldn't hire black sale representatives to sell there. He also sold all of the businesses that needed the products.

At meetings I would talk to other managers and they couldn't understand why they decided to change the top rep in the office just because I was black. I had been doing very well where I was. Black business owners would either stroke me or pretend they were going to buy and then back out with checks that bounced. I was also trying to protect the precious trip to Hawaii by not having any office products charged back between January 1 and April 15 because one chargeback would have made me ineligible for the trip. Back when James was in the area, his customers were charging back between $20,000 and $30,000. That was not encouraging for me because even though he had cleared the trip by $70,000, he still lost thousands of dollars in commissions.

Then to top it off they were sending me to collect from James's accounts, which meant either picking up office products or picking up unpaid checks. I started to get depressed because it was obvious race had stepped into the picture. But the trip was going to solve all my problems because it meant everything at OBT Co. to earn the trip. It finally came in April. Me and Donna, Ron, James, and all the other superstars went to Maui. Donna, went although she was six months into her pregnancy. Because James and Ron were single, they had to go.

Of the top 100 reps on the trip, about four were black. One black rep won the trip for two years straight and still hadn't been promoted. I knew racism existed but again I said, "No, that's not going to happen to me. I've worked too hard. Besides, maybe this guy had done something wrong."

The Key to Stopping the Violence

Maui was wonderful, peaceful and a dream. Because James, Ron, and I were from the same district, we did most things together. Ron walked over to us one day and he was steaming mad. He said some of the white guys said that they noticed he was hanging with the blacks and called him a nigger lover. Ron always thought of himself as a fair person, but he could not relate to this black experience. His family lived in the south suburbs and he had moved to the city to prove that he could be integrated. But his biggest claim to blackness was that he knew James Johnson and me. It took a lot out of the trip because I knew these same people who were smiling in our faces probably said James and I being there was a fluke. And, some of them would be the same people hiring and firing others in the future. I tried to put blinders on for I knew after we returned, they would be approaching me any day about a management opportunity.

However, I was struggling, trying to make this new territory work for me. Paul would work with me and hold the carrot in front of me saying how fair the company was with him and how they had moved him from Florida to Chicago after just 15 months. At the same time he always tried to get into my head to see what I was thinking about. He would especially try to question Donna about me at company parties and picnics, so she tried to avoid him. Paul had told my wife that promotions come about three months after the trip. That was the carrot.

Time passed and no one had talked about promotion, although people in other parts of the country were moving up, even people in my sales class. Frustration set in when James Johnson started to avoid me because I was always asking him and Paul to put me back into my old territory.

As June blitz, 1987 rolled around I explained what happened to Jack, the supremely confident sales manager, and he couldn't believe it, but he wasn't in a position to tell Paul what to do. However, after he worked with me on a blitz day and we couldn't sell to anyone because no one had any money, he knew I was right. I was selling enough to eat, but my big commission months were not coming.

My attitude started to deteriorate and I gradually became part of the Breakfast Club (salesmen who complained about everything, never worked hard but always wondered why their numbers weren't working). We started renting videos during the day and hanging out at game rooms or watching Oprah during the breakfast hour. That's when I knew things weren't going to happen for me. My emotions ran high because I started seeing younger sales reps not being able to cut the mustard. They were purchasing vans and six months later, they were out the door. I would take a lot of these guys out on the initial interview and would do all that we could to make them successful, but you had to be a certain breed to last.

Despite the adversity I was still on target although a long shot for the President's Club during my second year, but I had decided it was time for me to make other career plans. But what could I go into that would give me an opportunity to move up and not be denied, but at the same time would not have the monthly pressure like at OBT Co.? I found my answer in a doctor's office in the South suburbs.

While sitting in the waiting room to see an account, there was an older gentleman with an extra large briefcase. I asked him what did he carry it for and he said he was a pharmaceutical salesman. I almost fell out of my seat. How could he be a salesman with gray hair? He told me he was about to retire he had been with the company for 25 years. I felt a sigh of relief because I had never heard of someone being in the field or carrying a bag so long. I asked him for a card and thought this is the industry I want to go into.

I started asking everyone I knew about the business, but I couldn't get any outstanding leads. Meanwhile, I called on a video store on the South Side. I met with the owner that evening for a demonstration. Video stores used office products for promotions, among other things. He thought it was a wonderful idea and could use the office product. The only problem was the same one I was running into all over the South Side: He didn't have any money. Nevertheless, he was very nice and seemed to be honest and up front. He complimented me on my presentation and started a conversation about how he had worked for a major corporation for years before deciding to venture into his own business. I listened as he talked about how tough it must be selling office products because of the competition between companies. At that point I had nothing to lose so I looked at him like a puppy with his tail between his legs and said, "Sir, to be honest I'm looking to get out of this market."

He said, "Well, what are you interested in?"

"I'd like to get into an area of sales that has repeat business, you know something like hospital sales or pharmaceuticals. To my surprise, he said his wife was a pharmaceutical rep.

The Key to Stopping the Violence

"I'm 45, but she's only 29 years old. And as a matter of fact she's going to be resigning in a few months to work in the family business full time."

Before I could say anything, he continued, "You're welcome to call her at the number here or at home. She comes home after 8 p.m. every night."

I thanked him, loaded my equipment and left. The next day I called her and we met at the store. She was more than happy to talk about how her sales worked and how to get into the business, but she said because she was leaving, it would be better if another person in the company referred me. Fortunately, there was a black guy on the north side and she would call him and ask him if he would refer me.

I called the black pharmaceutical rep at his home and we spoke for a few minutes. I told him I would get a resume to him and figured he would want to meet me because it's hard to refer someone you don't know. He didn't have time to meet with me, but said to send my resume anyway. A week later, I called and he said he had presented the resume to his boss and he wasn't interested at this time. I asked the brother how long had he been doing what he was doing (five years). He was placed by a headhunter, Rick Chaney, at Chaney and Associates. He didn't have a number, but he said to call and use his name. I thanked him, looked up the number and called the next day. Rick Chaney asked me to send my resume. It was late in the year, around Christmas. Rick said they were really slow and to call back after the new year.

The managers at OBT Co. were really coming down on everyone because we were gearing up for the December blitz. Things came to a head when I called a meeting with Paul and his boss. I asked why I couldn't assume my old territory, which was open because a new rep had left. I was granted the territory change and during that transition month, in November I made $6,000 in my old territory. But I had no leads going into December. By this time, I was burned out. No one had talked promotion, but the rumor was one of the sales managers in the north office would be moving to a new district manager spot. So I figured I had to be a front runner because all of the superstars in that office had been promoted. The new superstar had only been around 11 months. I had been around for two years.

In December the north office managers started the interview process. I put my sales in a booklet and my co-workers wrote and signed endorsement letters that I put in there. Three people interviewed for the position and I kept hearing the word that they were not going to put a black manager in that office because it was one of the best on the country.

During the interview, the two managers said they had never seen a candidate more organized. I was questioned about my slipping productivity as if they didn't know I had been switched three times that year. After leaving the interview, I didn't hear any word the following day. Then Paul pulled me into his office the next day. He asked me how I felt the interview had gone. He wanted to break some news to me.

"E.J., this is difficult for me to say because you have done an outstanding job. But sometimes you have said things that lead people to look at you a certain way. Let me put it this way, if you're on the phone a person should not be able to tell if you're black or white. I've been meaning to talk to you about this, but I hadn't gotten around to it."

"What are you saying, Paul? That I'm too black for the job?"

"I'm just telling you that played into their decision."
Paul was suffering from what a lot of white people suffer from: They want you to be them.

So I said, "How was I salesman of the year in my territory if I could not get along with my customers?"

I left his office pissed off. The next day, Paul pulled me back in his office and apologized. He said that he had made a mistake and he had not spoken to his manager beforehand. He made assumptions. Then he said what he had to tell me was not good. Ron O'Toole would be moved from our office to the north side office and Sam Winters would be the new manager, and he would be my boss.

I sat there in shock and repeated what he had said to me because I didn't believe that Ron O'Toole had interviewed for a job with anyone. Ron was dating the district manager's sister-in-law in the north office, so his future would be taken care of by his future brother-in-law. Sam Winters, who had been around for only 11 months, was going to manage me. It was fair to say that it was a slap in the face. Then it was explained to me that Sam Winters had military experience.

All of the white sales reps in the office were blown away. I had done everything and more. I won the trip, the ring and I had changed territories. I had worked with people, trained reps and I was a family man. But I had the wrong skin color. My wife and others in the African American community had warned me,

The Key to Stopping the Violence

but I didn't listened. I called Rick Chaney the first day after the new year. Rick said it was going to be difficult to get together because of the holiday. He had to get back in his routine and that would take at least two weeks before he could get me in. I was at the office the morning when I called and asked again about meeting. Finally, he had some time around 11 a.m. I was on my way.

Once I got there, Rick took my resume and started asking questions. He was very impressed with my training and interview skills. He brought in his partner and we talked for an hour. I looked up and three hours had passed. Toward the end, Rick said he was ecstatic to have me as a candidate and that he knew I would get placed with my track record in office products. Most people respected office product sales reps because they knew you had to be a closer to sell.

As Rick and I were about to part, Rick was rumbling through his papers and wondered aloud why hadn't he thought of an interview earlier in our conversation. He asked me if I had ever heard of Star Inc. Who hadn't heard of Star Inc. He said they would be in town soon and I would be perfect for their new product. He said a headhunter from the West Coast would call that night with details about the interview.

A New Beginning

I went home fired up because I had interviews with two major Fortune 500 companies. The headhunter called that night to explain the Star Inc. position. She said they were promoting a new product that would revolutionize the market. They were looking to fill slots in two territories and needed people who could close. The sale would be repeat business but the rep had to sell to get in. I told her I was the right person for the job. She said according to Rick, he thought so too. The next day, I went to work but the day after, instead of working with Tom, I blew it off because I had nothing to say.

The morning of my interviews finally arrived. I had studied all of the information on the two companies. I wore my best suit and I had read a book called "Knock 'em Dead" referred to me by a OBT Co. salesman. I was ready to go. Both interviews were out north, so I drove out in my van. I thought everybody I saw was somebody who worked with me. I was ducking at stop lights and almost pulling off the road. I arrived at the EFG Co. office and saw a few brothers with Jerri curls.

SILENT CRY

"Cool. They hire some of us here," I thought. While waiting for the district manager, I went to the restroom, looked in the mirror and exclaimed, "It's showtime. Let the show begin."

The manager came out and escorted me back to his office. He spoke very candidly. The job, he said, consisted of a great deal of travel, including downstate Illinois and into different markets. I could handle that. Then out of the blue he said, "E.J. I'm going to be honest with you because I don't want you to waste your time. I don't think you're the right person for the job. Don't get me wrong, you have excellent credentials. But I don't think they will fit in this environment."

"Can you give me a little more feedback," I asked.

"Sure. This interview is over."

It had only been 10 minutes so I said, "What could I do to show you my capability to do this job?"

"Nothing," he said.

"Based on a scale of one to 10, one means you will throw me out and 10 means you will have me come back for a second interview," I reasoned.

The manager assured me his answer was one. He gave me the standard line that I'd do well, but just not for their organization. But he had to doubt that I really would be successful. He kept reiterating "not at this time with their company." Then he escorted me to the door. He almost had to push me out because I was still trying to close from the parking lot. I was walking to the van not knowing whether to cry or not. Because the interview had been so short, I had a lot of time to spare between interviews, so I wandered into a restaurant, feeling sorry for myself. I was losing confidence because I felt that big companies don't want to deal with black men. I sat in a corner booth and cried as I ate my lunch. I felt totally worthless and defeated. I wanted to go home. But on the other hand, I really wanted the Star Inc. interview to go well. This is the job I want, I told myself. I started firing myself up, saying that I would not leave the interview without a job. I walked in the bathroom, wiped my face and again said, "Showtime!"

I got to the interview early. Rick had said they would be interviewing all day for three days and would choose people that week. I was totally jacked up because I could walk away with a job in a major corporation this week. I started the interview in a hotel suite with John Francis, the district manager. I was wired when I walked through the door. I asked him how his day was

The Key to Stopping the Violence

going and told him I was having the best day of my life. I told him how I had succeeded even though I grew up in the inner city of Chicago. John was engulfed by my stories and I sat there on the edge of my seat giving him exactly what he wanted to hear. Then we talked about the industry I was in. He, too, had sold office products. I felt at ease with John and the interview seemed to be more like talking to a friend rather than a stranger. Toward the end I asked the $64,000 question: Between one and 10, would he hire me today. John said 9 1/2 and added that if I could do the same thing in my next interview, I'd be own my way.

He sent me on to the next room with another manager. I took John's advice and used the same enthusiasm and fire in my interview with him. He seemed to question why I made more money my first year than the second. I told him that I'd changed territories three times, but I was still making the best of it. Again, I asked him the $64,000 question and he said "9" and sent me on to another manager, who was the most relaxed.

I was going on my third hour of interviews. I felt pretty confident and I showed him all of my "Brag Book" information. He stopped me and said he had never interviewed anyone who seemed to be so inspired to get a position. I took the compliment as a sign to go for the close. After the interviews I met with Rick Chaney in his office. He said that he would get feedback the next day and that he'd call me. Later, I received a call from Rick, who said the interviews went extremely well. I skipped work on Friday and John Francis called Friday evening to make a job offer.

That Monday was payday at OBT Co.; we were to get our draw checks. Paul put my check in my mailbox, but the next time I walked by it was gone. Paul had taken it out. I had never missed my draw in two years and because of one month he decided to treat me like that. I went into his office to question what he had done, knowing I already had a new job. It was the second week in January and I planned to continue working because the training class for Star Inc. wasn't until March. I had taken enough bullshit from Paul so I told him I would be taking a position with another Fortune 500 company. He said I was making a mistake. Star Inc. wasn't that good of a company. He said he didn't understand why I would leave him when he had given me an opportunity. I let Paul know that everything runs its course and this job had played out.

As I left to enter my van and pull away Paul walked outside as if to check it out. He started pouring through my stuff in a last-ditch effort to humiliate me. That showed me his lack of character. Everyone who left OBT Co. was called a slug and a bum. They couldn't just wish you well without trying to drag your name through the mud.

Quitting early gave me two months to stay home. I enjoyed the time with my 3 year-old daughter and 4 month-old boy. John Francis called periodically to see if things were going alright. I finally let him know I had left OBT Co. early. He asked me if I wanted to start in an earlier training class. I turned him down.

A New Experience

Training started with 30 people, 29 whites and me in Dallas. The people always said, "E.J., I heard about you." I wondered what they were talking about. What had John told them about me? On the first day, the trainers asked each new person to give his name and background. I gave my nickname, "Leading Edge,"and said that I wanted to be, and would be, the No. 1 salesman in the company. Everyone looked amazed, as if I were crazy. I was the only African American present, yet I stood tall. It was my first experience working with white females. OBT Co. didn't have any because of the heavy equipment involved. Now half of the people were women.

Training lasted for two weeks. Star Inc.'s training was very intense and there was some very good people there. My roommate was from another office product company. Whenever companies train you, they keep you busy morning till night. As the week passed I started to feel the pressure of being the only black person there. From the time I got off the plane to entering the hotel the only black people I saw were shoeshine boys, maids, waiters, waitresses and bus boys. The blacks in Dallas seemed to have a certain noticeable, submissive attitude. The whites were extremely comfortable having a black person wait on them and call them "sir" or "boss." To me it was an insult. I called home and told Donna it was modern-day slavery. The brothers wore outdated Jherri curls. The blacks looked surprised when they saw me enter the hotel or airport. Our eyes would meet because we were black. When I spoke to the people around the hotel, my white peers asked if I knew them. Why did I speak to them. I let them know that it is customary for us to speak because there are so few of us. One of the waiters was walking by and I asked him how things were going. He said he was proud

The Key to Stopping the Violence

of me because he noticed how I could sit at the table and deal with those white folks. He was 22. I told him he was young and that I was only 26. He could deal with them, too, if he believed in himself and his abilities. He looked as though I was telling him something he had never heard before.

"Don't look to just work here all your life. Find a way to own it," I told him. Then I said laughing, "Well let me go deal with these white folks." I questioned the blacks I ran into about where blacks party. I found out there weren't any nightclubs for black professionals in Dallas. It was nothing like in Chicago.

Throughout the training I was treated well, although I still felt a difference. There was always somebody in the group who wanted to say something pleasant but often seemed to say the wrong thing. Everybody said I reminded them of Michael Jordan because of my dark complexion and short hair. I became close to several people, but I felt the need to be seen more than heard. No matter what I did I couldn't fit "the image" like a white boy could. The white girls said things like "You must really make your wife happy." The white guys would make statements about the size of my private.

Going to the dance hall on Saturday night was a trip because I'm not known as a dancer by any means in the black community. But, when in the company of whites, everybody wanted to dance with me. I realized that a lot of stereotypes existed and a lot of whites in America had no clue to what we are about. I also had many stereotypes about them.

I even felt the tension that some people in training had just holding a conversation with me. But all those things could not stop me from doing my job and being the best that I could be. Don came to me as we spent more time together and said he couldn't imagine being the only white person somewhere for two weeks. He asked me how I was dealing with it. I explained that I stayed focused with a purpose, knowing this time would pass. But inside, I missed my friends and family, often calling home to tell Donna that I was ready to go home that day.

We were learning more about the product and the people in management had been very nice. The second week of training promised to be more interesting because John was coming down and he was a manger in the central district, along with Brian . Star Inc. was a company that worked hard and played hard. But a black person could never fall asleep and think he or she could get away with the same thing the whites got away with. The second week was even more pressure-filled because everyone was trying to earn brownie points. I heard people talk about others; who they felt was doing well or worse. It was strange that whites would talk to me about other whites, as though my strategy was not to come out on top myself.

After an afternoon session we had a night out where everyone started drinking and partying. John Francis walked up to me on the beach and said he had something he wanted to talk to me about. He spoke casually. "Edge, I know how you grew up in the ghetto. Well that is something that, being a white man, I will never understand. What's it like to be black in America? I happened to noticed when you spoke earlier today you said the word '"ax"' instead of 'ask'. Now all that hard work you have done to make it. That statement put you all the way back in the ghetto. Maybe we can find a speech class to help you."

Having said that, one of the nice-looking ladies in the company walked by and John turned to me with a beer in his hand and acknowledged her nice breasts. Then he started talking about how he was committed to helping me be successful and if the company had to send me to a speaking course, he would do that. Someone called his name and he said we would talk later. He ran off,toward the beach, leaving me puzzled and in limbo. If he said I pronounced a word incorrectly, I wouldn't deny it. It was how he said it. I had heard many whites who had mispronounced words. Pay me a penny for every white person who does that and I'd be a rich man.

I was depressed and distressed that night. I went back to my room and stayed in for the rest of the night. I didn't get much sleep, so by morning I was throwing up from stress. I had just left an asshole at the other company and I'd gotten into this situation again. When I asked John about his comments, he said he couldn't remember anything because he had too much to drink. At that point I hadn't met a black manager yet -- maybe there weren't any. Back in training, the class voted on who they wanted to be the class speakers for the training graduation ceremony. I had learned from OBT Co. during their training that it is difficult for whites to vote for any black first in anything, unless they had to. Back in college I had learned a difficult lesson: A black person has to be twice as good to win half the praise, but if you are on the same level as whites, they will call your success a fluke or accident. In the voting, the winners were considered the leaders of the future. I looked at it as those who would be put on the fast track to management.

The Key to Stopping the Violence

At our banquet I sat there and looked around the room and realized I would be one of the best in the room. I knew nobody had worked as hard or had been through as much as I had. I also knew that I had a tremendous opportunity but I had to take full advantage of it. Then I said a silent prayer for Ray and all the brothers in the 'hood who didn't have a chance to live this life style.

During that week John mentioned to the Chicago rep, and me that he was looking for another representative for Chicago. I thought of Mark Carls from OBT Co. I walked over to John at the dinner banquet table and asked, "If I had a person with the same background in sales as mine, would you be interested in interviewing him?"

John said, "You're not trying to promote all the brothers, are you?"

"This guy, for your information, is white."

John looked at me and smiled. I knew inside he was saying he had hit his quota of blacks by hiring me.

Family Values Over Corporate Dreams

Because Donna and I had just had our second child in 1987, my first decision regarding the company wasn't necessarily the perfect career move. Everyone in my class was offered the chance to go to test markets in Florida or California and continue distribution of the new product. Star Inc. would put you up in the best hotels and fly your spouse or significant other out to see you every weekend. I would have loved to go but my son Mario was only five months old and Deanna was three. Donna was working in downtown Chicago. The commute for Donna was over an hour and a half one way . I couldn't imagine not being home to assist with the family. Although they said we didn't have to go, it was made clear that this extra service would show your commitment to the company. Management looked at commitment as a sign of loyalty. It was also said this would go a long way in deciding promotions in the future. Instead, I headed back Chicago to be with my wife and kids. Selling the old products of Star Inc.

I didn't know what to expect in the field because it was a totally different setup from my previous job. Instead of going into the office each day at 7 a.m., I worked out of my own office at home. Instead of straight commission, I earned a salary plus commission. Instead of me buying a van, I received a company car. I sold my van and bought office equipment.

SILENT CRY

I started building my new territory which began close to Iowa , across Illinois to South Bend, Ind. John Francis told me to use the phone book to locate clients. Clients who had not seen a Star Inc. rep for years said they were disgusted with our present product.

I went to the library and pulled out 10-15 Yellow Pages looking for new accounts. My own eyes started crossing as I sat there with migraine headaches, wondering what in the hell I had gotten myself into. I was suffering anxiety attacks because I had left a job that I knew and now I was the new kid on the block. I and trying so hard to get all this new information together. Too often when I talked to accounts about our new products, they wanted to talk about returning the old ones. It was like baby-sitting people day in, day out.

John sent me up to Minnesota to work with a white rep who lived in a suburb of St. Paul. She said I reminded her of a black sales rep in the company in Florida. She even called him and he gave me a call once I got back to Chicago. She taught me a lot about selling our old products and I stayed close to her in our tenure at Star Inc. In June 1988 we had our first meeting with the entire sales force. I met the black rep from Florida, an ex-football player who was very straight forward in his approach to whites. He was very overpowering and I would see him almost turn whites into black people when he was around. They would smile and slap him high five and then as soon as he left they would whisper about him. I remember John telling me about the company's other black reps. He said the black guys had their own way of doing things and that the female black sales rep. in Virginia had a unique way of selling. Whenever he talked about the few blacks in the company he would always end with something that made you have a little doubt about their abilities. Then there was Vernon Turner, a brother from the south, who walked up and said we all need to stick together. Then he walked away.

Star Inc. launched the new products at a convention in Chicago. With their order accounts would receive free samples, posters and, of course, a Star Inc. representative to service the account. But our accounts were not buying the program. They were concerned about buying a new product from a company. When they were not sure the product would work. That led to a great deal of anxiety among the sales force. As frustration set in people started talking about leaving. But the sales reps stayed strong.

The Key to Stopping the Violence

But the Chicago management was in complete chaos. There was no manager because John Francis was promoted to national sales trainer. His mentors, were moving him up the ladder. Chicago ranked last. The territory boundaries were not defined, so on paper I could sell some product but another rep would get credit. Our territories were being change almost monthly. But as frustrated as we were we continued to sell and do our best, figuring in the end things would work out.

As months passed in 1988, Star Inc. changed some of the programs to give customers a better way to afford our product. The company continued to add sales reps. In downstate Illinois, two reps were added, one black, one white. Don Carr was hired as our new district manager. Don came in to straighten out the Chicago market by bringing direction and stability. He had us do reports and maps to justify what was going on in Chicago. There were certain people that Don didn't get along with. But he went on with his job. His philosophy was if you work your ass off he would work his ass off for you. Don was big on doing analyses and making sure everyone in the company knew what his reps were doing.

At the meetings, I found out, most of the blacks in the company were having major problems. A black in Kansas City left and called his manager a fag. Downstate Illinois was asked to leave. The sister in New York left. Indiana rep was asked to leave. The black in Florida was fired and the sister on the East Coast had never been promoted and wasn't getting promoted anytime soon she eventually left. The only blacks who lasted were Vernon Turner and me.

Back to the Hood

Ray spent a year in jail for stealing some gold chains while staying with Ivory in Blommington, IL. Then he flew to California where he beat up Gertie. Once back in Chicago, Ivory got Ray a job and tried to get him back in school. Ray saw Eric on the CTA bus and handed him a letter he had written to me. He told Eric that he wanted to talk to me and was sorry about not contacting me while he was away. Eric threw the letter away and never told me about his conversation with Ray until it was to late.

As I drove back to the Ida B. Wells projects, everyone kept telling me I had just missed seeing Ray. Everyone in the neighborhood knew if I was down in the 'hood, it was to see him. I was always thinking about him in the back of my mind, wondering what he was up to. I admired him for his courage to fight, but I objected to his excuses. Some of the things he was fighting about had gotten old with me now that I had reached the next phase of my life. Ray didn't want to walk that road with me and I knew that I couldn't follow him, for death was waiting around that corner and I had too much to live for.

This last visit was on the spur of the moment. I was in my sales territory in the south suburbs. It was close to 5 p.m. and I figured what the hell, I hadn't been down to see Ray or the fellows in a while. I headed to 39th street in my new red '88 Grand AM company car. In the back of my old building, across from the park, I pulled up next to Hank's house in the spot where Dad parked for years during the '60s in his 1965 New Yorker. I didn't see anyone, so I turned toward Frankie's house. He wasn't there, but Debbie, his younger sister, was. Frankie was 28 and Debbie was maybe 25 now and had a son. They still lived with Martha, Frankie's mother. Debbie and I started talking. As they praised me on how successful I looked with my suit and new car, people started to come around who I hadn't seen in years. Martha was making a big fuss over how nice I looked and how I had grown up.

Debbie was saying that some of my friends seemed to be stuck in time. I heard about how bad things were, about how everybody was doing drugs. I was standing there like some out-of-touch politician, nodding my head in agreement. Debbie introduced me to her son, who was 8-years-old. Then Carla walked up and joined the conversation. We would occasionally break our conversation because Carla would have to run to her apartment. I began speaking to Carl, who was going through some tough times. Carl had lost his mother and sister to murder on consecutive days. I hadn't seen him since their double funeral. Carl, 26, looked like he had been through hard times. His hair was knotted all over his head. He pulled me to the side. "Damn Ersk, you look good man. You must be making some nice cabbage."

"Well, I'm hanging in there. Trying to take care of the family. How are you getting along nowadays Carl?"

"Shit ain't going well because I need a job. You're making good money man. Can you give me a job?"

I looked at Carl with confusion. I looked at his beaten down body and his rotten teeth, listened to his bad grammar, and said, "What do you mean, give you a job?"

The Key to Stopping the Violence

Then Carl told me he was living with his woman and five kids, and he was getting pressure to feed them. Again, sounding like a politician, I asked Carl if he had been filling out applications. Then he got mad and said he couldn't pass the GED to get his diploma.

"I have tried to pass the motherfucker, but I can't. I need money and I can't make it flipping burgers!" he continued in a frustrated voice.

I looked Carl in the eyes and said, "I remember when we were kids and I would tell you to get an education. This was what I was talking about. Brother, I want to help you, but no, I don't have a job to give you. I can help you get your GED though."

Carl turned and walked away, saying something under his breath. Carla came back and talked until some dudes pulled up on the street in a car. Another childhood friend, Floyd, walked up. Floyd was always the boy the girls loved. I was elated to see him.

"Floyd, what's up! Good to see you." I said reaching for his hand.

Floyd was chosen to attend Lindblom High School, but chose another High School instead. Floyd looked almost the same, but because he was still around, I thought it would be better not to ask what he was doing, so I asked about his family. Floyd said he often saw Ray in the neighborhood and that Ray had really cooled out and was just taking it easy. As a matter of fact, he said that Ray had just left and he thought he would be upset because he didn't get to see me.

I made a statement about how troubling it was to find out about all the drugs and murders going on in the low end. Floyed agreed and said that he had to go. Then M.C. walked up and a big smile popped on my face because M.C. was one dude that I had chased and beat up all my childhood. The first thing M.C. said was that it was a damn shame what had happened to Floyd.

As I watched Floyd walk away, I asked, "What happened?" "You know, those drugs almost got the best of him, but he recovered well after going into rehab."

I stood there feeling like a fool because I had just condemned people around the neighborhood for doing what he knew he had done. That's why he left so fast. I knew at that point to keep my mouth shut, but I didn't. I asked M.C. about his brothers, and sister. As he started telling me, Debbie interrupted like a big sister and started telling M.C. he knew he shouldn't be around when he knew the police were looking for him. I stood there with my mouth hanging open. When M.C. saw that I couldn't get a word out, he started telling me in so many words that he was sneaking back and fourth from in and out of state because he was selling drugs just to get the things he needed, then he would quit. In the middle of the conversation, Frankie finally walked up and I immediately brought him into the conversation.

"Frankie, do you know about what M.C. is doing?" I inquired.

"Yep, but M.C. don't know how to run his game right because he is too open with his shit. I'm not involved in all that shit." But take Carla, for example."

I looked at Carla. She had gone back into the house again. A few moments later, she handed something in a can to two men. Carla had been going back and forth from her apartment. During the entire time I had been there talking, it never occurred to me to turn around to see what she was doing.

This time I managed to ask Frankie if Carla was also selling.

He nodded yes. "But she's smart about it, because she don't sell it from the house. Carla won't let MF'S knock on the door of her apartment."

I thought, "I am in way over my head." Carla, M.C. and Floyd, the list includes almost everybody! Most of the people I talked to about the problem, were part of the problem. Carla had a job. Why was she selling. That's when I knew that talking to Ray would probably bring even more disappointment. I had heard it all too often. Ray had been giving me the "I'm going to get it together" shit for far too long. Times had separated me and Ray. There were too many things that had made me make a decision not to come back down to the projects. Donna felt that my life was at risk trying to save Ray's life. But in the end, he was still my boy and my friend.

Reflections on The Old and The New

T.D. and I were downtown, where we met to go out for the night. T.D. worked for a major corporation as a salesman, and I had just been hired as a salesman for Star Inc., earlier in the year. We always liked to clown and kid a lot, and this was going to be a good Friday night for us. We were middle class guys who had "made it," the nice wives, beautiful children, new cars, expense accounts and suits. Ray had fallen on harder times;

The Key to Stopping the Violence

no college degree and no job. He had returned to 37th Street to hang out with the fellas. Some of them weren't bad men. They were in their mid-20s but without an education and jobs to fall back on.

I hadn't seen Ray in a couple of months because we had an understanding that his direction was not mine. I would tell Ray that independence is not just a word, but an action that you repeat until you get results. I tried to talk to him time and time again, often running into his famous words, "I know man, I'm going to do better."

Ray continued to go to the low end even after he had been to jail and back for beating up Gertie. Ivory helped him get a job, which Ray only kept for a short time. He could not take orders from the white man. In the back of my mind I knew that was the dual burden all black men faced. Knowing some of the bull shit I had gone through in corporate America. He asked, "E.J. why should I give that white man the pleasure of making me his slave, they fuck with you are your the best." I told him we had to start somewhere, then later we'd start our own business. I repeatedly asked him what he was going to do without a job. "Just hustle" is all he would say.

Ray called my house in the suburbs, during the 1988 baseball playoffs. I hadn't spoken to him since Ivory's wedding. I didn't know that would be the last time I saw Ray alive. At the wedding reception Ray was high as we talked about Deke. He explained that while he was in prison, he had seen Wayne Foster. Ray had to do extra time because Wayne told the guards that Ray tried to attack him. As I talked to him, I sat there holding my son. It hit me again how different our lifestyles had become. All I had to say was the wrong thing about anybody and Ray would have a reason to take matters in his own hands. I told Ray to take care and didn't pretend that it was good to hear from him.I was mad that I lost my dearest friend not because he had died but because mentally we were worlds apart. I had heard later he got into a big fight with Ivory on his wedding day. I was so tired of the excuses and of him blaming everything on everybody else, then telling me what I wanted to hear. Ray was two different people. The person I knew and the person that everyone else saw. Friends on the low end would always tell me that I was the only one who Ray respected and acted civilized around. Maybe they were right because Ray didn't even as much as show anger toward me since before college. They said he was wild and out of control when I wasn't around.

SILENT CRY

Homicide

Ray and some partners were living out of a hotel. Lamar had just seen Ray a couple of days earlier. Ray told Lamar he didn't have to work because he made more money in one day then we had in a year. Ray and some of my other partners would go to the low end to sell drugs at night.

One of the known dealer's used runners as young as 15 and 16. A rule of the game was not to use your boss's drugs or profit, which could get you killed. The young boys started using this dealer's drugs and to protect themselves, they had to make it look like someone robbed them. Then they had to give their boss a name, and that name was Ray's.

Ray knew how that game was played because drugs have no friends . The dealer became Ray's enemy, even though they grew up together and had been friends for over twenty years. Ray knew the dealer wouldn't walk up on him. Ray continued about his business, hanging out, with the fellas. His family knew and tried to talk him out of carrying a gun. But he told his aunt he had to but not to worry because death wasn't the worst thing that could happen to him. Ray also let her know he wasn't afraid to die. On that Friday night in October 1988 Ray went to the meat market, a nasty store that smelled and sold rotten meat. Ray would walk there sometimes to get lunch meat and crackers like we did as kids. From there, Ray and some of the fellas went to the Lake Grove buildings across the park. They broke into a Jamaican's house and held him up at gunpoint. The Jamaican owed them some drugs and money. When he couldn't produce the money, Ray took his one-year-old baby and held him out the window by one leg from the fourth floor apartment, telling the Jamaican he would drop the baby on his head. Then Ray and the fellows went back to Ida B. Wells.

It was a Friday night. I was in a suit and tie in the downtown area about to attend a black middle class, after-work party. I was living the so-called American dream with a house, two incomes, working for a Fortune 500 company, driving a company car and using an expense account. Less than 10 minutes away, my childhood friend was living the American nightmare, in one of the worst crime infested neighborhoods in the city.

Ray and the boys had already done enough damage for a lifetime and it was still early, around 9 p.m. After they left a

The Key to Stopping the Violence

friends' apartment, they walked toward the car where they were met by the dealer and the two teenagers who had accused Ray of stealing their drugs. An ambush was next. Out of nowhere the Dealer came from one side and the two teenagers came from the other side of the car and started shooting at the crowd. Everyone broke out and ran, except for Ray, who hesitated and then jumped into the passenger side of the car. Ray almost seemed to know that he didn't want to run anymore.

Earlier that day Ray and the dealer had words with each other. The dealer told Ray that he would have to pay for stealing his drugs. Ray walked up to the dealer and said if he was a man he would do what a man would do. Ray was not afraid of the dealer and he was not afraid to die. At that point, the dealer was planning Ray's murder.

The dealer walked up to the passenger side and shot through the window. The bullet struck Ray on the right side of his head, and lodged in his brain. The dealer and his boys ran. My other friends returned as the ambulance arrived. I was still downtown on the phone with T.D., calling up friends to see if they planned to join us at the party. Donna paged me. When I called her back, she said, "Lamar just called. He said Ray's been shot." My heart fell to the floor because it was a call I never wanted to get. I told T.D. and the thought "here it goes again" raced through my mind.

Since we where already downtown, we made it to Michael Reese Hospital before the ambulance. I was waiting in the hallway with T.D. when I saw them rush Ray into the hospital with blood gushing from his head and mouth. His body was trembling out of control. Hospital personnel wheeled him up to a large room with other black gunshot victims and walked away. They never cleaned off the blood or covered the wound in his head. I got some paper towels and began cleaning the blood when it hit me that a black life was of no concern, even to hospital workers. I became outraged at the treatment and started to curse and demand service. Finally, a nurse apologized and began doing her job. Other old friends began coming in, but not one of the homeboys who was with him that night.

Ray's brother, Ivory, who had just graduated from state troopers academy, told me that Ray was supposed to be at his graduation in Springfield, Ill. Ironically, Ivory was becoming a law enforcer, keeper of the peace, role model and protector of the law while his brother Ray was fast becoming a statistic; a statistic that says black men are 15 times more likely to die of violence than white men. All of the things I had talked to Ray about were staring me in my face.

Coma

After Ray was shot there was a coldness in the air. It was the time of year when the season starts to change, the days get shorter, night comes earlier, and the wind forces you to wear a fall jacket. I was struggling at work with Don Carr, the new district manager, and my visits to the hospital to see Ray were long and tedious. Tedious from the standpoint of looking at him in that condition. Ray stayed in a coma for three or four months. His eyes would open slightly when I called his name and a painful grimace would crease his face. His family and I watched his body slowly deteriorate to nothing. I would come to the hospital and read the paper to him. Somehow I felt he could hear me.

The Unthinkable

The next morning after Ray was shot, my oldest brother called and said we needed to go to another hospital because my father's brother, Uncle George, was going through some tests. So I drove by and picked up both Eric and Eddie. We speculated what could be wrong with our favorite uncle. Once we got to the hospital, the tension set in because I've always hated hospitals and I didn't like it any better this day. I had been planning to see Ray later that day anyway. Dad had already been there and gone. "Well, what's going on?" one of us asked. I looked at my uncle, who looks a lot like my father. I admit I wasn't ready for his response. Uncle George said, "I've been in here getting tests run on me because I had a cold that I couldn't get rid of. When I coughed, I spit up a little bit of blood." Then he hesitated. "They told me I have cancer."

As he spoke I began to get weak at the knees. He put his hand on his head and said, "The cancer has spread through my lungs and they say it has spread all over my brain and body." As he spoke I looked into his eyes and listened to his voice. I felt as though I was running a slow motion film. My mind was trying to make sense of what he said. He was telling us that he was going to die. All I kept thinking was this is the day after Ray was shot, and now my uncle has cancer.

The Key to Stopping the Violence

Uncle George was being optimistic. They didn't know how long he would live, but he would go through chemotherapy anyway. Then he said he would be around for a long time, so not to worry.

He returned home from the hospital and continued to complain about his kids as I had heard him talk about his kids all my life. He seemed to be really beat down by all the years of having family around who didn't care about him or his property.

My cousins, his two sons and daughter, were all close to my age. Their mother died when they were under 5 years old. Uncle George didn't make much money, so he had to work a lot in order to make ends meet. Consequently, he didn't have a lot of time to spend with his kids.

My uncle managed to purchased two houses in the Englewood area, close to Lindblom High School. He bought them in the early '70s and left the projects on 43rd and Cottage to raise his kids in a better environment. The area started to deteriorate a few years later. My Dad finally decided to leave the projects in the early '80s, so my uncle gave him one of his houses, which was right next door.

Things always disappeared from Uncle George's house, little things like money, lawn mowers, saws, thousands of dollars in tools and even food. Over the next three months, I watched my uncle sit up in a chair in constant pain, not sleeping for weeks. He passed away in early January 1989. After he passed his kids were fighting over the house the next day. Ray's coma finally ended and he died while I was at Uncle George's funeral. So that week I attended two funerals, my favorite uncle's and my best friend's. Ray's died at the age of 27, just five years after Deke was fatally stabbed.

None of the fellows who witnessed Ray's murder could go to the police station because they would have been arrested for their own crimes. One of the boys saw the shooting and wanted to testify, but he would have had to wear a bulletproof vest because the dealer's boys would try to kill him. That really didn't matter because he changed his mind about serving as a witness for fear of being arrested himself.

Ray's funeral was at the same place as his mother's, father's, the Hudson's and other neighborhood funerals. Within two months after my uncle died. My cousins rented the house out to drug dealers. The drug dealers had kicked my cousins out and were looking to kill one of them for trying to collect the rent.

SILENT CRY

There were no lights or heat. Everything had been stolen from the house even the furnishings.

I would stop by to visit Dad on the weekends and little shorties would be selling drugs in front of my father's house. I pleaded with Dad to move because I could see this stuff tearing his heart apart. But my dad, being from the old school wanted to stay because this was his brother's house and he felt no one would run him out.

Finally, Dad had the city come out and board my uncles house up. Before they locked the door the evicted at least 20-30 drug dealers, women, and children who were living in the house with no water, heat or lights.

Back to The Grindstone

Don Carr came to Star Inc. with an intense work ethic. His background including an unusual amount of paper work. Don made us do the very things that burned him out. He wanted color-coded maps, business analyses, reports on everything. He felt this was the key to showing upper management what you knew or didn't know. Working with Don in the field became an intense experience. He wanted us to memorize all of our competitors' products. Don had to have everything his way because he had to bring Chicago up to speed.

I was scheduled to work with Don Carr the Tuesday after Ray was shot and my uncle was diagnosed with cancer. I had been at the hospital every day since the shooting and Star Inc.'s color-coded maps were not an issue in my life. Up to that point I had talked very little about my personal life to Don. I knew he would want to drill me on my knowledge of product and everything else and I wasn't feeling up to it. But instead of canceling the day I decided to go on with it.   That morning I met Don and we were about 15 minutes away from my first scheduled appointment. So we jumped in my car and headed out. After a few moments into the ride Don started in on the material he requested. "Edge, let me take a look at your territorial map, he said." I drove on staring at the road, preoccupied with the events that had taken place in my life over the weekend. I told Don that I didn't have the map prepared because of some things going on right now. I still avoided talking about my personal life, figuring Don would not understand. But instead of asking me anything else Don said he wants what he wants and doesn't want to hear anything else. I got very upset inside because I knew this

The Key to Stopping the Violence

white man could not imagine what my weekend had been like. Don asked me how did I feel about what he had just said. I couldn't say anything because if that was the way it was, then that's the way it is. Don wanted me to talk about it more but I said I didn't have anything else to say.

Don was upset and said, "Well you can turn around and take me back to my car. I'm not going to work with a salesman who won't talk. I've been a manager for seven years and have never had this happen. Just take me to my car." Now I was smart enough to know that if I took Don back to his car I might as well give him the keys to my company car because he would find a reason to fire me. I looked at Don with a tear in my eye, pulled the car over to the emergency lane and told him what happened to Ray and my uncle over the weekend. Don turned red as his mouth dropped opened. He couldn't say anything except, "Go home for the rest of the day and take care of business." I told him I would rather work, but I needed time to complete some of the projects he wanted. He said to take as much time as I needed.

We completed the first call because we were so close then I dropped Don off at his car. Then I made another call and took the rest of the day off and went by the hospitals.

A Need for Diversity

1988 ended in disappointing fashion for me because even though I sold a great deal of product to end the year, many of my orders were not credited to me; they were going to other representatives. I figured I would be able to make up the credit the next year. Don told us to be patient and that the company would take care of things. But starting in 1989 things were not as he promised and a lot of reps were mad. But halfway through '89, Don had become a much happier manager because Chicago was coming around. We were moving up in the company ranks and that meant he was getting the monkey off our backs.

Our national sales meeting and awards banquet was held in Hawaii and it was the first time all 100 plus salesman and management would be their together. It was a beautiful meeting site. I had a chance to meet all the different people in the company. The politics were evident as Don made sure everyone in the district behaved.

I had three unpleasant experiences at this meeting. One happened when I spoke to the only black district manager in the

221

company. Just hired, she had a problem with speaking and making eye contact. I tried several times during the meeting to speak to her. The second incident happened when I decided to sit at the swimming pool. All of the whites were sitting in the sun getting a tan and I walked by heading for a tree to sit in the shade. After passing a group of white managers, someone hollered out, "Hey Mr. T.!" because I had a chain around my neck. I turned around ready to whip some ass, but then I remembered where I was.

The third incident was the most upsetting. Going into the awards banquet, I didn't know what to expect. Star Inc. had a spectacular set up with all the excitement and thrill one could expect. The first awards were given to all the sales reps who hit 100 percent of quota or better. As they called names I waited for mine to be called. I leaned over to Don and said I had hit my quota last year. Don said I missed my quota in some minor product lines. I sat there watching my peers, knowing that part of my territory numbers were given to them, but nobody wanted to hear about it. And if you complained too much you were likely to be called a troublemaker. So I sat there the rest of the night and watched others win such awards as rookie sales rep of the year and sales rep of the year. I felt like a total failure. Nothing was going right. I couldn't even win the one award I thought I should have won. I had every reason in the world to say this is not the company for me.

I especially paid close attention to the salesman of the year for the entire company. That was the award I wanted. So instead of dwelling on all the negative things, I called Donna and told her I hadn't won anything. Then I told her she had to get ready to face a year of not seeing me too much because next year I wanted to be up on that stage as the sales representative of the year. I wanted to dedicate this year to the people in my life that I love and who were dying.

I came back to the awards dinner and told John Francis this year would be my year. John said if any one could do it I could. I set myself up to have the best year possible. Many of the other reps -- white and black -- didn't have the same focus. I knew I wouldn't see them again after the national meeting.

After the awards banquet, I walked with my old training roommate along the beach. He was having some problems with his manager that he wanted to discuss. We started our walk in front of our hotel. About two blocks later we came upon two

The Key to Stopping the Violence

sales reps making love in the sand. He couldn't tell who they were but I saw both faces and their naked bodies.

Upon leaving Hawaii my performance numbers from the year before continued to haunt me. In my evaluation Don had ripped me a new asshole and he thought I should have been happy with the fact that I received a raise.

The week after Star Inc. revised our quotas for the year because of high projections, things started to take off for me. They called this the year of "closing," the year true sales skill would shine. I started by knowing who in my territory needed our product. I concentrated on closing whoever and wherever. Then after they put the product in, I made sure they understood what I wanted to do for them. I listened to their needs and then let each and every account know that I wanted to be Star Inc.'s top rep in the country. In order to do that I would have to service them better than anyone else had ever done. I wanted it and felt it could be done.

A Reality Check

Mr. Henry Daniels was one of the leading professionals in his field. John Francis told me I would have as one of my accounts one of the largest buyers in the state and a leading authority in the business. He gave me a few articles and explained Mr. Daniels' relationship with Star Inc. I felt overwhelmed having a renowned buyer in my territory. I challenged myself by making him one of my first sales calls.

Walking into his office, I saw evidence that he and his staff were successful. Mr. Daniels had award after award hanging in the long corridors by the supply rooms. His staff was courteous and the they made me feel at home.

Mr. Daniels was extremely nice to me and always took time out to see me. Many of his peers would frown if I mentioned his name. So as we became closer I asked Mr. Daniels why they reacted as they did. He would smile and say, "When you're at the top other people will probably hate you, too." Working in the business with him was one of his sons and two others associates. We became good friends because his son, like myself, was an avid Chicago Bulls fan. Michael Jordan opened a lot of doors for me in handling my accounts.

Mr. Daniels shared my dreams throughout 1989, often asking me if I was hitting my goal and if they were helping me get there. I handled his account with kid gloves. He was my eyes and ears to Star Inc. He knew more about new products, the direction of the company and what the competition was doing than I could ever know. He would tell me things that later happened as he said. Mr. Daniels had close contacts to the higher-ups, including the president of our company. He would always say he was putting a good in for me. I would sit back and listen to him with a reverence for what he was saying.

The real value of Mr. Daniels came with the lessons I learned from him about life. Mr. Daniels would say, "E.J., Star Inc. could really benefit by utilizing your talent the right way. You're nice looking, articulate and perfect for their company image. You have a lot going for you because whites trust you and Blacks need you as a role model." I would always leave Mr. Daniels' office feeling special.

Jeffery Davis, Mr. Daniels' son, and I had a good but different relationship. Because I was not aware of his ethnic background. I never thought of him as being anything other than white. But it was Jeffery who brought it to my attention that he was Jewish and his people are faced with just as much bigotry as blacks. He wanted to know why there was so much violence and destruction in the black community. I tried to explain that self-hate and years of exclusion were part of it, but the final key was self-reliance. Jeffery said that the only difference in racism perpetrated against blacks and racism against Jews was that he could hide behind the color of his white skin and I couldn't. "People don't know what I am walking down the street," he noted, "but E.J., they will never mistake what you are."

There were other instrumental accounts in my life that have given me a lot of satisfaction in knowing; Cary Herzberg, Stephen Steinmetz, John Sims, Garry Masterson, Joseph Digorgio, James T. Day, Harold Davis, Leo Prentice and Jordan Beller just to name a few.

In 1989 I learned what and how to deal with people from all walks of life without feeling intimidated or frustrated. It was a strange source that help me gain that insight. On normal days I would spend a lot of time in the car, usually listen to music. One day I heard a man who almost made me pull off the road because I was laughing so hard. His name was Jim Shorts, and he was a sportscaster. By listening to his Kevin Mathews show and then a show called "Steve and Garry," they were actually teaching me certain things about the way white people thought. Some talk radio would be more main stream, but these guys dogged everybody.

The Key to Stopping the Violence

Other talk radio programs including Rush Limbaugh would get me mad. Although he has some valid points, most of his views were just the opposite of what blacks experienced. I started understanding that most of white America's impression of blacks came from t.v. They had no understanding that my life revolves around family, family values and making a better life for my children. I started becoming more of an ambassador for our people, trying to build relationships on common ground. That put me at a great advantage in sales and life because I wasn't going to lose a good person in my life because of color.

"Hands Up!" in Hyde Park

T.D. and I considered ourselves pretty successful. He was doing well at his company and I was making my mark at Star Inc. We knew black men were getting bullshitted everyday, but we would pretend like it didn't exist.

After work one day we decided to go to the integrated Hyde Park neighborhood in Chicago to visit his cousin before she moved to the West Coast. Hyde Park was -- and still is -- an area for buppies and yuppies, so we felt pretty safe as we jumped out of my company car wearing our nice business suits, and walked to his cousin's apartment. It was a Friday night and she was excited about taking her new position. She gave T.D. an oriental carpet as a token of friendship, and he rolled it up under his arm. I suggested we head downtown for an after-work drink. As we started out the door toward the car, two policemen jumped out of a squad car. Two more police officers came flying down the street, jumped out of their squad car and pulled their guns. One was a white male and the other was a black female. They shouted for us to throw our hands in the air and for T.D. to drop his carpet. Instead T.D. asked what we did and why should he drop this carpet. The black lady cop looked at us as she pointed that gun nervously and said, "If you don't drop that carpet I'm going to blow your fucking face off."

I never looked at the white cop. I put my hands so far in the air I though I would touch the sky. T.D. continued talking about his rights. Finally he dropped the carpet as they rushed us and turned us around and spread our legs. Then they kicked the carpet open and didn't find anything. They said they were looking for two black males carrying a shotgun who committed a robbery.

SILENT CRY

T.D. asked the cops, "Did they say the brothers had on suits and worked for two of the biggest Fortune 500 companies in America?" They told us we could go as they jumped in the police car and pulled off. They never offered an apology, only a simple explanation. Two corporate men by day were nothing more than society's prey by night.

Going for the Gold

After the halfway mark in 1989, Don let me know that I was in the number. 30 spot in the company. I figured I was in striking distance because I ranked No. 4 in the region. I decided to do things I knew other salesmen weren't doing. I consistently made sales calls after 5:00 p.m. Accounts told me they had never had a salesman call on them after 5:00 on Friday. Then I would share my strategy about becoming salesman of the year with them. I carried my pager with me to give the account an added feature to my service. I guaranteed a response in 30 minutes. I did everything to make my clients know I was working for them. I started carrying a large photo of my family in the front of my presentation binder. That distinguished me from anybody in the practice. I also decided to be non-confrontational, the peacemaker, the one that no one hates.

Don and I grew from our working relationship and I listened to him because he had been a district manager for seven years, although he was only two years older than me. He always preached getting his people promoted was the key to his success. If you promote others you look good because you're developing your people, and if your people are promoted you must be doing the right thing to get promoted yourself.

Don had become a good person to work for and also a person to learn from. He would tell me what people considered a weak point. I asked what characteristics did the top sales rep and others of great success have. He gave me a list, along with his personal beliefs. He would also share investment tips. Don never spent a commission check he earned. He invested it. The thing I was most impressed with was how this 29 year old showed me how he would be a millionaire by 50. He put it on paper and showed me a plan. I have since incorporated that in my lifestyle.

By the end of the third quarter I was in full gear. I had picked up where I left off at my previous company. I was confident that I could win the major prize. Don had invited me to work a convention in Denver. He grew up there so he wanted

The Key to Stopping the Violence

me to see his hometown. On the plane, Don told me I had won sales rep of the quarter in the region and that I had moved to No. 7 in the company. Three months left and I smelled the finish line.

In Denver I met Don's grandparents and saw the house he grew up in and its swimming pool. Don explained how you could tell a low middle class white community: look at the cars, everybody has model a from the early '80s and late '70s. I still use that as a barometer. He told me how he had videotaped his grandfather as Don asked him questions about his life. I later purchased a video camera and did the same thing with my loved ones.

On the flight back I asked Don if he were shooting for the No. 1 spot what strategy would he use. He gave me a list that included strategies to get accounts to buy products. I took what he said literally and started selling like a mad man. After October, I was No. 3 and in November I was No. 2. December arrived.

I felt nervous. What if I actually reached my goal? I gathered myself and worked morning until night, making sure everyone ordered everything. There was no tomorrow. I willed myself to win, I had to. For the second time in my sales career -- the first being when I won a trip at the other company -- I checked myself into the emergency room suffering from exhaustion.

Victory!

Right after December ended I knew I had made the President Club but I wanted more. I didn't know if I had won salesman of the year. I woke up thinking about it. I slept dreaming about it. This would correct the wrongs at OBT Co. Plus, it was a perfect way to show myself and a Fortune 500 company that a black man could deliver excellence by doing the things that my white predecessors had done to get to the next level. I knew by being No. 1 nobody could refute the fact that I did everything possible to make my career go forward. I would be the best in the country.

Don called an emergency meeting at a restaurant in the south suburbs. The meeting included all the members of our district. I figured Don would announce me as salesman of the year along with my promotion to field sales trainer. Don pulled us together after dinner and announced that he would be leaving the district as manager and would take a higher position in another end of the business. We all wished him well. He said they would be interviewing for a new district manager and the position would be filled in January.

Then he announced that a member in the district would be getting a promotion to senior sales representative. Me. I sat disappointed because I had never heard of anybody getting a promotion to Senior Sales Rep. What was this, a promotion that had no added responsibility? How could all these other people get field sales training positions and district management positions and I got this bullshit promotion. I walked over to Don and asked him what the promotion was all about. He basically blew over the question. I still didn't want to bring race or other factors into the picture.

The next month Don was gone and Brian, a region manager, called a meeting to introduce us to our new sales manager, Vernon Turner. I was happy because he was black and figured he would be able to understand my efforts.

At our meeting Vernon seemed to be very tense. Brian said that he promoted Vernon because he liked him. Vernon was the last candidate from the old sales reps to get promoted. If this opportunity had passed him up he would have probably quit.

In our first meeting Vernon knew he had walked into a hot market. Chicago was the second-ranked district in the company. He had a full staff of reps who had been around more than a year. He had the No. 1 and No. 2 reps in the company, Sally and myself, complemented by good, solid reps. In our first conversation I told Vernon that my career was geared to become a district manager and I wanted to work toward that as soon as possible. He looked at me and said, "I'm not interested in your career. I'm interested in making you a better sales rep."

I looked around as though he didn't understand what I said. I was one the best sales rep in the company and I wanted to get to the next level. But Vernon again replied that his job was to make me better in the field. So I knew right then something wasn't right, but I figured he was new and nervous and I would work it out later.

As time passed, we geared up for the national sales meeting, and I went down to Atlanta, not knowing what to expect. They still hadn't confirmed that I had won the company's biggest award. That afternoon before the national sales meeting/dinner. Brian, my region manager, pulled me to the side to let me know I had won the big one! It was finally

The Key to Stopping the Violence

confirmed: all the things I had worked for had come together. I was the first black in the company to be recognized as the best of the best. That gave me enough time to think about what to say on stage that night. That night during the ceremony other events built up to the big award. I had won several awards earlier, including The President Club, Sales Rep of the Quarter, Winners Club and a company gold ring. The, vice president of sales, introduced me as the hardest-working person he had ever met. As he invited me to speak before the president and other board of Directors and the entire sales force. In that speech I generated a feeling of team and opportunities within one of the world greatest companies. Tears flowed in the audience and the speech ended with a thunderous response. Managers and sales reps alike complimented me on the speech that I came to be known by. I figured then my road ahead would open up like it had for other sales reps.

Don and Brian said they were down at the bar later that night and cried again because of the unfortunate things that had occurred in my life. After this I knew I would be on my way to management. Ranks again changed when John Francis got another promotion to regional manager. It was a move that I felt favored me, because after, all John did hire me.

John came back to Chicago. He started getting reports of representatives who didn't care too much for Vernon's management style. John called me at home one morning and asked about Vernon's interaction with me. I felt like I was between a rock and a hard place because I didn't want to dog a black man. I told John that Vernon was working hard and I was being patient with him. But the whites in the district had no patience for him.

After Vernon had been on the job about six months, I decided to go back to him to discuss development and career advancement. What motivated me to do so was when I went on the President Club trip with the top reps in the company. Donna and me were the only blacks there and some of the white guys told me how their managers were developing them and how their careers had to have goals and timelines in writing.

I listened to the top managers talk about certain employees and I realized they had handpicked certain people to be managers. I spoke to several people about Vernon's style and they said it wasn't consistent with the company credo. So after coming home I sat down and worked out a strategy. John had picked up some of his old tricks at meetings. At a party after a meeting he called out during the night that he wanted me to show my teeth because he couldn't see me. John was known for making racial and sexist remarks after he had a few drinks.

I went back to Vernon and asked again for him to help me develop a strategy to get promoted into management. Vernon said he felt I wasn't ready yet and that wasn't his focus.

A Corporate Nightmare

I was having another great year, as I made the President Club again and was the region's No. 1 rep for the second year. It was becoming very obvious to the sales reps and others that I wasn't getting my due. After the new year I decided it was time for me to make a move to another company to get what I had worked so hard for. I called a meeting with John and invited Vernon to attend because it was obvious that Vernon didn't know what his job entailed. When I got to the office Vernon and John had already been meeting. I called for a win-win agenda that would get some questions answered. I asked Vernon what he thought his job consisted of. His answer wasn't like what he said before. His job, he explained, was to develop his sales people and help move their careers ahead. Then John and Vernon started making excuses about how they were both new in their positions and they were pleased with the way I approached this situation because it was productive for them. I let them know that I had been there for 2 1/2 years and the past year was a waste because we didn't do anything to develop my management skills. They promised to get an agenda to me in two weeks that would put me on the path to be a sales trainer. There were people who were trainers after their first year. I was the most successful rep over the last two years and I was still a senior sales rep.

After two weeks I didn't get the development program so I sent a follow-up memo to both of them. Finally, in April 1991, I received the program and the development items went into September. Up to that point I was doing all types of assignments. The paperwork was intense but I wanted to move up. Vernon said he was extremely impressed with all of my development work and reports.

At the same time I was being honored in *Dollars & Sense*, a national magazine that honored the country's Best and Brightest Top Business and Professional Men for 1991. The president of Star Inc. told John to sponsor a table at the event to show support

The Key to Stopping the Violence

for my achievement. John, Vernon and their wives were to join my family during the celebration.

A week before the dinner, we had a sales meeting in Florida. Vernon told me that he knew I had worked extremely hard for the sales trainer job and that he hoped I would be promoted in September. Then he said, "By the way, Steve has just been promoted. I wanted to tell you before they announced it."

Steve was another white sales rep. I barely knew who he was, except that he had been asking me what made me successful.

Vernon handed me a pile of papers and said he needed all of the work redone because John was looking for improvement from him so he had to pass it on for my development.

"You've been telling me for the last six months that my work was impressive. Now you're going to hand me all this work at once and say redo this for you." I told him he was just playing a game and walked away.

Later, I was still mad, I pulled John over and asked what had he thought about all the work I had done for my development program. John said that he was satisfied, but it would probably take until spring 1992 before it was complete.

"I'm not working on anything for a year because a year is forever," I responded. "I don't know anyone else in the company who worked a year. Plus, how could you know what's going on with my development when Vernon just gave me all the paperwork to do over again?"

John sat there looking like an asshole caught in a lie. "You know Edge, nobody can question your sales ability but you have a certain 'E.J. way' about doing things. "You have a certain ability that's almost to natural." I knew at that point he was trying to say you black people know how to sell anything. I see the way you people sell drugs and stolen goods on the news. But I had to address him intelligently even though he was addressing me like a fool off the street.

"John I disagree. I can sell the Star Inc. method better than anyone in the company. I don't appreciate your belittling my years of work."

John backed off and promised to look into what was going on. Later that day John had Vernon cornered and was breathing fire. All I wanted to know was what I had to do to reach my goal. Vernon wouldn't look at me for the entire plane trip home. At that point I didn't care because what they were doing was wrong. I didn't see them again until the night of the *Dollars & Sense* magazine award. Vernon, John and their wives shouldn't have come because it was obvious they didn't want to be there. Donna said not only did they not speak to anyone in my family, they all got up and left early without saying goodnight or anything. I noticed it from the honorees' table up front and took mental notes. These were the representatives of a major corporation.

Donna and I flew to Germany the next day for the President Club trip. From there we flew to Italy and met the other winners. We even rode in the gondolas. That night we had dinner with the Stars of Star Inc. and their wives, including, the company president.

The president and his wife were magnificent the entire trip and I listened to him with a careful ear to understand what made him successful throughout his career. Here I am again traveling around the world, learning about new people and cultures. But at the same time, while I'm at home, I can't get the monkey off my back. The same monkey that has held down so many black corporate types. I figured I had battled with these two clowns enough and I would move on to the next phase of my life. But there was also a side of me that didn't want to give in this time. Vernon and John had never done what I've done. They hadn't won anything. Why would I do all this work and then give up.

We left Italy on the Orient Express and went to Paris. It was a beautiful journey with the best that life has to offer. In Paris, we stayed at one of the finest hotels. We visited all the landmark sights and had dinner at the Eiffel Tower. I networked with the top managers and salesmen. Many of us had made the previous trip together, so our wives knew each other well. The managers would always ask about Vernon and John. Rumors spread quickly in the sales arena, especially when there was not a solid manager. There were reps who were shocked that I wasn't at least a sales trainer. It became very embarrassing to answer the same questions, including the infamous "Why aren't you promoted yet?" Many times on that trip I was going to discuss my concerns about the situation with the president. On our flight back, Donna and I were given first class seats. I returned home on Saturday afternoon, and after unpacking, I opened my mail to find that most of my problems were still ahead of me. Vernon had sent me a letter titled "Customer Complaints and Unsatisfaction." I read this letter in disbelief as it outlined what a terrible job I had done in taking care of my customers. Then I

The Key to Stopping the Violence

received a phone call from one of the customer service people who said that Vernon had all of my personal phone mail calls directed to him while I was in Europe. He took my calls and pretended that these people had called him to complain. When in reality, they were calling for me just to request routine service. What made it so bad was that he sent the letter to John Francis and his new boss. This was the first information she received about me. At the end of the memo, it stated that he knew I wanted to be a trainer but how could I handle that job without being able to take care of customers.

I was so pissed that I almost thought about going to the projects, looking up a few homeboys and ending this bullshit. I knew Vernon and John had gotten together and covered their asses. They were setting me up. I called some of the top people in the field to get different opinions and advice. One rep gave me the best: I couldn't win a head-to-head confrontation with management. He advised me to get so positive that they couldn't stand it, even if I had to fake it.

The first thing I did was explain to John and Vernon that my mother had undergone heart surgery while I was in Europe and was living with me and Donna during her recovery. I also explained that because of this and other factors, I would prefer to be responsible for only my regular duties at this time. That threw Vernon and John off. The slave nor his master knew what to do. Vernon almost seemed to nervous to talk to me. He tried to apologize for the memo because he knew he was wrong. But I already knew that he was wrong. I also knew that he had done the worst thing you could do. He was a "sell out brother" who had no back bone. I continued to do my job and they constantly tried to check my head. They wanted to see what was going on and make sure I wasn't going to sue. I had put all my ducks in a row by contacting the NAACP, Urban League, Operation Push and Star Inc.'s Human Resources and Personnel Department. I knew I had a strong, documented case in my record.

No Justice, No Peace: Rodney King Verdict

My sales calls sometimes took me to a small town in Illinois called Bourbannais, near Kankakee. Three or four of my smaller accounts were located in a mall there. One trip on a sales call, I took my brochures, calendar folder and small briefcase, as usual. After the visits, I planned to head home, which was about 45 minutes away.

SILENT CRY

I decide to sit down in the mall and review my call schedule. Two security guards, one white middle-aged female and one white late-middle aged male, approached me. The normal response for a happy-go-lucky salesman would have been, "Hi, how is your day?" But before I could get that out, the female officer said very harshly, "What are you doing here?" I laughed as though she had made a mistake. Then she asked again, "What are you doing here?" I explained my job and what I did. But she quickly accused me of solicitation and asked me to leave. I told her that I was doing my job and handed her a business card. Surely this was some kind of mistake. I walked to my first account. When I came out, they were standing right there. I said to myself, they are not following me, so I went to my next account on the other side of the mall. They followed me the entire length of the mall. When I came out of that appointment, the two security people were standing right there. So as I started walking I turned around and asked, "What is the problem? "The white lady said, "You are the problem," then they called the head of security.

At that point, my accounts were watching me, the white shoppers were watching, and kids pointed at me like I was on crime watch. The security guards had done just what they wanted to do: aggravate a black man then make him look like a trouble maker. They knew I hadn't done anything, but embarrassing me made their day and was a way to say that I didn't belong there.

After their boss got there and assessed the situation, he confirmed that I hadn't done anything but he didn't reprimand them. He had a smirk on his face as he walked away. I felt humiliated and powerless.

Unknown to me, my lack of power in that situation was echoed more than 2,000 miles away. I walked out of the mall angry and upset. To cool my spirit, I turned on the radio just as a special report came over the airways about the four Los Angeles police officers responsible for the Rodney King beating. They had been acquitted and the people of the Los Angeles had taken to the streets.

Why do white people say "go to school and get a job?" You only become what some whites call "a high priced nigger" -- white America can't have it both ways.

The Key to Stopping the Violence

Omitted Facts

Vernon had a meeting with me in the fourth quarter of 1991 to go over year-end business. I always knew that he was being set up by John to get me out of the picture. John figured if Vernon fired me I would fight him and with all the other reps hating Vernon and filing complaints that would leave John in a good position to fire Vernon, killing two birds with one stone. I understood that, so at my meeting with Vernon I told him my life was based on good things and bringing a black man down was not one of them.

In my view, Star Inc. was not exactly a progressive company when it came to blacks. There were no blacks on the board or in upper management. There were only two blacks in management, period, and neither of them had ever hired another black person since I had been with the company. As a matter of fact, a black district manager was promoted to regional manager and blocked the first hire in her new position, that of a black guy. White manager, said he didn't understand why the black would block the hiring when he wanted the guy desperately." Anybody could tell the company had a serious problem when it came to hiring minorities." The white manager stated.

In our meeting, I told Vernon that I didn't think the company would promote any blacks. John entered the room at the end and he said he wanted Vernon and I to work out our differences. I told John that everything was fine and that I couldn't be better. After I left Vernon told John all of the details of my private conversation with him. He told John that I said we didn't have enough blacks at Star Inc. Management called me and said that I was right, they needed to do a better job in that area. Vernon decided to take credit for that observation. John ordered him to write me a memo that said I was not promoted because of my development, not because I was black. I took the memo in stride and didn't fight back.

What amazed me more than anything was the number of people who were aware of Vernon's strange behavior. The other reps left because they had had enough. My attitude was that I deserved to be there as much as anybody else. But I had no one backing me, nor did I have a mentor. Case in point: A position opened in another division under Don Carr, but before I even found out about it, Don and John had filled it. I asked Don about the position and he said everything had to start with your manager. I knew that Vernon was never going to help me and that John was the overseer of the plantation.

A Successful Change of Direction

The status quo continued at Star Inc. until spring 1992. That's when they added another black sales rep in the Midwest. He asked why so many people had numerous positive things to say about me. He also asked, "But why are you just a senior sales rep after four years?" I told him I didn't have an answer. As he watched and learned, it became apparent that John had a problem with all blacks and Vernon felt good because he was the only black in the company in his position.

I stayed at Star Inc. because it allowed me to do other things. I had always enjoyed speaking to kids, so I went to the schools and community centers and spoke about issues dealing with life and death. I started to do more public speaking until my brothers and I decided to develop a company that would help young people find the proper resources they needed to help them through high school and college. I continued to use the company name, even though I was being treated like dirt. But I was telling the kids they could make it and be what they wanted to be. At that same time, I had to create this wall around me to keep my sanity.

After speaking on one campus the students said I reminded them of someone named Les Brown. I had never heard of him, but they said he was a motivational speaker. Around that time, he was holding a seminar at the UIC Pavilion. Tookie invited me to attend and that's when I decided I wanted to speak for a living. I saw Les Brown in front of thousands of whites and blacks, doing exactly what I had a passion to do: I knew I wanted to speak for a living to teach and help others reach their potential. The only reason I ever wanted to be a trainer or manager was to help others obtain the success I had. The only thing I couldn't be was white. I knew all the time that if I had been a white male with the same track record, they would have made sure something was done.

The new black sales rep continued to ask me why I wasn't promoted. I assured him if he hung around long enough he would see why and also experience what blacks in corporate America were facing. In many ways, I had become a trailblazer by being the first inner city player recruited in college. I was the one who forced my previous company to send two blacks on the trip. Also

The Key to Stopping the Violence

the first black to win salesman of the year at this company. Continuing to push forward puts me in control of my own destiny. The new black rep realized what I had been going through when he returned from training and the national sales trainer said that he wasn't a team player and that he used unprofessional language in the training sessions.

I learned valuable lessons over that five-year period and it made me stronger and more humble. At the same time I continued to strive for excellence because that's what makes the difference between best and average. Success is a long road, and I knew I couldn't be afraid to challenge racism, apathy or even my own complacency.

The Letter

I would always think about all the people I knew who were dying. It seemed like I had attended over 100 funerals and I was getting mentally and physically drained. Ray and Deke were constantly on my mind and I knew I had promised Ray that I would write the book, "From Ghetto to Glory," that we talked about our entire lives. I didn't believe that I could write it, but I was telling everybody I knew that I would. I used this as a tactic to psych myself up for it.

One day in the summer of '92, I found a letter that Ray had written to me back in 1982, after he left W.I.U. The letter talked about how he didn't think he would make it, but he knew I would. Ray said that it reminded him of "From Ghetto to Glory." I knew at that moment I had to write our story. But, because I'm not a writer, I came up with more excuses about needing a ghostwriter or someone to help me.

I called T.D. and Vince and asked them to have all of the Thee Family Brothers meet to talk about Deke and all the others who died. We never got together so I started writing and with the encouragement of Donna, I continued. As time passed, the newspapers were continuing to fill up with other stories of violence, black victims and bodies.

Mandatory Layoffs

In 1993 Mr. Rose another one of my accounts who had a very successful business and a successful outlook on life. I was fortunate to know him and sell his account. Mr. Rose was a very straightforward person who let you know exactly what was on his mind. I wanted to know what and how he did it, so often times I would take him lunch. That way I had his undivided attention.

I decided to open up to Mr. Rose because I wanted his advice. I told him I had interests other than working for Star Inc. He said he wanted to share some reality with me.

"E.J.," Mr. Rose said, "it's time your people look past just working for these companies because there are signs that say times will be very bleak for black people. Hell, my next door neighbor is one of the top men at a major corporation. He makes a lot of the key and final decisions when it comes to cutbacks and downsizing jobs within his company. He told me the other day that the order in which people will be fired is black men first, black women second, then white women, and white men last.

"My neighbor sits in a very influential seat at the top of this company," Mr. Rose continued, "and he said black people had their days in the '60s and those days are over. This is the reality you have to live with and deal with."

I knew he was telling me the truth because he had no reason not to. I respected what he told me. Those are more reasons why black people, including me, have to utilize all of our talent and resources to make the best for ourselves.

The Boss From Hell

Vernon took away the very things that kept me going. While training, some of the new trainees commented the exceptional job I had done. One young lady said that her training with me was more effective than the previous three trainers she had worked with.

The news reached the top executives and they gave me high praise. However, Vernon and John stopped me from training in all of 1993. Again, my complaint to upper management went unnoticed. I kept trying to give Vernon the benefit of the doubt because he was black. I learned the hard way that just because you're black, doesn't mean you're a brother.

After several episodes of career sabotage, Vernon did the unthinkable. He went to the white establishment and said that my community involvement was interfering with my job. He said the very opposite of what community was all about. Even the company was in favor of improving the places in which they live. To have a black man forget he is black and abandon the people and area he came from is unacceptable.

The Key to Stopping the Violence

I knew Vernon was a bigger part of the problem than a man putting a gun to my head because he was doing a character assassination. He tried to take all I had done and make a joke of it or make it appear to be a mishap, even my love for my own people.

My resume spoke for itself, but I learned the hard way that there were few blacks commanding what I was qualified to earn - well over six figures. There were even fewer companies that hired blacks in their highest-paying sales positions. So, I became trapped between being too good and too black. One interviewer even had the gall to ask me if my qualifications were real.

Depression

I knew that the violent ending of all the people before me could be my fate if I didn't turn toward God and family. What happened to Ice Cold Cool Slick Curtis, to Ray and the many others, happened because they lost view of that light at the end of the tunnel. Without that hope there was nothing.

I was losing focus. After all I knew and had learned, I too felt smothered by the pressure and became seriously depressed. Vernon and John were applying the pressure so easily because they had the power. It's like telling a baby what he can and can't do because it's your house, your candy, and your everything else. The only thing the baby can do is cry.

I still felt that there were enough good whites in the company that if I got to the right ones, they would have to respond. I explained how Vernon was destroying my career. I wasn't going to run even if it was one of the largest companies in the world. I said to myself, "Damn it, I'm black in America and proud of it. All they can do is fire me, they can't kill me, because as a people, we're already dead."

I had to get away from the corporate violence, its vicious system and all of its ponds. I had to make my own dream as I made it through to the finish line. I had to do what God intended me to finish because the stories I wrote needed to be told.

PART V
In Memory Of

Ben Wilson -- Although I never met Ben Wilson, our stories crossed paths because of a number of events. Ben grew up in the inner city of Chicago and basketball became the game that would give him his dream of becoming a winner. He attended Simeon High School, where he became a premiere big man on the basketball scene. Ben was going into his senior year, and was the No.1 player in the country.

Ben was a very generous young man, but above all, he was a son and a true gentleman. However, like a lot of other soon-to-be-successful young black men, Ben had one thing that worked against him -- ignorant brothers running the street. And that ignorance played itself out in one of the most tragic events in Chicago's sports history.

On Tuesday, Nov. 20, 1984, at around 1:00 in the afternoon during school Ben and some friends decided to walk to a small candy store that was popular with Simeon students. He went in the store, made his purchase and intended to head back for practice, after walking his girlfriend to the bus stop. Meanwhile, some gang members from a rival school had come up to Simeon to harass the students. As he left the store, he encountered two teenage gangbangers who flashed their gang's signals. One of them made a comment to Ben about what could happen to him if he chose to violate the gang by walking past them. Ben tried to go out of the store but one of the young gangbangers pulled out a pistol and shot him twice in the chest.

The Key to Stopping the Violence

Ben fell in the doorway while his girlfriend frantically screamed for help. An ambulance took Ben to a hospital emergency room on the South Side, but he had to wait a long time before being treated. Ben died that next mourning. The suspects tried to flee, but were picked up later.

Ben's death and funeral was a reflection of what had gone wrong with our city and the country. As I watched his wake on TV, I thought about Deke and the other tragic things that happened in my life. I thought about how fragile life is. I watched Mrs. Wilson as she appeared on TV, trying to address the gang problems. I watched her talk with pride and confidence about what her son had accomplished and how she felt the country needed to respond to stop the senseless killing of black boys.

Around that time, I had just graduated from college and was working on the South Side, involved in the community. I worked with three young 6th graders -- who passed out flyers and assisted me with other general jobs that kept them busy and off the street. They were adorable boys who I treated like little brothers. They would spend Christmas Eve with me, helping me put my daughter's toys together.

Ralph, one of the little boys, was bright and fun. As I got to know him better he opened up and shared some information that hit me right between the eyes. He talked about how his cousin was his hero. I asked what made his cousin special. "He killed Ben Wilson because Ben was the 6'8" giant." Ralph told me that his cousin had a lot of bragging rights (rank) in prison because of what he had done. I could tell that as much as Ralph admired me, he loved his cousin. I struggled to find the right words to express that Ben's life was taken by a thug and that his cousin should rot in hell.

I continued to work with the boys. When I moved on to OBT Co., I stayed in touch with them as much as I could. As they entered high school, I still felt I couldn't say enough to change Ralph's mind about his "role model." A few years later, while they were still teenagers. I learned one of the other boys was in jail and Ralph was doing time for murder. Looking back, I feel I could have done more to help save them both.

At OBT Co. I met Mrs. Wilson. I sold her Ben Wilson Community Foundation an office product. She told me how much she missed her son and how I reminded her of him. She seemed preoccupied with making sure her younger kids were protected from the violence that Ben died from. It hurt to think that my own mother left and didn't stick with me through thick and thin. But Ben's mother was standing tall, even in his death. I always wanted to do something special for her to show that I cared. But then there was a part of me that felt terrible because I knew the person who killed her son probably had no remorse.

Eight years after Ben was murdered I listened to Nick Anderson from the NBA's Orlando Magic, who was discussing a group he helped start in Chicago called "Boyz From The Hood." The organization was started to help the young men in the community. I went to a meeting and heard what Nick, fellow NBA player Marcus Liberty and pro football players Mickey Pruitt and Russell Maryland had to say. These million-dollar athletes were suffering from some of the same problems I encountered in corporate America and those faced by blacks in the street; ignorant brothers. They couldn't escape the silent cry of death and destruction that was taking place with their friends and loved ones. Nick and the rest of the athletes wanted to make a difference. They have a commitment to make a difference and give back to the community and I have a commitment to help them. Ben you will always live in our hearts.

Michael Bey--I hadn't seen Michael or Jerry or Reggie since Western IL. days. But I kept up with them through T.D. and Tookie. T.D. was just telling me that they both still played in the semi-pro and the USFL. I was disappointed that with all Michael's talent I had never seen him play. Michael was in the suburbs what Mitchell Brookins was in the Public league the best. Our birthday was the same day, March 19th. We always joked and said we would celebrate together and turn Chicago out. We never had a chance to because a tragic event almost took 12 family members of the Bey family. The family was living in North Chicago when a carbon monoxide poison over took them. When one of the family members opened the door to the house he found his entire family sick to their stomachs or unconscious. Everyone on the first floor was saved, but Michael and a companion were found in the basement. His friend recovered but Michael never regained consciousness. This was another gifted brother who died at 25-years-old for no reason.

Marie and Danielle "Nookie" Hudson -- Marie was a very slender lady, about 5'2", 105 pounds. Her family moved into Ray's building on the corner. The oldest of Marie's children was Loretta, then Carl, Paula, Nookie and Leslie. As we grew up, Ray and I became a thorn in the sides of many people, including Marie and her kids. Once Ray threw some eggs and

The Key to Stopping the Violence

messed up all of the Hudson kids' Easter clothes. Carl told Ray's mother, Mrs. Grandberry, and Ray beat Carl up for telling.

I'll never forget the time Marie yelled at Ray and me for fighting her son. In anger she hollered out that we were going to wind up dead or in jail for messing with so many people. I saw the frustration in her face and although I had heard her say those words before, this time I know she meant it. We would fight one hour and be friends the next.

I always tried to show Marie that I was growing up, especially later in high school and college. Marie kept her job at Spiegel where she had worked for years. Nookie had her first baby and dropped out of high school.

Whenever I was home from college I would knock on Marie's door to catch up with what was going on with her kids. Nookie, Paula and Loretta were all nice girls. Marie eventually moved out of Ida B. Wells projects and moved to a apartment complex. Nookie stayed in the old apartment, in the 'hood.

One night Marie went out and when she returned she was met by a unidentified person. Marie started screaming for help but was dragged into an abandon building. She didn't show up for work the next day and her body later was found after an anonymous phone call. Her body had been badly beat.

The news devastated the Hudson family; everyone knew except Nookie. She had left her kids with Debbie and was gone on a short trip with her friend and couldn't be reached. Nookie had always told Debbie that if anything ever happened to her mother she would die.

As they arrived home, Debbie, in tears, met Nookie and her friend on the sidewalk to break the news. Nookie went into a panic, crying, and put her head in her hands. Out of nowhere a man appeared, walked up behind her, called her a name and repeatedly stabbed her in the back and chest in broad daylight. Nookie fell to the ground as he took off running. Some of the men took off after him, caught him and beat him. Nookie died in Debbie's arms.

In less than 24 hours, two family members were murdered in different parts of Chicago by two different people. Marie left five children and Nookie left two boys. There was a double funeral that left the community in shock. One of Nookies sisters has her two boys as she takes care of her own kids.

Michael King -- The first time I saw Michael King we were little boys, about 9 years old. Michael was on 37th Place, across the street from where I lived at 628 E. 37th Pl. He was being beaten up and cursed out. Over the years Michael's name became synonymous with ass kickings. People would pick fights with him wherever he went. The thing that amazed me was the gracefulness with which Michael accepted the ass kicking. He was even beat by a girl one day. If he ever hit back, everybody in the backyard would have thought they were justified in beating him up some more.

Michael was the oldest of what we called a "weird family." We made it part of our day to belittle him with names and everybody talked about his mama and daddy. Michael's eyes and face had more scar tissue than a boxers. There were so many times over the years that I saw even Michael's father beat him up as they had heated arguments. As he grew older, he became an alcoholic. His face and body became even more a mountain of scars and abuse. Michael had death written all over him.

Michael never had a bike. I never saw him play baseball or football. The only time we let him play with us was when we allowed him to chase us when we played games like "Funky Michael King." If he touched you, you also became funky. Most of the time if he touched you, he'd get beat up again for touching your cloths.

Then one day the unthinkable happened. His family moved next door to my family in the same front hallway. As I grew older, I had a sincere fear of Michael because I had to see him in the hallway our apartments shared. He would tell me that he would catch me in the hallway, so while the other brothers harassed Michael, I was skeptical of what he would do to me if I was caught in the hallway. After they moved, the verbal attacks from Ray, Lamar, Frankie and me became more vicious. One day we decided to play karate with Michael King. We started playing gently until Ray got carried away and struck Michael in the back. Michael bent over on one knee, crying as I went over to help him up. Ray picked up a garbage can and dropped it on Michael's back. I stopped Ray, feeling bad for the things we had done to Michael. He cried and shouted that all he wanted was to be accepted not have everyone always beat on him. I tried to stand there even though Michael smelled like hell. I walked him to his back porch.

The one thing that Michael had a passion for was swimming. When we were younger you couldn't keep him from the pool. You couldn't get me in because the big boys always dunked us and tried to drown us. Besides, people would piss in

The Key to Stopping the Violence

the water and sometimes you'd see shit turds floating in the water. Or somebody would cut their feet because somebody would throw broken glass in the pool at night.

As I grew older, I would see Michael, bottle of liquor in hand, at Madden Park, watching us play baseball. He had become an alcoholic. We started talking more and he complimented me on my play. He would drift off talking about what it would have been like to be "normal." He would tell me how good he could swim and how swimming was the best thing in the world. He also told me how he wanted a job with the Park District in Madden Park. Eventually he got a job as a lifeguard at Madden Park. However, he said the only problem was that the gangbangers knew when he received his check, so he had to pay them to work there. He enjoyed his job, but only made enough to buy whiskey; the gangsters stole everything else.

By my senior year in high school, oftentimes I would come home and find him sleeping on the cold concrete stairs. I would plead his case with his mother. By his early 20s, he had no teeth and looked like a 50-year-old man. One day Michael was found slain in a pool with a knife in his heart. He died doing what he loved most: watching over other peoples' lives.

"Munchkin" -- Unlike Mitchell Brookins, Chris Hinton and Lamar Lewis, Munchkin was recruited by a Division III school. I went to his apartment one day and he discussed his life and concerns. He wanted to help his family and friends to escape from the streets of Chicago. Munchkin did escape, but like many of us, drugs had permeated people close to him, specifically a close friend.

After he earned his college degree, Munchkin relocated to a different city and got a job in corporate America. The wrong crowd was after his friend and Munchkin knew that if he stayed on the low end back in Chicago, he might become a murder statistic. So he sent for his friend to come live a peaceful middle class life. Once there, however, the friend began hanging with the low lifes until drug money was owed to some people-- just like the people in Chicago.

Desperate and in need of drugs and money, the friend was willing to set Munchkin up, the person who saved him. A time was set when the robbers could come into Munchkin's house and rob him. They did just that, and also robbed him of his life. Muncskin died for the love of his friend.

Darnell Harper #33 -- "Harp" was what the Lindblom crowd called Darnell. He was a senior when I was a sophomore

SILENT CRY

at Lindblom. Darnell Harper was a tall, slender running back with long steps, almost like a gallop. In my sophomore year, I worked hard to become a starter. Harp gave me a running style I could identify with because he was so thin, like me. The sophomore team would go to the varsity games with our jerseys on and sit at the Public League stadiums. Once, Harp ran an interception back about 50 yards. Then he ran a touchdown from scrimmage in the backfield. From that time on, I wanted to be just like Harp, #33. I would talk about him all day at school. Sometimes I followed him around to see how he acted. He seemed to be quiet and in the background, never taking credit for the things that he did well. He always dressed in a T-shirt and blue jeans. I went and stood in for the same spot he stood in the yearbook varsity team picture. I had to have that number, #33, in high school and in college. That next season after he graduated, and I wore his number. He played for Lindblom in the prestigious Public League versus Catholic League all star game. I would go down to the practices the summer after my sophomore year to watch what was the best talent in the city. Harp and my good friend, Lindblom's captain, Frank White, were Lindblom's selections to that team. In practice, I remember Frank White, a linebacker, plugging the hole and Harp dove up the two hole, over the guard. I saw a cloud of dust come up and heard the loudest hit, I have ever heard in my life. It was so loud that I was actually afraid that Harp was knocked out. As the dust cleared, Harp was knocked back three or four yards but he stayed on his feet as he broke around the corner for a touchdown. The crowd applauded both Frank's hit and his teammate's run. I stood there with a mixture of excitement and pride for those two.

I'd heard that he was working in Chicago. He would have never known of this kid who came behind him with an abundance of love and respect that had developed over the years. People did remember my admiration for him. That's why I received a dreadful call from a former Lindblom student who said he knew Harp "was" one of my heroes. I asked him what did he mean by was. That's when he explained that Harp had died and the cause was not known. We attended the funeral to pay our last respects to whom I felt to be one of the best athletes I've ever seen play. He was 32 when he passed away. "We love you, Harp, though you are not here. Your courageous play in the game of football helped me make courageous plays in the game of life. Thanks for it all. E.J."

The Key to Stopping the Violence

Toni Borders -- My wife Donna always talked about her look-a-like cousin Toni and showed me pictures. She described the wonderful summers they spent together on the South Side of Chicago as kids. Toni was now living in the extension high-rises across from where I was raised. I finally got a chance to meet Toni before Donna and I got married. I didn't say much but I appreciated her because she was Donna's cousin and I understood the closeness Donna had for her cousins since Donna is an only child.

Toni was supposed to be in our wedding but couldn't for financial reasons. Donna noticed Toni didn't attend the wedding. The next time we saw her, she visited us at our apartment on 119th Street. Donna didn't recognize her; neither did I. She looked so bad, I actually thought she was a boy. Her skin was bad and discolored. She looked hard as if the streets were getting the best of her. Donna said Toni's boyfriend had taken an iron and burned her with it and tied her up and burned her body with cigarettes. Toni was afraid to tell the police because she thought he would kill her.

At age 25, she had been introduced to drugs but had been clean for some time and was trying to get her life together. One night her male cousin stopped by the projects at 2 a.m. He wanted her to walk with him and some friends to the Alco drugstore on 35th Street. As they walked, a jeep pulled up and a group of men jumped out and started shooting. Everyone began running, but Toni was struck in the back and fell face down on the ground. The jeep sped off and Toni died before the ambulance could get her to the hospital.

Toni left behind three children who will barely remember their mother. Her youngest was five months old when she died.

Mooney -- Fred's older sister was fine, wearing her skin tight jeans and pretty smile. They lived in the building behind me. Arlene was one of the first girls in our age group who had a baby. Arlene was a sweetie pie, but she would curse you out if you said the wrong thing. All the younger boys my age had a crush on her. We called her baby boy Mooney. Mooney was a cute little kid who was kind of chunky. He would always be with his little buddy, Booger, who lived in my building. Booger and Mooney were little shorties that seemed like men in little boys' bodies. They would walk around holding their privates at five and six years old. I would always tell Booger to take his little butt in the house because he would be out way after dark. Even though they were shorties, they had seen and been around a lot.

SILENT CRY

One time when Booger was about seven years old, we saw him standing close to my father's car. I thought he was between the cars pissing or something. So Ray, Lamar and me hollered,"Get away from that car." As we said this, a little girl ran one way and Booger came from around the car zipping his pants. I asked him what was he doing and he said that he was trying to get some ass. We started laughing and asked him what did he know about ass.

Mooney would also curse at the older boys. If we told him to do something, he would tell us to kiss his ass.

By sixteen, Mooney was dealing drugs and Arlene was using them. Mooney and the young boys had started selling on their own, cutting out the drug dealers they worked for. That caused tensions because the profits were being split too many ways. Mooney knew that he was marked to be taken out, but that was the nature of the business in the low end. The day after Arlene's birthday, Mooney gave her $20 to buy herself a present. Instead, she went out and bought drugs.

It was an unseasonably hot 80 degrees that November day in 1990. Mooney sat in the bathroom for hours, just staring at the floor. Finally, he walked out of the house wearing a huge Starter jacket. Mooney walked over to the spot where he and his boys sold drugs. One of his enemies spotted him and started walking toward him. Mooney's boys told him to run. Mooney looked at his boys and said, "I'm tired of running, let him do what he's got to do." His boys took off running. The shooter walked up in broad daylight and shot Mooney three times, once in the jaw, the neck and thigh. Mooney fell to the ground. Arlene came running over and put his head in her lap as Mooney took his last breath. The shooter had been out of prison for two years and during that two-year period had managed to murder over 15 other people.

Arlene has been off drugs for four years and has a new son, and a chance to start over.

Nate Chamberlain--Ray always talked about Wes Chamberlain because he felt Wes would be the one to make it to the big leagues. Wes name was always coming up because he had been drafted out of high school and we knew that he had the desire as a little kid to play baseball. The last time I saw Wes was at Ray's funeral in '89.

Wes also had seven brothers and four sisters. His closest brother was Nate. I grew up with T.C., Juan, Larry, David and Wes. Nate was younger, but he would come on my front porch

The Key to Stopping the Violence

and talk to me about Africa and black civilization. "Where did you learn this stuff?" I would ask him. "At school," he would reply. I was impressed with this 7-year-old wonder boy. Nate attended Northeastern Illinois University for grammar school and spoke five languages. He studied under the direction of Dr. Jacob Carruthers and a host of other black scholars.

High school became boring because Nate was so advanced. By age 21, Nate had attended college and was back down in the 'hood hanging out when he was ambushed on the fifth floor of one the Darrow Homes high-rises. The men shot Nate in the shoulder and chest, robbed him and left him to die. Wes was at the center playing basketball when word got back to him. Nate was pronounced dead at the hospital. Four months later, Wes was called up to the big leagues where he still starts for the Boston Red Sox. Nate was loved by many, especially his strong bonded family.

Morris "Buzzy" Ellis -- Buzzy's Dad, Morris Ellis Sr., heads one of Chicago's most successful orchestras, "The Morris Ellis Orchestra." Buzzy came from an upper-middle class family with good values and a strict upbringing. He attended the best schools. His family opened the first black book store in Chicago, where Buzzy worked as a youngster. His younger sister recently graduated from Yale.

I got a phone call and on the line was a long-time friend from high school; she had some bad news. "I just heard that Buzzy was killed over the weekend and his funeral is tonight."

The friend couldn't give me any more information, so I hung up and I began dialing numbers frantically to find out the location of the funeral. I couldn't find anybody. I sat on my bed upset because a high school and college friend had died and I wouldn't be there to pay my last respects.

I sat in my room and prayed for him and his family. I was in disbelief as images of Buzzy flashed through my mind. How could Buzzy be dead? He has a wife and kids who love him. He had been trying to pass the CPA (accounting exam) for a while and finally did. He was one of the brothers who "made it." How would Tracy, and his children manage without him?

The next day I finally had a chance to talk with someone who knew what had happened. They said Buzzy had fallen victim to drugs. The day of his death, he was seen in his old neighborhood. Buzzy was found behind his parents old house with a gunshot to his head. The death was classified as suicide.

SILENT CRY

Buzzy attended a private grammar school, where he excelled. At Lindblom High School he was always well-liked and appreciated. He was popular with his classmates and one of the ladies' favorites. Back in college, Buzzy and his running buddy Gerald "Squirrel" Allen will go down as the most well known members of Kappa Alpha Psi in the school history. When people talked about the Kappa's they really meant Buzzy or Squirrel. In high school Deke wanted to pledge after visiting the campus and seeing Buzzy pledge.

Then I remembered the Buzzy who tried to pull away from the trappings of popularity and influences of his peers partying and ladies. In his heart he wanted to get away from the fast college life, but like many, struggled with what starts off as just college fun.

Recognizing something was wrong in college Buzzy came to Brother Thomas and me after we gained control of our lives. He asked us to pray with him because inside he wanted the moral strength to walk away from the things that could ruin his life.

In Buzzy's last days I can't help but believe in my heart he tried to fight those same negative influences that started innocently in college. But he eventually lost. His father later shared with me that indeed the negative influences in college eventually ruined his son's life. I feel Buzzy represents the battle we're losing in thousands of black men's lives. Buzzy was one of our more intelligent leaders. His life is another example of the urgency with which we have to address the struggle and battle to save our men by helping them handle their problems. Buzzy, you are not forgotten.

Rick Thornton--I met Rick in 1980 at Western Illinois University. I admired everything he stood for. There was something special about him. He was reflection of the best of young black America. First, he was handsome at 6'2", 190 pounds, with a look that most young ladies would die to be close to. He had a kindness that let people near him because they knew his intentions were good. Rick's education was the best of a black middle-class family. He went to St. Catherine Elementary School and Brother Rice High School.

That summer of 1980 I knew Rick was relied on by a lot of people. Rick was there with a large following of friends that depended on him. We needed his courage, his compassion, his friendship and leadership. Rick and Deke pledged the same Phi Beta Sigma Fraternity in 1980. There were women that leaned on him for what he had and what they thought they could get.

The Key to Stopping the Violence

I believe we, unknowingly, could have had a hand in Rick's downfall. We are the people who received so much from him being around. We received his goodness and his love. We received his smile and his willingness to say it was alright. But some of us sat on the side and watched a magnificent man try to tackle his personal problems. We watched a man struggle with having the world at his feet, now barely able to stay afloat. We heard the nasty rumors about his problems, but how many of us sincerely address those concerns?

I say this out of my own regret of not speaking up. I last saw Rick at an art show at Tookie's house. I was late because of family commitments, but I was unable to talk at length with Rick. I was aware of his problems with drugs. And I raised the question to myself: Was I qualified to ask him about what he was doing and why. Well, I was! Because if I love that person I have an obligation to address any concerns to let him know my support is there. I told Rick I came by even though I had other obligations, because it was his art show and I wanted to support what he was doing. Rick, the superstar to everybody else, was just a man himself.

When anyone loses focus of what they need to do, it's like entering a dark hole. Once in that hole, they will wander around in a state of confusion because they can't see. This very state can put some men in the state of suicide. I believe that's what happened to Rick. With his problems, he felt he didn't want to burden us any longer. We didn't rally behind him to let him know that we were there for him, would take care of him and that we loved him. Rick couldn't see that light at the other side. He decided to take his father's gun to a hotel on the South Side of Chicago and end his life. The next morning the fire department sent a limo to his father's house. When it arrived, Mr. Thornton knew that his son had done the unthinkable. Yes, Rick is a small sample of the growing problem in black America. We see the gifts that our youths accumulate and carry with them. We know the world is there if they want to receive it. The youth has given us so much. Their very existence on Earth is a blessing. But when all of our expectations are not met, we continue on with status quo, knowing that our young men are suffering. We fail to give back what they have given us.

Rick was aspiring to become a lieutenant for the Chicago fire Department where he worked for six years as a fireman. He was a loving husband and father of two kids.

251

SILENT CRY

Rick committed suicide in December of 1992. His body was found in a small South Side motel with a gun shot wound to the head. We must learn from this tragic mistake.

Mitchell Brookins-- Mitchell was labeled one of the world's ten fastest human beings, as he dashed the playgrounds of the projects to the pro football fields of the Buffalo Bills. I remember in the eighth grade throwing a touchdown to Mitch during lunch time on the school playground and watching him out run everyone in sight. Racing him as kids was a joke because he left me and the others dazed trying to understand where his speed came from. All of us wanted to play pro ball. Dreaming a dream that so few would ever get to fulfill. But Mitch In grade school was determined. As he watched his favorite football player, O.J. Simpson on T.V. He turned and looked at his mother and said, "I'll be out there one day running touchdowns in the pros. His mother also remembers Mitch telling her the first thing he would do is buy her and his dad a house. Mitch delivered on both promises after running up yardage in the Chicago public league. He dazzled fans at the University of Illinois by becoming a big play specialist and playing in the '82 Liberty bowl and the '84 Rose bowl. He also became a Big Ten wide receiver. He excelled in track as the indoor 60-yard dash champion and finally being drafted in the fourth round and the 94th pick overall. And one of the few men that would have ever beat his hero O.J. in running a 100 yard dash. Most of all Mitch was a good man and a family man that believed in God. On July 20, 1993, on his way home from work . Mitch was killed in an automobile accident while a passenger with a work associate. These are the words I wrote for Mitch at his funeral. "Travel a path that makes you wiser so that the next man following that path may learn from your steps. For your steps may be long but because of you his steps will be shorter. Love all and that love will multiply. Because you are not just any man but you are a black man in America. "Mitch your mother, father, sisters, brothers, kids and friends miss you dearly.

Robert Hurst--I first met Robert in the spring of 1994 at Northern Illinois University. We were both scheduled to speak to the minority graduating class. While we sat next to each other waiting to speak, he introduced himself to me and handed me his business card. During his speech, he stated that it was important for him to be a role model and to take time out of his schedule to show black students the level of success one could attain. After my speech, Robert complimented me on the importance of my

The Key to Stopping the Violence

message, but said that I sounded a bit angry. He didn't know the hell I was experiencing in corporate America.

He extended an invitation for me to visit him at his corporate headquarters to discuss other opportunities for sharing my message. About one month later I took him up on that offer and we had lunch. He explained that he was the president of Ameritech's largest division, with over 42,000 employees. I listened carefully as he gave me pointers on what was needed in black America to achieve success. He touched on many topics such as the need for role models, helping our youth create their own dreams and realizing the consequences of failure. He discussed the tremendous stress of his high-profile career. Toward the end of our meeting, Robert asked me to come into his office. Then he opened his desk drawer and there lay, already opened, an old *Jet Magazine*, dated 1963, with a photograph of some civil rights demonstrators. Robert pointed to a young man in the picture and said, "E.J., that's me. I went to jail for what I believed in. This is the one thing that keeps me focused." I left that day knowing that I had met a brilliant man. More importantly, a friend and role model.

Over the course of the next several months I would send him information about my upcoming book. However, one day, I received an unfortunate call from a student at Northern Illinois University. She explained to me that Robert Hurst had died one week earlier of a heart attack. I called his home to express my regrets to his wife, Joyce. Although I had only known Robert Hurst for a short time, the impact of his conversations will stay with me forever. This was a man committed to helping African-American people of all walks of life. He proved it with his life.

PART VI

The Keys To Stopping The Violence

Achieve Success

I've learned that the only way we will be successful is to create opportunities for our young people to dream. Our youth and many adults have lost that hope. Although I was being smashed against a wall, I still had to find a way to see my dream and purpose fulfilled. I wanted to complete this book more than anything, so I made it a mission and stuck to it even in the worst of times.

We must also learn to trust each other and feel comfortable with seeing another black person achieve success, even if that means passing us up. The only way independence will happen is through family values, respect for our family and the ability to spend and build each other economically. There are white business organizations that network and do business with each other in order to create wealth.

An excellent example of this is a gentleman I met named Brian Hays. Through an international network, called Crown Enterprises, he shows people how to build their own businesses by purchasing products they normally used from themselves. Why does it appear natural for whites to service each other and create wealth, but blacks don't take advantage of the same opportunities? And if we were doing this, our communities would show it.

There are those who would want to work for corporate America and everywhere else. But we need more people who

The Key to Stopping the Violence

want their own businesses and are willing to create opportunities. That means leaving the comfortable job and taking a risk. For example, Wendell Davis and Thomas Sanders, both former football players of the Chicago Bears, are using their star status and business intellect to score big in the business community with their company, ALLSTAR Sports. They are also two excellent examples of good parents and husbands.

The motto for the '90s is not "How much I get paid" but "How many people I employ."

To Ray and Deke, I'm going to go on and live my dream because you've taught me with your lives and deaths that nothing works without trying. If I'm trying, that means that I'm still alive. I LOVE YOU BOTH!

Alive and Trying

I joined the National Speakers Association, Toastmasters International, American Management & Training and Professional Speakers of Illinois. These organizations and a host of others have helped me develop my speaking ability as well as introduce me to key contacts in launching my speaking career.

As I started picking up speaking engagements, the college campuses became a targeted market area of opportunity. Donna assisted me in looking up all the colleges in Illinois. Then we sent brochures out to all the colleges and universities in the state. After getting the brochures out, I followed up with a phone call to make sure the right people on the campus received the brochure and the information. I'm talking about schools and places I had never heard of, like Southern Illinois of Edwardsville University, a pretty big school, but I had only heard of Southern Illinois of Carbondale. These brochures led me to several speaking engagements at places like DePaul, Northern, and Eastern. Phone call after phone call was made to reach the right person or people. The first target was sent to the African American centers or cultural centers. My speeches were geared toward what it would take to be successful in corporate America, plus trying to be a role model, what you can do to focus yourself with studying, family and just being fair to yourself. Because if you treat yourself well, you will treat others well. One lead would usually get me more information about another place. I learned that the black students had the same concerns I had when I was in college. They had a high dropout rate during the first two years, fighting on campus especially on weekends during the parties, and poor study habits that manifested in poor self esteem. Many black students still had unrealistic expectations about life after college. I knew my message was good for high school and college students, young corporate sales people, and married couples.

Keys to Stopping the Violence

To stop something you must first recognize that it must be stopped. Then you must identify what it is, understand why it exists and what negative effect it has on your life; then be strong enough to come up with the solutions to stop it. Ask God for the courage to use those solutions in your life to make a difference. A silent cry does that with violence, which is defined as a destructive force. It is not always physical. Mental violence can be just as destructive. Violence can be tracked in the inner cities of America in the form of gangs, drugs, high school dropout rate and ignorance.

There is also violence on college campuses: lack of self-esteem, misuse and disrespect of other cultures, campus fights, etc. Then there is corporate violence in the form of prejudice, unwillingness to achieve diversity, insecurity, companies stifling employees' growth and a lack of respect for family.

No one can take all the blame for this violence, but at the same time no one can be let off the hook. We are all guilty of perpetuating violence in some way. That is why we must all stop pointing at the next person and find the key to stopping the violence.

1. We must understand what violence is. Violence is the outward symptoms of an inward hurt. Usually this hurt is caused by a need to belong or be loved that has not been met. This causes a person to lash out at others.

2. We must truly want violence to stop. No one can deny that violence is a growing illness in our society. However, if we sincerely desire to stop the violence, we must be willing to sacrifice for those outside of our home, community, church or workplace. The sacrifice may be in the form of time, energy, money, knowledge, love, job creation, and general support.

The Key to Stopping the Violence

3. We must admit that we are the root cause of violence. If you are not actively working toward a solution, you are in fact, part of the problem.

4. Make time to learn more about and understand yourself, your family, your history, and other people of the world. You should be able to answer questions like what do I want to do with my life? What direction do I want my life to go? Do I like me? Why am I the way I am? What habits do I need to change or keep to become the person I want to be, and get the things out of other people and out of life that I need to get?

5. Have a purpose in life. Proclaim a selfless mission to help someone or something worse off than yourself. What mission would you be willing to live for or risk death for.

6. Find a mentor or role model to pattern yourself after. Overcome your fear of rejection and ask questions. Often times people are more than willing to share what they know with someone who has common interests. Be sure only to emulate the positive characteristics you are trying to achieve.

7. You must have ownership - land, business, schools. Without ownership you are still a slave to your circumstances, credit cards, jobs, apartment owners, school systems, etc. When you own, you control what goes in and what comes out. You have the power of making results come out in your favor and the favor of your children.

8. Start building a financial structure. Develop an avenue to regenerate income in the community. By doing business with each other and creating wealth, you build a strong economic infrastructure. These dollars can then be reinvested in the community in the form of jobs, parks, tourism, youth programs, better equipped schools, etc.

9. Educate yourself and share knowledge. We must learn to love God and life. We must teach unity self-respect, respect for others, the value of quality education, unity, and how to empower ourselves, network, and how to plan and organize. We must also teach how to live - diet, hygiene, exercise, child rearing, etc.

10. It is our duty as a people to protect and execute our right and the rights of our children to do everything mentioned above. We must be willing to lie face down in the mud so that our children may cross over on our backs if that's what is necessary for them to dream, create, and achieve success. A black-controlled military presence will neutralize drugs and violence. Training camps can teach young boys and girls what it means to be men and women. Camps can also provide role models, rights of passage, jobs and job skills, sports, enrichment, and much more.

Self-Exam/Workbook

The following 10-question self-test is designed to help readers assess the values, standards, experiences and opinions that have shaped their life and continues to mold their life experiences. Answer each question honestly to gain a deeper understanding of who you are, why you are the way you are and where your aspirations might lead you.

1. Are you as familiar with your family/cultural history as you would like to be? Yes   No
If no, why not?

The Key to Stopping the Violence

2. What is your purpose in life? Why were you chosen to do this?

_____

_____

_____

3. Are you getting what you want out of others? Yes   No

4. Which of your habits would you like to keep/change to get what you want out of life and the people around you?

_____

_____

_____

5. How are you viewed by your peers? (positive/negative and why)

_____

_____

_____

6. What are your short-term (1-3 years) and long-term (4+ years) goals?

_____

_____

_____

7. Who are your mentors? Who do you want to be your mentor(s) and why?

_____

_____

_____

8. Do you look for the positive out of all things? Yes   No   Why or why not?

_____

_____

_____

9. Do you share your money, time and
   resources with those not as fortunate as
   yourself? Yes No

10. List all the things you want to achieve
    in your lifetime and how you will
    accomplish each of them. Make a goal
    sheet if more space is needed. Review it
    each day to stay focused. Make sure
    that you work on your goals each day to
    make them a reality.

_____

_____

_____

Epilogue: To The Black Man

It's sad the way we live in this society. When I say "we"
I'm talking about the black man in America. When I talk about
society I'm talking about a society that is not obligated to help,
but should assist another man to get on his feet. America is the
wealthiest country in the world. America is also a country of
cowards. Cowards are men who have economic and military
power, but choose not to use it for the good of all people.
Cowards are sneaky murderers or those who see weaker, people
drowning in their own blood and turn their heads, pretending not
to notice. Cowards are men who set the laws to ensure that one
race will always be behind the game. When that race does catch
up, the rules of the game change, so that race is left to do things
itself and set rules in ruleless situations.

Black men have to raise their heads up and realize our
destiny is in our own hands. Although I'm a white collar worker
by trade, I still have to be a counselor, teacher, doctor, judge,
law enforcer and guardian, all according to the way the game is
played. It's just like sports. Former Chicago Bulls superstar

The Key to Stopping the Violence

Michael Jordan, one of the best athletes of all time, was whatever his teammates needed at a particular time. He was a scorer, rebounder, point guard, shooter and defensive specialist. Michael was indispensable because he had value that was created with his game and education.

Black men have to raise their heads and not be so proud as individuals, but as a team. We are not winning when babies are dying in gang shootings. We are not winning when crack cocaine is in our babies' systems. We are not winning when our lives are at risk because of the varying colors of our skin. In a white town like Naperville, Ill., you can walk untouched, but in another "town" like the low end, you can kill and walk the street to brag about it.

We have not grown comfortable with our situation because you can never get comfortable with murder and poverty. We have grown complacent with what is going on. We must understand that one cry can be heard by another cry and those cries must stop the killing. We cannot continue to have a silent cry. We must make a difference.

Every man must start with himself. I'm starting with myself. I must be part of the solution. By being neutral, I can easily be viewed as part of the problem. Let's all be the key to stopping the violence.

Where Are They Now?

Eric Bassette - Totally recovered from the church and is married. He and his wife Annette are entrepreneurs in fashion design. We are good friends and brothers.

Ivory Grandberry - A social counselor dealing with abused children. He and his wife live on the South Side of Chicago and are expecting their first child.

Lamar Lewis - Working for a major vending company. He is also married with four children and living in a South suburb of Chicago.

Vince Currington - Works for the Board of Education in Chicago. He married his high school sweetheart and they now have two children. We are still close friends.

SILENT CRY

T.D. Davis - Owns a successful real estate company in the South suburbs of Chicago. He and his wife have two children.

Jerry Bey - Works with youth and is sharing a message of hope in the north suburbs of Chicago. He's been married 14 years and has two daughters.

Eddie Bassette - Owns the B Elegant Clothes for Men at 1718 W. 95th St. on the South Side of Chicago. (312) 233-5000.

Mrs. Kennedy - Moved from the house where she raised her sons, but still lives on the South Side of Chicago. She never has recovered from the death of her youngest son or the loss of her husband.

Tookie Tompkins - Branch manager for a major bank. He also married his high school sweetheart and they have three girls.

Momma - Our relationship has grown. She is still deeply involved with the same church and lives in Chicago with one of my older sisters.

Dad - Lives on the South Side of Chicago and will be celebrating his 75th birthday in 1994, but doesn't look a day over 50. He is still my heart, soul and biggest hero.

Scholarship

Thee Family members have founded The Garry Dean Kennedy Scholarship Fund to help Lindblom students purchase books for college. It is my hope to create other scholarship for some of the sons and daughters of the victims of violence. You can help with donations and time. Together we can make a difference.

For more information, call or write

Garry Dean Kennedy Scholarship Fund
C/O 3B Publishing Company
1517 Western Avenue
Chicago Heights IL 60411

1-800-424-EDGE (3343) or 708-747-6822

The Key to Stopping the Violence

ABOUT THE COVER

The photograph is a portrayal of an African-American man who believes he is successful yet his sons are falling prey to the streets. The message is simple. In order for our sons and daughters to succeed we must open our eyes and help create opportunity. Because our success means nothing if our children have no future.

Ray Jr. is now living on the west coast with his mother, step-father and two sisters.

Featured (left to right) E.J.'s son DeMario Bassette, age 7, godson, Ray Raheem Grandberry-Shores Jr., age 11 and E.J. Bassette.

ORDER FORM

☐ **Yes!** Please send my personal autographed copy of the book:
SILENT CRY:
The Key to Stopping the Violence

Name _____

Company _____

Address _____

City _____

State _____ Zip _____

Telephone: Day (_____) _____

Evening (_____) _____

Order Information:

_____ Books at $21.95 each = $ _____

Illinois residents add 7% tax

Shipping and Handling   2.75

TOTAL $ _____

Thank you for requesting your personalized copy of **SILENT CRY: The Key To Stopping the Violence** by E.J. Bassette.
Please complete and return the attached order form. Use the space below to print the name(s) of the person to whom this book(s) should be autographed.

1. _____

2. _____

3. _____

4. _____

☐ Enclosed is my check/money order
(Please make check payable to 3B, Inc.)

Mail this form to:
3B, INC.
1517 Western Avenue, Suite 252
Chicago Heights, IL 60411
(708) 747-6822   (800) 424-EDGE

Allow 6-8 weeks for delivery